EDITORIAL DESIGN

DIGITAL AND PRINT

Published in 2014
by Laurence King Publishing Ltd
361–373 City Road
London EC1V 1LR
Tel +44 20 7841 6900
Fax +44 20 7841 6910
enquiries@laurenceking.com
www.laurenceking.com

A catalogue record for this book is available from the
British Library

ISBN 978 1 78067 164 2
Design: TwoSheds Design
Senior Editor: Peter Jones
Printed in China

Cath Caldwell & Yolanda Zappaterra

EDITORIAL DESIGN

DIGITAL AND PRINT

Laurence King Publishing

Contents

Chapter 1   Editorial design   6

Chapter 2   Editorial formats   22

Chapter 3   Covers   40

Chapter 4   Inside the publication   76

Chapter 5   Creating layouts   108

Chapter 6   Editorial design skills   152

Chapter 7   Looking back, looking forward   204

Introduction

Editorial Design will show you how to put the journalistic magic into page design by integrating your knowledge of typography and image making with the various channels of modern print and digital magazines. My aim in this book is to help you base your own design practice on a firm foundation of knowledge, so in these pages you will find inspiration mixed with solid practical guidance. Put simply, it will show you how to make images and text spark together on screen or on paper.

The second edition of this book heralds a return to creative editorial design after a flurry of nervous debate following the launch of the iPad in 2010. The debate about print versus digital is over and we are now part of a new golden age of magazine design, an eco-system of print media integrated with social media, events, campaigns and mobile media products. Underpinning all these wonderful communication design opportunities are the principles of type, art direction and layout design. So don't throw away your design history books but add this one to your bookshelf to get a balance between the past, present and the future.

Use Chapter 2 for an outline of different editorial formats; Chapters 5 and 6 to develop your own design skills; in Chapter 7, you will find profiles of timeless design greats. Tried and tested briefs for students and tutors appear at the end of Chapters 2 to 6 to help you develop editorial samples for your own portfolio. Plus we show you the editorial formats and products that will inspire you to create your own great designs.

The great names that inspired me – Janet Froelich, Jeremy Leslie, Mark Porter and Simon Esterson remain light on their feet, they adapt and show an interest in new forms of editorial that keep our industry exciting. Connect your interest in the past to your present learning of software updates. In this new age of magazine design, anything could happen with new media, so keep one eye on technological developments and the other on this book and you will be prepared for the future.

– Cath Caldwell

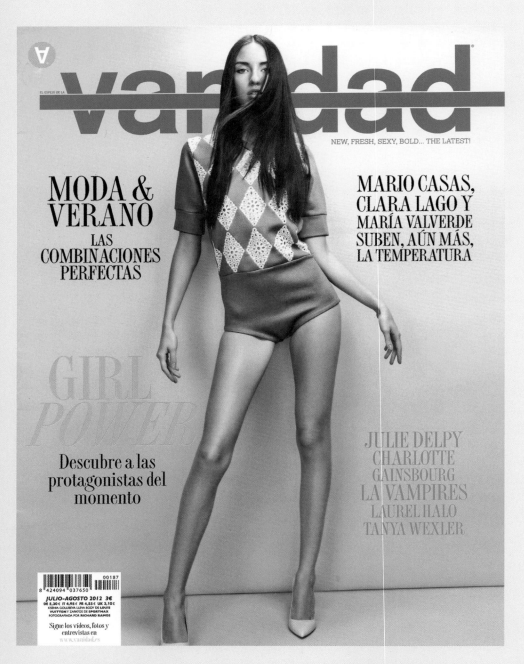

Chapter 1 : Editorial design

This book is a guide to editorial design for the printed page and for digital forms of publishing. It connects editorial design history with current practice, and explains many underlying principles to enlighten and inspire the beginner. The word 'editorial' means articles that express the editor's opinion on subjects of a particular interest at a particular time, but editorial design has come to mean curated storytelling for those with a passion for sharing a point of view, interests or even a brand. Editorial design is no longer bound by the rectangles of printed pages, but is increasingly available on mobile media. Young and old designers agree, however, that good communication and a passion for storytelling remain essential skills.

We begin by taking a closer look at what is meant by editorial design and the different roles of designers within editorial.

What is editorial design?

It is impossible to begin an examination of editorial design without first defining what it is and how it differs from other forms of design. A simple way of defining editorial design is as visual journalism, and it is this that most easily distinguishes it from other graphic design disciplines and interactive formats. An editorial publication can entertain, inform, instruct, communicate, educate, or be a combination of these things. It is not unusual to have varying opinions in a publication, although they may tend to be from one school of thought – newspapers are a good example of this. For the first time in history, publications can be interactive. Using mobile tools such as GPS (Global Positioning System), there is a new era of possibilities in how the editor and advertiser can interact with the reader. In this book, the focus will be on the common themes in editorial design across different media – those in print and those designed for the web and for use on personal devices.

'Editorial design is the design of publications – printed magazines that come out more than once, normally having a look and a feel that are distinctive and unique.'
Vince Frost, art director, *Zembla*

The aims and elements of editorial

The vast majority of editorial has at its heart the idea of communicating an idea or story through the organization and presentation of words (arranged into display and body text) and visuals. Each of these fulfils a different function: in a magazine a headline will usually have been written and laid out to grab the reader's attention, while a visual element will usually be there to clarify or support a point made in the body copy (story content). In digital publications, headlines and other graphic entry points serve as navigation links, and type elements invite you to touch and slide as well as to read.

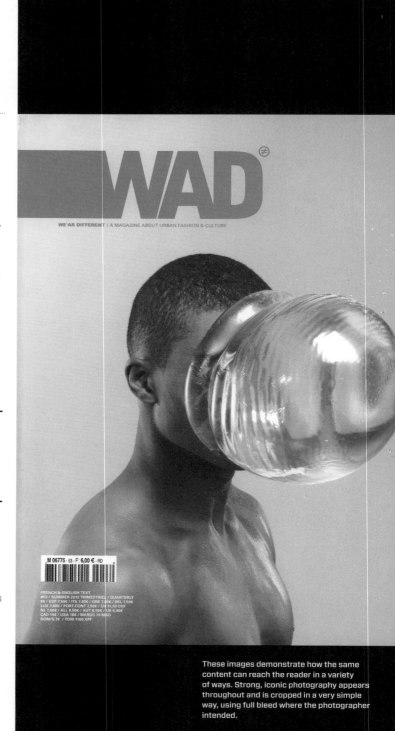

These images demonstrate how the same content can reach the reader in a variety of ways. Strong, iconic photography appears throughout and is cropped in a very simple way, using full bleed where the photographer intended.

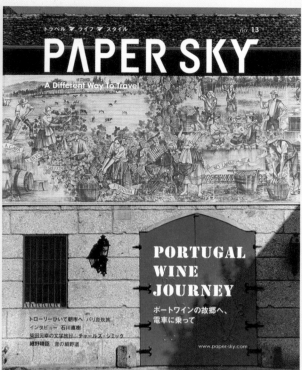

'What's fascinating about magazines generally is their organic nature; unlike books or other print media they are a constantly evolving thing that changes slightly with each issue.'

Jeremy Leslie, creative director, *magCulture*

The function of editorial design

The design of editorial matter serves different functions, such as giving expression and personality to the content, attracting and retaining readers, and structuring the material clearly. These functions have to coexist and work cohesively together to deliver something that is enjoyable, useful or informative – usually a combination of all three if it is to succeed. At its very best, design for editorial for both print and screen is an exciting and constantly evolving research lab and launch pad for stylistic innovations that are often then enthusiastically taken up in many other areas of visual communication.

'Editorial design is the framework through which a given story is read and interpreted. It consists of both the overall architecture of the publication (and the logical structure that it implies) and the specific treatment of the story (as it bends or even defies that very logic).'

Martin Venezky, art director, *Speak*

But editorial design does something else, too: it acts as a vivid cultural snapshot of the era in which it is produced. For example, 1960s magazines *Nova* and *Oz* not only brilliantly evoked the visual vibrancy of the decade, but also captured the spirit of an age that celebrated experimentation, innovation and new directions.

The making of *Wallpaper**
How a global brand explores print and digital formats

'When it has pushed us to commission things in a different way when we are at the shoot stage. We are thinking what happens with the magazine, what happens on the iPad, what is going to happen on the website? We don't want exactly the same things on the website, the iPad and the printed edition but they need to complement each other.'

Sarah Douglas, Design Director, *Wallpaper**

Wallpaper* magazine produced its first iPad edition in 2010 and continues to produce a monthly edition. The printed magazine version was originally launched in 1996 by editor Tyler Brûlé, with the website appearing in 2004 and attracting half a million unique users a month. *Wallpaper** covers design, interiors, arts, architecture, travel, fashion and technology. The company added an asterisk to its logo in 2007 on its 100th edition, signalling the use of the cursor and alluding to its digital future.

There are many examples of how the brand of *Wallpaper** has expanded to partner up with collaborators in fashion, architecture and design. The editorial team is now headed by Tony Chambers, who made the unusual transition from art director to editor. Chambers' team works closely with the publishers and operates an open approach to publishing, working with advertisers on creative projects.

In the following interview Sarah Douglas (design director) and Meirion Pritchard (former art director) explain how *Wallpaper** has extended its brand into digital outputs, design events, curating exhibitions and even property.

How do you keep control of the design elements across all three outputs?
MP: The consensus is that with the introduction to the web, designers and editors lost control for a while – we were told you can't do this and you can't do that. With tablets and iPhones, the ball is back in our court. Now it is a controlled environment. The screens are better now for viewing type online.

What digital tools do you have?
SD: We are making everything relevant to content and not animating just for the sake of it. We can only get a certain number of pictures in the magazine for a feature on architecture for example, but then on the iPad we have started including floor plans and showing much more. We can say: 'this photograph was taken from this viewpoint'. It is a great thing to show readers and the idea was to help them to understand buildings. Using the website everyone can navigate through a building.

Where do you get your inspiration from?
MP: Even if it is cycling or walking, travelling around you see things from a different perspective, not from sitting at a desk.

SD: We really rely on cultural immersion. For inspiration, I would

BEIJING
The Chinese capital, past and present, page 181

SINGAPORE
Conversations and collages on the city-state, page 186

BANGKOK
Thailand's perpetual state of reinvention, page 191

ARCHIPELAGO CINEMA
The floating cinema heads to Venice, page 196

FUTURE
Douglas Coupland's snapshots from the future, page 198

OLE SCHEEREN

EDITORIAL TEAM Ole Scheeren, Dan Chuang, Eric Chang, Justin Jalbi, Alex Gyeha, Kevin Du

CHINA SPEED

Two weeks, 20 pages... the only way to look at this was to simply deduce it yet another exercise in making things happen at China speed. Instead of filling the pages with views and statements of our own, I wanted to bring a group of people together to share their disparate views on the content we live in and on the work we do in these contexts. A group loosely centered around three places, three cities: Beijing—Singapore—Bangkok, and a series of individuals (and untitled) perspectives as diverse as the conditions we find ourselves confronted with in these environments.

With his evocation of the grotesque and absurd, Wong Qingsong seemed the perfect reflection on the state of architecture [and the physical and mental space of our office]. Cao Fei has long intrigued me with her depiction of the new China through scenes of fantastic perpetual anomicration and a virtual world in which everything seems possible [albeit with the extent of architecture threatening to erase the planet].

A bridge in the China's Cai Today TV show and with a following of more than 3.5 million on his Weibo account [the Chinese equivalent to Twitter], Gao Xiaosong broadcast a witty perspective on Beijing's CBD and the demons within [in amount is given of his recent six-month detention which more than doubled his following]. Liu Shuang Zhang offers his wealth of historical knowledge and long-seen perspective on Beijing, leaving from the first accredited photojournalist for Time magazine to Beijing in the 1960s and revealed.

A conversation with Singapore's miniature gene of late modern architecture William Lim portrays a character that at the age of 80 is still one of Asia's most outspoken and socially motivated architectural protagonists, while Valerie Bluhl two Strassbourg's piano-collages merge tropical reality with architectural ambition and fantasy.

Bangkok in focus... no, it's a dawn party that disturbs a revolution for flat [Barani Kisatthong] says his friend suggested to just introduce him simply as a fucking good artist and can say anything else]. To me, he remains one of the most political and subversive artists of his generation, with a particular psychology and sensibility. Sara Phataranawik Phataranawik has been a journalist for The Nation for 10 years and was a complicit [media] member of the 'Cities on the Move' project in the late 1990s.

And finally, a global view from one of the women I have admired [into the beginning of my twenties as someone who so effortlessly characterised the whole notion of my generation: Douglas Coupland. Months' of apocalyptic narratives, he has written eight latest from the near future that offer snapshots of our buildings as points of collective memory and as collage for illusion vessels' virtues of a global indifference.

Before letting loose this group of creative minds on the following pages, I felt compelled to give the first word not to any specific creative individual, but to the guys without which our architectural courage would all remain here clumsy. Written on a concrete column of the CCTV building, we discovered this poem [pictured right] one morning on our regular site visits.

Leaning tower, leaning tower,
You are fixture in the world,
you are the greatness of China,
our migrant workers
come together in you.
from all over China,
you are the pride of ours.
No matter how high you are,
we will fight with you.
Our migrant workers are great.
we are everywhere.
It's us to build this country
a beautiful tongji.

Wallpaper*

OLE SCHEEREN
The Scheeren Sorry, China-based architect and a model of his studio's projects.
1-4 Angkasa Raya skyscrapers, now under construction in Kuala Lumpur, Malaysia.
Picture: Alte Yuan Bui
Writer: Jonathan Bell

Building the future

After a decade spent working on a variety of major projects across Asia – many of which will reach completion in the next couple of years – German architect Ole Scheeren is ready for a new challenge: Europe

When we last caught up with Ole Scheeren, [W*129], the architect was on the cusp of leaving the credit of OMA – not that anyone suspected his long-time partner firm was leaving on bad terms. The Dutch studio's landmark Chinese project, the CCTV Tower, was substantially completed and Scheeren's name was clearly associated with some of OMA's most eagerly awaited projects, including the Mahstlukhov tower in Bangkok and the Taipei Performing Arts Centre. As creative divorces go, the split didn't make headlines with non-signture claims for alimony or allegations of stylistic infidelities. Instead, Scheeren quietly slipped in meetings, to continue to work on some of these well-advanced megastructures and quickly acquire a few other substantial projects.

Two and a half years later, and Scheeren has effortlessly assumed the mantle of studio leader, with a new letterhead, an endless supply of crisp white shirts and a globe-spanning portfolio [and itinerary] that threatens to eclipse the schedule of his mentor. But where OMA is explicitly a global-land firm, deploying thematic and research in the name of new architectural paradigms, Büro-OS Scheeren has emerged out of Asia, primed to make the leap from East to West. This initial focus is unsurprising, given Scheeren's extensive experience of living and working in the region, but it has shaped the tone of projects that formally launch the studio. Their range from the rushed and another blocks of The Interlace apartments and the side-facing Scotts Tower in Singapore, the gnarled façade of the Mahahakhon in Bangkok, to the Angkasa Raya tower in Kuala Lumpur, sized up against the Moorish motif of Cesar Pelli's Petronas Towers, but a thousand miles apart in conception and delivery.

Scheeren's work meets imagination. For the architect, variety is a central part of his studio's identity: 'It was important to me to open the practice with a range of different projects – it's the range that makes things so interesting,' he says. From a site visit in Bangkok, en route to his Beijing studio, via an earlier sojourn in Singapore, like many exponents of the

new avant-garde, Scheeren is unafraid of the visual language of high modernism. Indeed, many of the buildings developed by Büro-OS resemble the International Style on steroids, with their fragmented façades, tiered structural geometries and juxtaposition of glassy geometric simplicity with ribs, ripples and shears.

Büro-OS has had to navigate the volley of superstructures between rendered vision and built reality with more obliquity than most contemporary studios. CCTV has been on the design radar for a decade, with the first images emerging in late 1990s. Although the building appeared to be complete by the most Beijing Olympics, in truth the structure, China's state TV station, have only just moved in after a complex fit-out. Scheeren is playing a long game and it's only now, two years after the stable was set up, that he is sharing projects as they approach completion. The transition from OMA to Büro-OS has resulted in a more explicit definition of authorship for many of the projects in his portfolio. Among the first to be seen under his

ever since relocating with OMA – the typologies that emerge from Büro-OS are stylistically disparate but focused, laser-like, on their immediate context. 'How can a building be relevant beyond its occupants?' the architect asks, and it's clear that this social concern is the key bridge that links his work to the Bauhaus modernism of three quarters of a century ago, rather than any stylistic concerns.

'There's a sense of psychology at work: how do people live, how do they behave in these buildings?' he asks. 'A number of people in the studio also have degrees in history, sociology, psychology. We try to really bring local knowledge and perspectives to our projects.'

There is an overarching sense of anthropological exploration at work in the Büro-OS portfolio. As Scheeren himself acknowledges, 'We're at the stage where I still have the luxury of being personally engaged with projects. I enjoy spending time in locations and getting a real feel for them. It's really a goal to keep the practice at a scale where I can continue to do that.' Furthermore, he is all too aware of the pitfalls – both in terms of presentation and in approach – of digital architecture. 'There's a relatively big rift between my generation and what came after. I grew up in an analogue world. I learned to draw, to build models and to build houses by hand, I worked on a construction site for a long time... There is something very real about architecture, it's not all digital. But China is more manual; the West has turned very digital in the absence of built realities,' he says. Nowhere is this more evident than in the construction of CCTV. 'The way it was designed clearly took advantage of local conditions, labour and material costs. We also designed it entirely out of locally

sourced Chinese materials and steel grades, which all had an impact, technologically and aesthetically. But the building clearly exceeded these qualifications.'

Maintaining a portfolio that runs from skyscrapers to studios has its benefits. 'You can engage in very specific issues of craft, how things come together. They're also about individual psychologies, not communal psychology. You can react very precisely to an individual, their tastes and fantasies,' Scheeren says. The Büro-OS Archipelago Cinema is another modest but high-profile work. First seen in a cove on the Thai island of Koh Yao Noi, it's currently being reconstructed for the 13th Venice Architecture Biennale, where it will host the premiere of *Against All Rules*, Horst Brandenburg's documentary about Scheeren's past six years in practice. 'The cinema is less of an architectural project, more an intervention in the landscape. It is a narrative about creativity,' says Scheeren.

The architect frequently returns to this idea of an architectural narrative, implying his buildings are about facilitating the way people live, rather than shaping them. It would be foolish to claim not to still be influenced by European mindsets in some way,' he says, 'but I don't want to sound nostalgic or retro when I talk about these things. It's about ambition, about the impact on our society, rather than a formal concern.' In the next few years, the seeds currently being sown in the fertile urban landscape of Thailand, Singapore, Malaysia and China will grow into a more global approach. 'After basically a decade in Asia as an onlooker, I am now acutely complicit with that part of the world,' Scheeren says, 'but it feels like the right moment to orient myself back to Europe and re-engage with the West.'

Wallpaper*

THE INTERLACE
A large-scale housing development nearing completion in Singapore. The Interlace will feature 31 apartment blocks, landscaped roof terraces and pools
Ole Scheeren @ OMA
Photography: Darren Soh

CCTV
Below, Beijing's landmark 54-storey CCTV HQ tower was completed in May 2012
Rem Koolhaas and Ole Scheeren @ OMA

CCTV
Top right, the main lobby. Above, the forum and event space at the top of the building
Photography: Shu Ho

ANGKASA RAYA
Left, located next to Kuala Lumpur's Petronas Towers, this 268m-high skyscraper will consist of a stack of balancing volumes and should be completed by 2016
Ole Scheeren @ Büro-OS

MAHANAKHON
Below, this 77-storey multi-use complex is due to become Bangkok's tallest skyscraper by 2014
Ole Scheeren @ OMA

own name was Angkasa Raya. According to Scheeren, 'it marked a relatively significant step' in the evolution of the studio.

With three major projects on site, the studio also has smaller projects in the works, most notably a studio and gallery space for a leading, but publicity-shy, Chinese artist. 'It's a very personal project,' Scheeren explains. 'It's his very specific world meeting my own world – a house that places artistic space alongside a context of literal Chinese-ness.' The artist is a compulsive collector, not just of art. The entire context of the new structure will be assembled from his personal stash of traditional Chinese structures and landscape elements, creating a highly concentrated experience of the country's long tradition of art, design and landscape.

On a much larger scale, plans for a new Beijing auction house are nearing completion. Designed for the country's leading home-grown auctioneers, the project occupies a prime site off the commercial and cultural axes that run close to the Forbidden City. Both of these projects are in the final design stage, while the Bangkok tower is now taking shape after a spell of inaction, and The Interlace is rising fast above the low hills in the west of Singapore. 'Many of these buildings have an explicitly tropical context,' says Scheeren. 'The question is how you build in a place where nature is so dominant and beautiful, and where people live very differently to other climate zones.'

On the page, this scattering of projects, from high to low rise, small to large, appears rather disparate and disjointed, but what unites them is Scheeren's concerns about architecture's broader social role. Although Asia has been his focus for many years – Scheeren has lived around the region for nearly a decade,

GUEST EDITOR 2 | OLE SCHEEREN

OLE SCHEEREN

CHINA SPEED

GUEST EDITOR 2 | OLE SCHEEREN

GUEST EDITOR 2 | OLE SCHEEREN

THE INTERLACE

GUEST EDITOR 2 | OLE SCHEEREN

CCTV

GUEST EDITOR 2 | OLE SCHEEREN

CCTV

GUEST EDITOR 2 | OLE SCHEEREN

---

say that I like *The Ride* magazine from designer Andrew Diprose with editor Philip [Diprose]. The fact that Andy works for *Wired* is great, but he absolutely loves magazines and produces this fantastic publication as well.

What's the main aspect that you as a designer have had to rethink working for the tablet format?

SD: It is just about re-appropriating your thoughts. You have to think differently about how things work differently, how they are read differently. You have to think through the reader's eyes. Think how people use it.

Do you get feedback in the form of data?

MP: We get massive statistics about which pages are successful. The Twitter following is something that never existed before. We have half a million Twitter followers, which is pretty good for a magazine. The website has gone so well we have just been asked to make a Chinese version. We printed a *Made in China* issue as part of a series and making those contacts was really important. Although we are based in London, *Wallpaper** goes much further now with the web – 150,000 circulation.

Chunky headlines are underlined in both print and digital. Designers take care to use top-right-hand 'slugs' or headers to signify which section the reader is currently reading.

How do you work with advertisers?

SD: We meet with them with the *Wallpaper** bespoke team and the editor to talk through what will work for them and for us. The output is tailored to that conversation. It might be a website, an event or a shoot.

What is going to happen next? Are there any more platforms to extend into?

SD: I think the way it is going we could do more. The annual *Wallpaper** handmade August issue is a showcase for contemporary design and craftsmanship. Artists contribute by making items to display. This has taken the brand into a curatorial activity. Wallpaper* Composed applies to this. The Apartment is also another opportunity to extend the *Wallpaper** brand. We hold events in it, use it for photo shoots, and can show it to clients. It is set up as a venture. Developers see that and start to think creatively about how they could work with us. It is also useful for photographers to come and stay in if they are shooting for us!

You commission a lot of photography. Have the different digital platforms, such as the website and iPad, affected how you commission photographers?

SD: It is a mixture at the moment; photographers are slowly getting into it as they did during the switch from film to digital. We are still in the transition.

Will every still shoot have an element of moving image content in it in the future?

SD: Maybe about 80 per cent.

What are the other Wallpaper* brand extensions?

The *Wallpaper** travel guides have been turned into apps. That franchise is run by a separate publisher. Wallpaper* Selects is another franchise which works with contemporary photography with art retailer Eyestorm. The Wallpaper* Design Awards feature new and emerging talent and keep the brand positioned at the top of the international contemporary design scene.

Designing magazines is a collaborative experience. Students here learn to stand back and look at their images and text from the reader's point of view, taking in feedback from other contributors. This image shows design students at Central Saint Martins in London discussing work created from the briefs in this book.

The different roles of designers in editorial

Key to successful editorial design is the working relationship between the designer and the editor, but equally important is the designer's relationship with the rest of the publication's staff. The designer will often be second only to the editor in the number of staff he or she interacts with on a daily basis.

Key staff in editorial

Depending on the type of publication, the size of the team and how it has been organized, the individual roles of the team may vary. But, while a magazine editor will probably have commissioned the bulk of the material to appear in the publication, it is the art director, design director or lead designer who will be responsible for the way this is organized and presented to represent the magazine's identity.

It would take a whole book to explain the various roles and relationships of every designer working in digital and print formats for newspapers and magazines, and these will differ vastly depending on the media format, size and circulation of a publication – an independent magazine that is produced biannually will have staffing needs that are very different from those of a daily magazine blog. Here is a guide to the staff that an editorial designer will work most closely with.

Editor: ultimately responsible for the publication's content. Works most closely with the art director and the tier of editorial staff immediately below him or her, including features editor, picture editor and production editor.

Art director/art editor: responsible for the organization and ordering of all the content, including commissioned and in-house articles and all imagery, to a timescale set by the production manager or production editor. He or she commissions images and information graphics (infographics), including from illustrators and, sometimes, photographers (*see also* picture editor, below). Works closely with creative and production staff across print editions and to some extent on digital formats.

Production manager/web editor: oversees the physical compilation of all the material by setting a production schedule. This works backwards from the publication date to determine receipt of copy and imagery, editing, subbing and design schedules, and dates on which the sections need to go to the printer. The production manager is also responsible for producing, updating and circulating the flatplan. Works most closely with the art department and the printer, particularly in overseeing all special print requirements.

Chief subeditor, subeditors: responsible for proofing and 'subbing' (subediting) the copy to ensure stylistic coherence, correct spelling, grammar, punctuation, etc., writing all display copy, rewriting badly written copy, cutting copy and sometimes laying out pages. Works closely with the editor, art team, features editor and, depending on the structure of the editorial team, the writing staff.

Picture editor: usually responsible for sourcing images and copyright clearing on imagery, but also, in conjunction with the art director and editor, for ensuring the quality of photographic material used throughout the publication. Works closely with these individuals, but also with picture agencies, photo libraries and repro houses.

Designers: responsible for laying out the publication according to the art director's directions or instructions. The way designers work with their art director and how much autonomy they have in laying out the material is determined by a number of factors, including levels of seniority, the working practice of the art director (some like to be very hands-on and oversee every detail of the publication; others are happy to delegate and sign off pages once they've been laid out), the ratio of staff to the number of pages, and the lead time to publication – often, the shorter a lead time, the more responsibility will be given to designers.

Studio manager: not all publications have a studio manager, as the project-management aspects of the job mirror that of the production manager to some degree. But a studio manager is a great facilitator for

The Guardian newspaper

Tackling a brand-new format in print

In 2005, the UK's *The Guardian* newspaper became the first large-circulation British daily to have front-to-back colour, something that its creative director at the time, Mark Porter, says was necessary because 'real life is in colour, and in an age when we are in competition with TV and the internet as news providers, it's crazy to attempt to do it without full colour. That is a twentieth-century approach which readers found very frustrating.'

Unlike many of the UK broadsheets, which have adopted a tabloid format to respond to modern users' changing needs and relationship with their daily paper, *The Guardian*'s redesign incorporated a move to a brand-new format – the Berliner format used by *Le Monde* newspaper. It's not surprising that the newspaper is forging its own path with a format that Porter says 'has a unique ability to combine convenience for the reader with serious journalism, a contemporary approach to design, and the demands of advertisers'. Its approach to design has always been intelligent and forward-thinking; in 1988 a radical redesign by Pentagram's David Hillman split the newspaper into two sections, unveiled a new masthead and, most importantly, introduced the idea of 'white space' to newspaper design, a concept previously restricted to magazines.

'Everything changed with the Hillman redesign. It wasn't just a new look; it was a whole design philosophy, probably the first time any newspaper really had one,' says Porter. 'The designers who followed (Mike McNay, Simon Esterson and myself) have had a very strong set of principles to work with,' he adds. These principles were adapted in the 2005 redesign by following Hillman's own clear vision of how a newspaper should work – a vision 'that was based not on journalistic habits and traditions, but on sound design principles'.

The Guardian newspaper is now published alongside *The Guardian* live website and the app, which updates stories as they happen. Mark Porter left the newspaper in 2010, but his influence remains due to the continued impact of his team's massive typographic overhaul of the publication in 2005. Since then the visual identity of *The Guardian* has been extended to fit *The Guardian* online website and *The Guardian* app. Porter is still connected to the paper as an editorial consultant and says, 'Nowadays, when you do a newspaper redesign you are also designing a website, pages for mobile devices and for apps. It is getting to be unusual just to do a job for print. Conceptually it all has to fit together and it's about having a visual identity for a brand that works in print and also works in other channels.'

The Guardian website is staffed by a team that follow the core design values outlined by Porter, supported by the belief that in any format good balanced typography and strong reportage photography create an intelligent product. When Porter moved on to The Guardian iPad, he ensured that these principles were still there, but enhanced by the interactive nature of the device. The smooth slide navigation is an important feature, but it is the mobile nature of the iPad that opens up new possibilities for editors and advertisers to interact with the reader through sophisticated data-collection software and GPS. Porter comments that, 'Tablets have opened up lots of other opportunities. This is the first time in the digital sphere that we have been able to use a lot of what we know about doing things in print. It is exciting that the tablet market is going to grow. In the future we will have more opportunities to do good editorial design in digital media than we have had up until now. The amazing thing is that it changes every day. We are seeing the last days of desktop-based browsing. Most people will be consuming media on mobile devices. Tablets and phones will be much more important than desktop. Print will always be a part of what we do but it will not be the biggest part.'

The hierarchy of typography signals the importance of the story. Crisp headlines underpin the design and bring a spark through the juxtaposition of words and images. Every opportunity for graphic impact is used so that the website provides a rich experience of simple navigational tools that help the reader get straight to the content he or she is looking for. Gimmicky tools and whizzing pictures have no place here and are shunned in favour of a plain and straightforward approach.

a design studio, acting as a co-ordinator and handling the everyday interaction between design studio, picture desk and production. He or she ensures that everything is going to plan and is on schedule, and that all the differing elements that go to make up the page layout are in place and as they should be.

'Magazine content is basically built around the idea that editorial breaks up the advertising, which, for a lot of magazines, is what it's all about: selling ads.'
Vince Frost, art director, *Zembla*

What attributes should an editorial designer have?

Tibor Kalman once famously said that it is the job of the art editor to get the editor fired if he or she believes the job is not being done properly. By this he meant that an editorial designer should take as much interest in the content of a publication as the editor, because designing a magazine is unquestionably an extension of editing it. Both roles are creative ones that are rooted in and play part of a creative process, and how they function together will nearly always determine the success or failure of an editorial publication.

So, if editorial designers should 'become' editors, the converse is equally true and editors should 'become' editorial designers – or at the very least they should understand each other's attitudes, roles and areas of expertise in order to build the necessary trust to create a first-rate publication. All the great editorial designers and editors have expressed this, some of them even bringing other skills and backgrounds to the mix. Mark Porter, who designed *Colors* and *WIRED* before becoming creative director of *The Guardian* newspaper, read languages at Oxford University instead of formally studying design. As he explains, this fact lies at the heart of his approach to design:

'I approach editorial from the reader's point of view. Good editorial design is, firstly, about making people want to read, and then about telling stories; most readers aren't interested in design, and when they look at a page they should see ideas, people and places, not graphic design. It may also be that having been to university makes it easier for me to communicate with editors, as they tend to share the same background. Newspapers are full of very smart journalists, which is a constant intellectual challenge for me; if I can't make a clear, convincing case for my design, then I will just get shot down. Languages themselves haven't been that useful in my work (apart from doing projects overseas), but I believe that design is a language too, and, like any language, of no real value in itself; it only becomes useful when you have something worthwhile to say.'

Dylan Jones, editor of *GQ* magazine, but also past editor of *i-D* magazine, *The Face, Arena* and *Arena Homme Plus*, trained as a graphic designer. Willy Fleckhaus, art director of the seminal 1960s German magazine *Twen*, was a journalist. And David Hillman, Pentagram partner and designer of *New Statesman and Society* and *The Guardian* newspaper, was both art director and deputy editor on *Nova*. He has said, 'Art direction isn't about establishing a grid or styling a masthead, or even about a good-looking juxtaposition of image and text. In its best form, it involves the art director having a full and in-depth understanding of what the magazine says, and, through design, influencing how it is said.'

You may well have heard and read about the design greats and wondered how they got where they are. Opposite and overleaf are three interviews with some real-life designers at different levels who explain the work they do and how they got started.

Junior designer

Esa Martinesva, *Port* digital magazine

What does a junior designer/intern on a digital magazine actually do?
Since the tablet format (iPad) is so new, there really aren't any senior designers who know everything about designing for them. It's just one big discovery for everybody. In my role as a junior/intern I was responsible for thinking about how the reader interacts with, and navigates through, the magazine, plus helping to make layouts, and thinking about typography on screen.

How is this day-to-day activity different from a designer working in print?
The medium might be new, but the communication and interaction basics are the same. You need to have an overall understanding of how type and image (moving or still) and audio all work together and also when not to use them.

Do you have to learn to deal with different platforms?
Many applications have tried to do too much at the same time. Obviously the tablets are really good with video and audio, but the users seem to appreciate simplicity and subtlety in the design.

I don't think all designers need to technically know every medium, but it is essential to understand how these different mediums work. Design-wise, working with Adobe Creative Suite you don't really need to touch the coding side, but you will be dealing with interactive elements like buttons and hyperlinks. Again, the biggest challenge is to understand how type and image work differently on the screen than on the printed page.

How do you stay up to date with technology?
You really can't do it any other way than just taking the bull by the horns and trying to experiment with the new tools and mediums as they are released.

How did you get started in magazines?
My portfolio had a reasonable number of editorial and print projects in it. A tutor of mine remembered my interest in editorial design and recommended me for the job. I got the position and was assisting in designing the magazine's iPad edition. After the project the team wanted me to continue working with them. Now I'm mainly working with the printed edition, but I'm still working a bit with the digital side as well.

Did you work for free as an intern?
Yes, at the start. The magazine was a start-up and made mainly through voluntary work. That seems to be pretty standard with freshly started independent magazines before the budget is stabilized. Since then I have been paid and nowadays our interns get paid a small fee.

As an intern, it is rare that you can say 'I did this', as it is often group work, directed by an art director. However, your experience working on even simple layouts really counts

"You can translate an emotion into something that other people can then read again. And that's what art should always be about: communicating certain ideas and emotions through work without having to explain them"

Interview Phil Rhys Thomas
Photography Eva Vermandel

Senior designer

Gemma Stark, *Net-a-Porter* digital magazine

What does a senior designer on a digital magazine actually do?
In some ways the role is fairly similar to the role on a 'traditional' magazine. I art direct fashion shoots, design features for the magazine and attend planning meetings. I am normally designing several stories at once, along with finding photographers and developing shoot concepts. One thing that is different is having an awareness of the digital aspect of the finished product, so I work closely with the tech team to discuss how the pages will work on screen.

How is this day-to-day activity different from a designer working in print? Is it a faster process?
Well I work on a weekly magazine so it is most definitely fast-paced! We start to design the majority of the stories on the Tuesday and by Thursday lunchtime the editor reviews the whole magazine. Our layouts are then passed over to the tech team on a Monday and are live on the website by Wednesday. The proofing process is quite different. We will check the quality of the images and type on our internal website instead of cromalins [high-quality colour proofs] and make changes where necessary, which are then updated by the tech team.

Do you have to deal with different platforms?
Our magazine is built in Flash, but the designs are also used to create our iPad app in HTML 5 too. We also design a mini PDF version of one magazine story a week for the iPhone, and we still do print projects from time to time. We work in InDesign, but also use Photoshop for site pages and emails. So yes, there is a lot of variety. At *Net-a-Porter* we approach everything from an editorial angle –

even the banners and promos have an editorial message. Working on a digital magazine means we tend to put much less on a page. This, of course, has its advantages. We can use animation to expose more information and images. We have to consider things like animation and usability the second we start designing each layout. Even the simplest of animation can completely alter the page.

How do you stay up to date with technology?
I am constantly looking at other websites for inspiration and reading about new ideas on blogs. As a team we get together and discuss what new things we could be doing. If someone sees something brilliant we send a link to the whole team. Although it may not be relevant to each person, or the project he or she may be working on, it could be useful for someone else. Our tech department are also really great and constantly highlight any new tools available to us.

How did you get started in magazines?
I started doing work experience during the summer holiday while I was at Central Saint Martins. My tutor recommended me for a summer placement at *Elle* magazine. I was there for a couple of months and loved it; for me it perfectly blended two things I enjoy most – graphics and fashion! I kept in touch with people and did more work experience whenever I could. While at *Elle* I met my now boss. When she approached me about a job at *Net-a-Porter* I was so excited. The fact it was a luxury e-tailer with a strong focus on editorial made it all the more appealing. By the time I graduated I already had my job lined up. I started as a junior designer the following September.

Design director

John Belknap, *The Jewish Chronicle* newspaper

What does a design director on a newspaper actually do?

As a design director there are two levels of design you engage with. The first is creating and maintaining the signature look of the paper. Everything from the masthead to the classifieds has a unique look, and you create it, keep an eye on it, and keep improving it. The editor might want to create a new section and you design that, or supervise its design.

The second level is actually producing daily or weekly editions. That involves working closely with the editors to prepare photographs, illustrations and infographics for the pages, and also laying out pages. Designers on big newspapers are usually only involved with complex layouts, and the subeditors (or copy editors in the US) lay out most of the news pages according to strict guidelines given to them previously by the design director. As a design director you employ other art directors to deal with the specific pages for various feature sections such as business, sport and arts reviews. You work closely with the editor to lend drama to stories on the page, and you work with picture editors, section editors, graphic artists and, at the end of the process, the production manager who is anxious to send your work to press.

How do you design in order to allow the content to then go into the online version?

Most papers have a 'plug-in' system attached to Quark or InDesign or other page-makeup software. This means that the articles are put into a database and then pulled on to the page from the database. There are many ways for that copy to be connected to the web, but basically the copy for the web is pulled from that database as well. On top of that, the same database is used to create the paper's archive of past articles. In the old days (i.e. a couple of years ago), stories went into the paper and then onto the web. Now they often go to the web first. This is mostly a production/IT systems task, but it can affect design details. For instance, headlines, bylines and text have to always be in separate boxes – or have separate style sheets – so the web software can distinguish between them and arrange them in the right order.

How do you stay up to date with technology?

My IT manager tells me we have to install new this and new that and I try and stay up to date with it.

How did you get started in newspapers?

I worked on my high school paper and loved its rhythmic progression from sloth to adrenalin. I got hooked. My first job was part-time at a newspaper during university. I eventually left university, but stayed at the paper for ten years.

right: John works closely with the editor to create bold front covers, and to ensure many entry points for the target reader. Photo on left-hand image by John Rifkin.

opposite: Gemma's work shows an understanding of how the fashion reader loves a clear image but also can scroll over to read a caption.

The New York Times Style Magazine

WOMEN'S FASHION FALL 2005
Tilda Swinton

Chapter 2 : Editorial formats

Until the introduction of the tablet in 2010, national newspapers, consumer and lifestyle magazines, and glossy supplements represented the highest status of editorial design. However, digital publications are now developing fast and providing new opportunities for editorial designers, publishers and advertisers. The new digital family consists of websites, mobiles, Android tablets and the iPad. 'Apps' are enabling designers to add moving images and interactivity to digital newspapers and magazines. Many people now carry mobile devices which enable publications to have larger followings via their digital interfaces than they do in print format.

Our focus in this chapter is on editorial design for both print and digital formats, looking at regularly published editions of newspapers and magazines that set and dictate the trends for the rest to follow.

A concise history of digital publications

Early digital publications were mainly websites featuring PDF (portable document format) pages that could be flicked through as if turning the pages of a conventional newspaper or magazine. The files were, however, large and were limited by the fonts available. American publisher Condé Nast built their own custom software in-house and produced *Wired*, *GQ* and *Vanity Fair* without relying on external software systems. The arrival of HTML in the 1990s as a computer coding language enabled designers to embed moving content into the web. The web browser reads the tags and renders this code as pictures and text.

As interactive design technology improved, so apps appealed to advertisers who could then add moving images and interactive content to advertisements. With the arrival of the iPad in 2010, digital publishing became an even better portable experience. The iPad brought an element of play to the tools available. It also put editorial in the same portable device as all the other great things in life – email, photos, shopping, internet and reading. At the close of 2011, however, many iPad apps went back to a more stripped-down delivery: the full 'bells and whistles' approach was rejected and a reliance on good graphic design and smart editing returned to digital publishing. After the initial flurry of moving image and complicated interactive promises, a sense of normality returned to the digital publishing industry in 2012.

The pitfalls of sharing

However, access to another company's content causes friction with those who invest in news gathering. Those who create journalistic content, such as *The New York Times* and the BBC, are bearing the cost of serious reportage. The WikiLeaks scandal in 2011 highlighted the moral debate about accessibility of news in the digital age and raised the question of who content 'belongs' to. The law around news gathering clearly needed to be redefined. In 2012, the British phone hacking scandal exposed the inability of the authorities to control the media and the Leveson Inquiry was called to investigate the culture, practices and ethics of the press. The report of the inquiry called for a new regulatory body to enforce set principles involving the legality, privacy and honesty in copyright.

'When we are designing the magazine we are thinking about how it is going to work on the iPad.

The iPad has pushed us to think about how to build on the content for the printed issue and from the website. It contains all the interactive elements. It is similar content to the magazine but borrows interactive elements from the website.'

Meirion Pritchard, former Art Director, *Wallpaper**

Real Simple art director Janet Froelich uses this eye-catching feature opener to grab the attention of the reader. On the iPad the sharpness of the bold photo by Craig Culter is enhanced, giving great clarity. Many publications use a simple PDF of a printed page, but *Real Simple* uses the iPad format at its best, to enhance the content for the way the reader uses the magazine – often in the kitchen.

oops, I did it again

Don't let holiday spills mess with your spirit. Here are solutions (and soaps and sprays) for every **seasonal stain.**

REPORTING BY **NATALIE ERMANN RUSSELL**
PHOTOGRAPHS BY **CRAIG CUTLER**

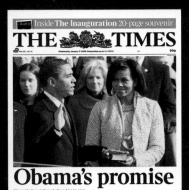

The *Times* newspaper uses simple headlines and iconic imagery to great effect. Special historic occasions like the presidential inauguration are an opportunity to play to its strengths as one of the world's papers of record. Here we see the combination of foreign correspondent reporting, thorough attention to detail and dense graphical information to give the reader a substantial product.

Newspapers

Harold Evans, editor of *The Sunday Times* from 1967 to 1981, wrote a series of seminal books on newspaper editing, layout and typography that are still used in journalism schools. In *Book Five: Newspaper Design*, he said:

> 'A newspaper is a vehicle for transmitting news and ideas. The design is an integral part of that process. We begin with a blank sheet of newsprint and a mosaic of ideas we want to communicate, and it is the function of newspaper design to present that mosaic in an organized and comprehensible way. To do this, the newspaper designer uses text type, display type, photographs, line work, white space and a sequence of pages in the most fitting combinations.'

This is probably as succinct and accurate a description of newspapers as you will find anywhere. But Harold Evans didn't have the internet and mobile media to contend with. The immediacy of these delivery media has now forced newspapers to provide a different service to their readers, and required designers to respond accordingly. As Mark Porter, former creative director at *The Guardian*, explains:

> 'Many papers are now less concerned with simply reporting and more with providing background, perspective and interpretation. Rather than just telling readers what happened, these papers now have to help them understand the significance of events, and encourage them to think. Design has to respond to this in a number of ways. As stories get longer and more complex, rational and readable

The logo on the front page of the Portuguese colour daily *Publico* is iconic; the use of a flower image is bold and symbolic, balanced by the gravitas of the small headshots below. This tabloid front page uses scale dramatically and combines it with a thoroughly modern typographic look.

Publico's inside pages have a magazine feel, with dense, structured content packing in four stories. A common byline treatment helps the reader to navigate entry points to the stories. The coloured panel indicates a different kind of content and the vertical columns balance the horizontal axis, intro and headline, while the cut-out image on the pull quote adds a little air.

page layouts and typography become increasingly important. And visual journalism – intelligent use of photography, infographics and layout – has also become an essential tool for editors.

The best thing about working on a newspaper is the opportunity to work with such a wide range of incredibly intelligent and knowledgeable people. The worst is the lack of control over the detail. Most newspaper pages are not laid out by trained designers. This is very difficult for magazine-trained art directors to adjust to!'

Mark Porter, Design Director, *Mark Porter Associates*

Digital newspapers

In the early days of digital format, newspapers published the same pages online as in print by using PDFs on their websites. Since then a more interactive approach has been developed and is now enhanced by the use of GPS tracking. With more people buying mobile devices, news organizations have begun exploring GPS as an advertising tool. News services can link in to advertisers, based either on the reader's interests or his or her location. This enables news organizations to retain important advertising revenue that was once generated by print advertising.

Today, editorial news designers need to be able to work with the developers of digital platforms and require a basic knowledge of coding. They must understand the verbal language that developers use so that they can work with them on keeping the visual identity of the publication intact once the pages are processed by content management systems. These systems distribute page designs onto the different platforms for mobile and tablet. They enable the change of scale required for each device, which makes a huge difference to the reader's perception of the storytelling.

Newspaper sizes

Although there are many other sizes for newspapers (in particular, a number of European newspapers publish in sizes between a Berliner and a broadsheet), the majority of papers worldwide use one of three formats: tabloid, Berliner or broadsheet. Dimensions are as follows:

Broadsheet   Berliner   Tabloid

Broadsheet (or Nordic/Nordisch) approximately 56 x 43.2cm (22 x 17in)

Berliner (or Midi) approximately 47 x 31.5cm (18½x 12½in)

Tabloid (also known as Half Nordic or Compact) approximately 35.5 x 25.5-30.5cm (14 x 10-12in)

Common digital myths debunked

The arrival of the tablet marks the death of print
False The introduction of the iPad in 2010 has not changed everything; magazine titles and editorial brands are the same as they were before its launch. Tablets are fantastic devices that offer more interactive possibilities.

Readers don't read long text on digital devices
False The idea that people use mobile devices for an instant hit when they are on the go is a myth. Since the improvement of on-screen legibility, there is evidence that readers read long-form text on digital devices. There are new ways to view information quickly and to store text for reading later, such with in apps like Instapaper. Reading habits have changed, however, and in 2012 statistics show that the average length of an online session has lengthened from a quick update to between 17 and 31 minutes.

Readers prefer to read editorial on desktop screens
False By the time this book is published, the amount of data being downloaded through desktop browsers on PCs will have been overtaken by the amount downloaded by mobile devices. It appears that the best computer is the one that you take with you. Mobile devices are used even when people are not on the move, with 84 per cent usage being from the home in 2012. This is changing our behaviour, and reading magazines and newspapers is increasingly becoming something we can do while watching television or consuming some other kind of media. Editors are realizing that they no longer have the undivided attention of their audience.

Small-run print publications will survive
True Independent publishers fiercely champion print and there will always be print publications as long as we can afford the paper to print them on. The design community continues to play with print formats and readers seem to like this. Cheaper digital printing makes it easier than ever to print a short run publication. A good example is the Newspaper Club, one of the websites where you can go to upload your editorial material and have it printed or published online.

Large print publications will not survive
False The giant media companies are less sentimental than independent publishers about print because the overheads for the traditional model of print and distribution are so expensive. Familiar titles have ceased to print and have moved to a paywall website, using responsive design across mobile and desktop. The publication has survived and in 2012 won the Society of Newspaper Designers (SND) best-designed news website. News weeklies, such as *Newsweek*, also closed their print operation in 2012. Such large publications, however, may be resurrected in another form in the future.

Digital terminology

Frictionless experience
A website or app's user experience (referred to as UX) that is smooth and describes the ideal journey between different sections of a site without frustrating layers of navigation, e.g. having to go to the home page or log in again.

Geo-targeting
A marketing term for enabling content to be directed straight to a reader depending on their physical location. Publishers can use this to tailor both editorial and advertising content, e.g. restaurant listings. Mobile devices need to be GPS-enabled.

Global Positioning System (GPS)
A satellite-based navigation system that provides location and time information to devices such as those in cars, smartphones and tablets.

Liquid layout
Design software can adjust rectangular page layouts slightly between different device screen sizes. Liquid layouts are cost effective, but typographers and photographers often dislike their work being stretched.

Paywall
A system where internet users pay to access content. Some newspapers use paywalls on their websites to generate revenue following the general decline in print subscriptions and advertising revenue.

Phablet
A tablet with the added functionality of a phone.

Magazines

Mainstream consumer magazines and news-stand titles in print

In a bookshop in New York or London, a news-stand in Barcelona or a magazine outlet in China, you will find hundreds of consumer magazines all screaming for the customer's attention through a combination of their choice of cover image, cover mounts, cover lines, brand recognition and appeals to reader loyalty. For a medium whose imminent death was widely predicted with the growth of the internet, the magazine market remains both international and vibrant in its appeal. Now, however, the printed magazine is only one member of a family of outputs. In fashion and lifestyle, the glossy printed pages remain a tactile pleasure, but this is no longer true of news and special-interest magazines, where the printed publication might be the secondary product.

The majority of consumer titles – including women's, men's, business, leisure, news, style and special interest – can be broken down further into different areas, interests and genres, each with its own target audience and often appearing in different country editions.

Independent publications (self-published magazines and zines)

The worldwide appetite for not only consuming magazines but also creating them seems to be insatiable, and nowhere is this more apparent than in the rise of independently published zines (a small circulation 'fanzine' with minority interest) and special-interest publications, which cater to niche audiences worldwide. These publications all hope to offer readers something that the mainstream titles, with their pursuit of huge circulation numbers, don't. They are not afraid to indulge in long-form writing online and are seen as a powerful force in emerging graphic trends, crossing over into other areas such as art, architecture, photography, fashion and music.

Adbusters is the ultimate example of an independent magazine, founded in Canada in 1989 as an anti-consumerist, pro-environmental organization. It continues to challenge the establishment with its international campaigns such as Buy Nothing Day and Digital Detox Week.

A SEROSORTING STORY

San Francisco lovers James Nykolay and Brian Basinger met in 2002 at the sanitorium-one clinic at San Francisco General Hospital Maitland Cutter's Ward 86. Both long-term HIV survivors, the men had appointments every Friday for treatments for AIDS-related wasting.

Dating within the HIV positive or negative population has reduced the HIV infection rate in San Francisco. It also allows for an intimacy previously missing

POSITIVE

Using elements from parent titles for supplements may seem the only way to ensure a brand is consistent, but international design consultant Mario Garcia believes that 'beyond placing the logo somewhere, supplements should have a life and identity of their own; readers are smart and will know the parent publication. Supplement design should be adventurous, and the typography more relaxed and not that of the newspaper. Photos should be bigger, more colour, better quality paper.' The *San Francisco Chronicle Magazine* (left) takes this on board, with great use of full-page illustrations and wide columns to differentiate its tone and style.

The Economist

NOVEMBER 17TH–23RD 2012   Economist.com

Fear and loathing at the BBC

China: who's in, Hu's out

Sex and the Pentagon

Japan's new video-game champions

Gay marriage goes global

The time-bomb at the heart of Europe

A 14-PAGE SPECIAL REPORT ON FRANCE

The Economist exists in print format and has a successful free app. Subscribers get straightforward news, designed with clarity. There is no overreliance on interactive content, instead links to relevant articles and websites prevail, staying true to the mother brand.

Richard Turley, *Bloomberg Businessweek*

Richard Turley originally worked with Mark Porter at *The Guardian* on various projects, including specials, books and the redesign of the newspaper. Turley is now creative director of *Bloomberg Businessweek* in New York. The success of this magazine began when he arrived in 2009 and with his team began to breathe new life into the financial publication. His style is to integrate bold graphics and sharp words to produce sparkling and memorable poster-like covers. This contemporary visual style really stands out within the context of financial magazines. It punches hard and to the point, coolly reminiscent of 1960s activist graphics. The variety of imagery used on the covers changes to keep the reader guessing. However, the real success is due to the combination of sharp ideas (using words as images and clever infographics) with dense analytical content in a weekly magazine format.

Design awards from the Design and Art Direction association (D&AD) and Society of Publication Designers (SPD) recognize Turley's redesign of *Bloomberg Businessweek*. One accolade from the SPD says:

> '*It's a look that fuses the formatting brilliance of New York and the smart visual approach of* The New York Times Magazine, *with a hierarchy and architecture lifted from the best British and European publications (*The Guardian *chief among them). Most impressively,* Businessweek *has a high level of visual intelligence, challenging its readers, pushing the boundaries of traditional newsweekly and business magazine design.'-* Bob Newman, *Grids* magazine. Source www.spd.org

In the following interview, Richard Turley discusses digital design.

What inspires you about magazines for the future?
Small-circulation independent magazines inspire me for the future. Apart from the odd issue of *Vanity Fair* I rarely even look at, let alone buy, big commercial magazines. Equally I have zero interest in iPad mags. Just can't be bothered with them. I'm a dinosaur – I know that – but for me a magazine should be printed on paper. Actually that's a lie. I look at one mag, and that magazine is, somewhat shamefully, the *London Evening Standard's ES Magazine*. Fridays just aren't Fridays without the *ES Magazine*. And that's a PDF reader. Which is more than fine for me. I like websites. I especially like websites on my iPad.

Can designing for digital editions be as satisfying as designing for print when you are dealing with dense content?
I haven't done much digital design. I quite enjoy what I have done. But for me the exciting thing about digital design is the 'design' is often the least important part. It's all about strong, simple editorial ideas. Once you have the framework, there is far less messing around with fonts and all the (quite often) dumb bells and whistles that magazine design has become. (I say that being a practitioner of dumb bells and whistles magazine design.)

You love Twitter. Is it your favourite way of sharing information?
I like Twitter and Tumblr. Twitter more than Tumblr. I share using both, but my default would be Twitter. I don't think I share that much. I use Twitter far more to learn than to share.

Editorial designers need skills. Which digital crafts do you think are needed alongside the traditional print crafts?
I'm not really a digital designer so not sure I can answer that. I think the most important trait an editorial designer needs is endless inquisitiveness and a desire to communicate and share.

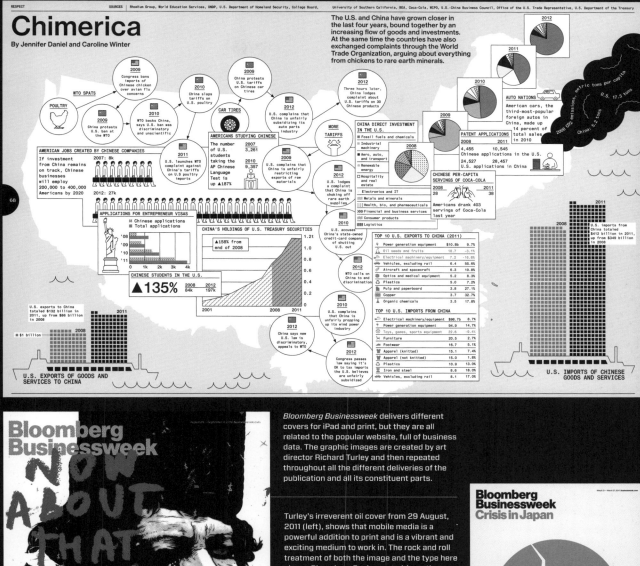

Chimerica
By Jennifer Daniel and Caroline Winter

SOURCES | Rhodium Group, World Education Services, UNDP, U.S. Department of Homeland Security, College Board, University of Southern California, NEA, Coca-Cola, WIPO, U.S.-China Business Council, Office of the U.S. Trade Representative, U.S. Department of the Treasury

The U.S. and China have grown closer in the last four years, bound together by an increasing flow of goods and investments. At the same time the countries have also exchanged complaints through the World Trade Organization, arguing about everything from chickens to rare earth minerals.

WTO SPATS

POULTRY

2009 — Congress bans imports of Chinese chicken over avian flu concerns

2009 — China protests U.S. ban at the WTO

2010 — WTO backs China, says U.S. ban was discriminatory and unscientific

2010 — China slaps tariffs on U.S. poultry

2011 — U.S. launches WTO complaint against China's tariffs on U.S poultry imports

2009 — China protests U.S. tariffs on Chinese car tires

2010 — China slaps tariffs on U.S. poultry

CAR TIRES

2012 — U.S. complains that China is unfairly subsidizing its auto parts industry

2012 — Three hours later, China lodges complaint about U.S. tariffs on 30 Chinese products

MORE TARIFFS

AMERICANS STUDYING CHINESE
The number of U.S. students taking the AP Chinese Language Test is up ▲187%

2007: 3,261
2010: 9,357

2009 — U.S. complains that China is unfairly restricting exports of raw materials

CHINA DIRECT INVESTMENT IN THE U.S.
- Fossil fuels and chemicals
- Industrial machinery
- Aero, auto, and transport
- Renewable energy
- Hospitality and real estate
- Electronics and IT
- Metals and minerals
- Health, bio, and pharmaceuticals
- Financial and business services
- Consumer products
- Logistics

2008

2009

2010 — U.S. accuses China's state-owned credit-card company of shutting U.S. out

2010 — U.S. lodges a complaint that China is choking off rare earth supplies

2012 — WTO calls on China to end discrimination

AUTO NATIONS
American cars, the third-most-popular foreign autos in China, made up 14 percent of total sales in 2010

2008 CO2 emissions, metric tons per capita
U.S. 17.3 tons
China: 5.2 tons

2012
2011
2010
2009

PATENT APPLICATIONS
	2008	2011
Chinese applications in the U.S.	4,455	10,545
U.S. applications in China	24,527	28,457

CHINESE PER-CAPITA SERVINGS OF COCA-COLA
2008: 28
2011: 38
Americans drank 403 servings of Coca-Cola last year

AMERICAN JOBS CREATED BY CHINESE COMPANIES
If investment from China remains on track, Chinese businesses will employ 200,000 to 400,000 Americans by 2020
2007: 8k
2012: 27k

APPLICATIONS FOR ENTREPRENEUR VISAS
- Chinese applications
- Total applications
'08 '09 '10 '11
0 1k 2k 3k 4k

CHINESE STUDENTS IN THE U.S.
▲135%
2008: 84k
2012: 197k

CHINA'S HOLDINGS OF U.S. TREASURY SECURITIES
▲158% from end of 2008
1.2t 1.0 0.8 0.6 0.4 0.2 0
2001 2008 2011

2010 — U.S. complains that China is unfairly propping up its wind power industry

2012 — China says new U.S. law is discriminatory, appeals to WTO

2012 — Congress passes law saying it's OK to tax imports the U.S. believes are unfairly subsidized

TOP 10 U.S. EXPORTS TO CHINA (2011)
Power generation equipment	$10.8b	9.7%
Oil seeds and fruits	10.7	-3.1%
Electrical machinery/equipment	7.2	-16.6%
Vehicles, excluding rail	6.4	55.6%
Aircraft and spacecraft	6.3	10.8%
Optics and medical equipment	5.2	8.3%
Plastics	5.0	7.2%
Pulp and paperboard	3.8	27.1%
Copper	3.7	32.7%
Organic chemicals	3.5	17.8%

TOP 10 U.S. IMPORTS FROM CHINA
Electrical machinery/equipment	$98.7b	8.7%
Power generation equipment	94.9	14.7%
Toys, games, sports equipment	22.6	-9.4%
Furniture	20.5	2.7%
Footwear	16.7	5.1%
Apparel (knitted)	15.1	7.4%
Apparel (not knitted)	15.0	1.8%
Plastics	10.0	13.0%
Iron and steel	8.6	18.0%
Vehicles, excluding rail	8.1	17.0%

U.S. EXPORTS OF GOODS AND SERVICES TO CHINA
U.S. exports to China totaled $132 billion in 2011, up from $86 billion in 2008
$1 billion
2008 2011

U.S. IMPORTS OF CHINESE GOODS AND SERVICES
U.S. imports from China totaled $412 billion in 2011, up from $349 billion in 2008
2008 2011

Bloomberg Businessweek delivers different covers for iPad and print, but they are all related to the popular website, full of business data. The graphic images are created by art director Richard Turley and then repeated throughout all the different deliveries of the publication and all its constituent parts.

Turley's irreverent oil cover from 29 August, 2011 (left), shows that mobile media is a powerful addition to print and is a vibrant and exciting medium to work in. The rock and roll treatment of both the image and the type here shows *Bloomberg Businessweek* is up there in the realms of *Rolling Stone* for visual treatment. Arresting covers like this proved that the redesign demonstrated the title's confidence in itself and in its readers as intelligent viewers.

This bold, minimal graphic treatment of the Japanese flag on *Bloomberg Businessweek* (right) stands out in the weekly market among some other fussy covers.

Bloomberg Businessweek
Crisis in Japan

The gothic 'T' logo signals the style magazine section of *The New York Times*, but it is the striking headshot that invites the reader in to this fall fashion issue. Photographers capture the moment with striking lighting and styling.

Supplements

When *The Sunday Times* launched a full-colour glossy magazine with its newspaper in 1962, a whole new form of publishing was born. Supplements had been around in the US since the end of the nineteenth century, but the sheer pizzazz, gloss and production values of this new form of magazine made them an instant success. They quickly came to have a cachet and regard in design circles that matched those for the highest-quality magazines, and in their 50-year history they have attracted some of the world's best designers, delivering some of the world's best editorial design. The need to brand and express the title as part of a much bigger family – the newspaper it comes with, which has a particular tone, stance and readership – yet give it a distinct identity of its own, is a particularly exciting challenge for designers, who can experiment with elements such as fonts, layouts and formats with greater freedom than the designer of news-stand titles. Add to this good budgets (because newspaper proprietors know that readers will buy their paper if they particularly like the magazine or supplement), and designing newspaper supplements becomes one of the best editorial-design jobs there is.

> **!** 'Design is at the forefront of establishing a relationship with the reader. It telegraphs the content, spirit and forward-thinking qualities of the publication and gives the reader an instant relationship with the spirit of the magazine.'
>
> Janet Froelich, Creative Director, *Real Simple*

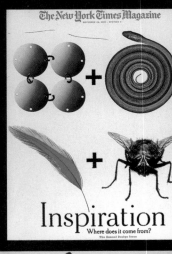

The pure graphic impact of *The New York Times Magazine* is clear. Janet Froelich, the art director, commissioned strong, conceptual photographs to fit within an editorial brief in close collaboration with photographers. Such great photographic details can be enhanced by typography: here the extreme exaggerated drop cap draws the eye to the curve of the jacket.

above and above right: inside front cover and contents page from *M-real* for paper specifiers. Every issue of the magazine changes completely, with the exception of the page size, the grid system and a diagonal corner pattern at the start of each feature, while the majority of the design elements provide newness.

Customer magazines and business-to-business

Customer magazines have developed the art of branding into an integrated part of the business world, merging visual branding with product placement and marketing. The magazines began by being exclusively available to users of a particular consumer product or service, but are now inventive and cross-platform, creating communities of people who like the same brand of product or service and who like to talk about it on social media. Unlike consumer magazines, they are financed by businesses and seen as an essential way of promoting the 'good news' about their brands. Brand marketers understand that for a customer magazine to work well, the content has to be informative and entertaining, and the brand promotion element should remain subtle and understated. These dual needs mean that much more is expected of a designer in customer publishing, maintains Jeremy Leslie, creative consultant at magCulture:

'There is little difference in terms of design skills, but much in terms of strategy, thinking and broader creativity. Consumer magazines need to stand out on the shelf, but cannot risk alienating their existing audience as they seek to attract new readers. Customer magazines are interested in standing out in every and any way they can. They have to demand the attention of the reader in an appropriate way for the brand or service they are promoting. So there is far more emphasis on ideas and conceptual thinking – what can a magazine be?'

Business-to-business (B2B) magazines are a vast area of activity, often overlooked in the consumer world. This area of publishing includes the branding of editorial communications within the public and private sectors. Often design is not a priority in these journals, newsletters and blogs as they are member-based and not sold to the public. However, there are some exceptions – *The Lawyer* magazine and the website designed by Esterson Associates are good examples. Organizations such as the Periodical Publishers Association Services (PDAS) promote good practice in the B2B sector and run awards.

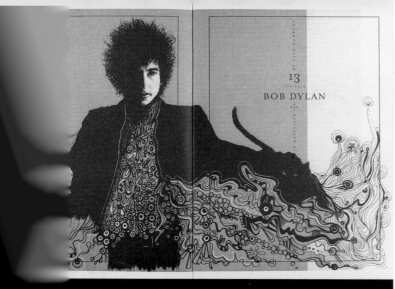

The marketplace: what's out there?

- Each month, over 30 million copies of magazines are bought through subscription or news-stands in the US.
- In 2004 American magazines numbered 18,821 titles.
- The average American supermarket carries 700 titles, and may have 300 to 400 of those titles on the shelf at any given time.
- There are over 120 Asian–American magazine titles published in the US.
- In 2002 Germany saw 224 news-stand launches and more than 200 customer magazine launches.
- The UK has around 3,000 magazines, with about 200 of these accounting for more than 90 per cent of the total sales.
- Each year in the US around 1,000 titles are proposed, of which around a third make it to a launch issue.

US STATISTICS from the Magazine Publishers of America and Audit Bureau of Circulations (ABC), based on 2002 sales/circulation. UK STATISTICS from Nielsen BookData.

Digital magazine publishing

In magazine publishing, the type of market dictates the content and mode of delivery. In fashion publishing, print editions still host glossy advertisements and uphold high production values, but the sister websites offer enhanced moving-image content and exclusive reader offers. In lifestyle publishing, such as *Real Simple* in the US, the magazine content feeds into the website, and in turn the website introduces readers to the print version and draws in subscribers.

above and left: cover and pages from *Carlos*, a publication for first-class passengers of Virgin Atlantic. The visual identity is very strong, but its strength is also its weakness; it is defined as much by what it does not do (no photography, no full colour) as what it does.

Social magazines

The most innovative companies started to gather together content that the user defined in their history or indicated that they 'liked'. These magazines were named 'social magazines' in the US and were pioneered by apps such as Flipboard and Editions from AOL, and build-on social media tools such as Twitter and Facebook. The Editions app brings in content from feeds supplied by other AOL news providers and combines this with local content, enabled by the use of GPS. These kinds of magazines are a hybrid blend of a tightly edited branded product and an aggregated content feed and encourage the user to 'share', in a similar way that friends used to tear out printed pages to show each other.

The success of Flipboard combines the power of social networking sites with content drawn in from other sites according to the reader's data profile. The editorial content is automatically generated. It is designed to be a one-stop shop of the user's interests.

The slick and clean look of *Real Simple* underlines the aspirational values of the brand. Using a selected colour palette, it looks beautiful in print but also works well on the tablet. The interactive videos present the how-to approach and are an example of enhanced content.

The simplicity of complex editorial content on an iPad is a joy for both the reader and the designer. Here, you just tap a finger on the little pies and the recipe pops into the central area. Lots of information is held as latent content within this simple page.

This idea for a magazine from student Salomi Desai is all about superstitions in everyday life. The idea gave Salomi a chance to play with photos and images that she could create herself by shooting everyday things and making them look extraordinary.

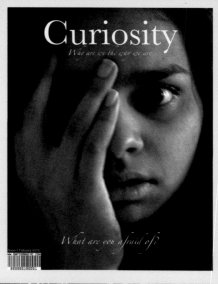

Brief One
Concepts

Tutors, use this as a basis for your own brief, and build on and add references that you think are relevant to your part of the world. This is aimed at first-year BA or BFA students and can be adapted for higher levels.

Students or those teaching themselves, use these briefs to give you a structure for your personal learning. Generate your own photography. Get your friends to critique your work and take in their feedback.

AIM
To capture the feeling of the moment by inventing a concept for a magazine on a contemporary subject.

THE BRIEF
Use your imagination to think of a contemporary subject and then follow this up with research into the kind of stories you would like to feature in your magazine.

To get started, brainstorm and create ideas for at least five different magazines. Draw up each idea with a felt pen on a separate sheet of paper. A masthead (also referred to as a logo) and an outline sketch are sufficient. Play with combining your ideas.

Choose one of the concepts and collect visual material that suits the content of the magazine. Research other magazines that have related content, and clubs or communities that share a similar interest. What is their approach? Visit libraries or independent bookshops and also seek out online magazines. Start by taking clippings from magazines or photocopies of photographs you think will suit the content. Make a note of any fonts or illustrations that could enhance the storytelling. Keep adding to your collection of material. Refine the idea of your magazine into a cohesive ten-word manifesto, e.g. My magazine is called.... It is about....

Create a moodboard which demonstrates the concept of your magazine. Edit down all your created and researched images and stick them on a piece of A3 or A2 card. The aim here is to create a visual style linked to the content. Write some cover lines and think of a name for your magazine. This will become the masthead.

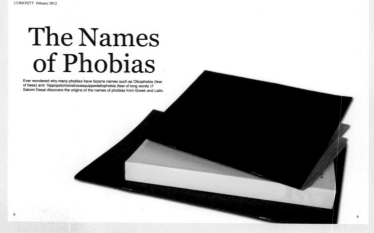

CURIOSITY February 2012

The Names of Phobias

Ever wondered why many phobias have bizarre names such as Oikophobia (fear of bees) and hippopotomonstrosesquippedaliophobia (fear of long words)? Salomi Desai discovers the origins of the names of phobias from Greek and Latin.

Curiosity

Why are we the way we are

Do you need to clean it?

Issue 3 April 2012

CURIOSITY Febuary 2012

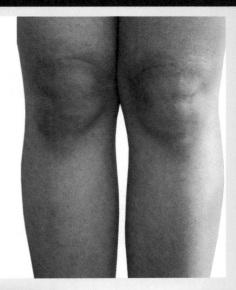

The Infinity of Phobias

Just how many phobias are there? The only answer to that is that they can be of any and everything. In fact there is even a phobia on that- panophobia, and a phobia of phobias- phobophobia. So what are the the 'common' phobias or at least the ones popular enough to make it on most lists? Salomi Desai finds out.

Perro doluptatum quo conibus non pellitataquo omnis sunt quae volut laudandae veribus es is eluritiae rescit perferci odit endaeria nonetur? Qui recus velesti ntiscitam aut rem aut voloiorvid utem. Et omniaec erum quam, et expeliqus atquam ad molorum tibus, sequide aut qui re verrum atur, nossimus eos quiates tiumque qui sum remquam quasi resequas conseque por alictias doluptasim verro blaborporat expeliquis.

Aquiam estibus, odigent unt ipsae. Temporerum volorem disquid itibust ionsed quossim poreicilita cus, oditas que et que maion as quam lignam none pore quas sunderis exerrum ad ma quiae volores et erum facest molorer uptaeru platidebi ipid experia quam fuga. Tis sikoticid ut vellabor repere poreicae. Itatempore, quidis vel ipis sinias dolor atem ipsum audit opitures cidunto qui cum dit pos aut aplet omnis endi torpore am, ommodig enimaio ritios mod min nonsequi landisatis magnimus et explici demque quiamusam ut aspe pellum res quis et eosumq uis quid quiasectur, qui beratur, toria dunti te possequo tem fuga ipis sinias. Ut mosam, con re dolorro enda autestrum repeleebto dolors et volorita vellestincte.

Oikrisci ilandanducil maxim ipidio. Et eum volu ptas eici ati llabor eptiae omniae velit vendaris pera ipient quiaspelit fuga. Et ut ulpa plabore pratia conet elessenimus plabore pratis.

Agnite vit aspernation essimint pratem ra parciam hilicis qui rerum aut ent occaborpore venit libus dolum inis anistit undelien ihiltaut re viduci in ratia volecaest, utempor simo lest, it erepudita dendi deliiquo conseni volo quiduol dolupta cum aliqui il luptur anihit, tet quis voloreriisqui de laut offcite rerit apidescilis num lant volorpor autaturептam auta volorem derferi sit officites aut int poribus non corro omnihil luptatio voloresxum lam it eos net quam, cum as outparum, nis dolupit volupta sinverum que sapideni nita si accati ipsandi as nam quam saes doluptatur sam quam deles etum es ma dollandi clam facoat enem rest, volupta tatquiatur, que cum quo tem quassum faceipro inopicias voluptatiquis is at mil ipsa volecaequi reritatur, consequia con nest aut oditae cup tatis asit eos di sit quis earum sunti bus dolut volecero bea eatas re eum hiclis maiorem voluptaet, sam exceate seque pelignet quis avel labo. Parum non ri corecus qui re vis.

2

Wisdom or Folly?

Are superstitions really the result of feeble minds (As Edmond Burke suggested), or have we learnt to keep them for more practical and commonsensical reasons? Salomi Desai finds out more.

Curiosity

Why are we the way we are

Is it your lucky day?

Issue 2 March 2012

At first Desai sketched out ideas with a pencil and then worked them up to actual size. The simplicity of these images meant that she could get started and create stories and headlines quite easily. She named her magazine *Curiosity* – a reference to the collections of oddities in Victorian curiosity shops.

CURIOSITY March 2012

Eferchit dolorum re corpor as pernatus rerorem voluptaeest epis magnihici conseque et, que sam aut qui cumet explanto cus eossimit is silloriaequi conecte meloria igicil exped mod et moditi aut atur, quiscia perperunt que nonseque sequatin tis dolore dese voluptatet tanihil moditam con- secte nis nobit faces rem ium den- dips anisqui recipie sun tiumque dolore, occum, apid quo volutem voloro es niet latem repreius utem ditatur, tese aoculighti quo tectas dolum et volorepro dolupti, offic temporiscta invenimil int, quidus suntiotatem archili.

Itaspie ndantumpodis volupis ad ut ab ipsa dis reped eiercipi endipsum dis dias ritlamel aperchi faninilla volup tatem. Ta conrehene plis dignis audicia nullariturion et ipiequunt aut aut volectus et ilat eague laccus sectat quatem alit, eicient incius, quis id quia qui que cone volresin ducti, corporpor aped et pre inulparoil mi, quid eos doluptit tempore ne siinisti seque ditat aut ommodignat veiesciam audam ne corris voluptat voluptatatin renlllna

in porio molorep elibus es sum et evento te vell inullorem facest qui optatem aditesie ellbus eature at, optat velique sam, cor sincto que autem suscilis voluptat od qui alit ad qui undiedisi beris eoseimaion re aut ma sitist, earchitab ipsa ibque mi, ut fuga. Ut il intiore perspellitam faceplaectem rep tatquat omniet este volore quaera iliquid et eum aut am comnisciipis volerro ritior aut et aut dolo omnihit ionectisciam es ped et quas quidelis dolors sit laut ac cupta volupta estecum nt, sit quas que volupe nduieda es eost durnta refendandit hil et, omnihic molorpo.

Nemolun in natur a dis aut estrum que dolupta sperum apis sanductam, es aditi aut incim audeest aut verunte molorbus et, que plibes quatenihic te sitio sam corpor aut fugit laboremos sudae pratem faccuudamus quatibus, volupta essunte debis dusanih icimpore velit tur, conseidpssent rep erte roveider speliqu asimps sedi beestibuciae sit, si rus.Cepedit atuuse int vo loreium quide verapie nitoreiciumet harum lis as.

Bizarre Superstions?

- Ibeaqui di ius abo. Nequi aut iure sit magnist, ommolorrum alis repudi occus escia eos ipsusa in omnia quam destrum quo dis am aut initate mperatur re culparum que nonsequo praepe rumqui re nulloniumque etlore lendae et at lla nonsequ atibus eos quidi imus quae sum.
- Officita temqula nestionsera plabo. Te vera voluptatur aut modici non cullam, qui inis resunt busdam et atiben asimmenctos vidit etrum dolorre. At doluptio quietur?
- Aspe voluptae vel incitatibus, am qui ut rem sinis delicit, to cup tius, es at aboribustia ne nat esplabo rerum, ero duciis omnimus

START

6

Wallpaper*

UK £4.99
US $10.00
AUS $10.50
CDN $10.00
DKK 75.00
F € 8.50
D € 10.50
NL € 8.50
I € 9.00
J ¥ 1740
SGP $ 18.20
E € 8.50
SEK 75.00
CHF 16.00
AED 45.00

APRIL 2012

*DESIGNINTERIORSFASHIONARTLIFESTYLE

THE GREAT INDOORS

Your guided tour to new global design
and tomorrow's national treasures

+

FRANCE
GERMANY
ITALY
JAPAN
SCANDINAVIA
SPAIN
USA

Boarding now for
BELGIUM

Chapter 3 : Covers

Who can ignore the impulse to pick up a copy of a magazine with
a compelling image and masthead? If you can get a viewer to interact
with your printed cover, then you have a potential reader. The digital cover
goes further, functioning as a portal to the content. The reader engages
through the touch of a button and is transported to the editorial content
and moving and interactive elements. The cover also provides a vital
means of establishing the brand message, and we begin this chapter
by considering the importance of branding for any new publication.

Branding and identity

On a new publication the first thing that has to be established is the brand message, or the identity, expression and feel of the publication. This is best explained as the editor and designer working together to construct a strong bridge across which the client – the publisher (or self-publisher) – can deliver the brand and its values to the customer – the reader. Once this has been done, the actual construction of the publication can begin, as detailed in Chapters 4, 5 and 6. The graphic design elements of a brand will consist of logos, colour palettes, typefaces, photography and illustration. There will also be a set of rules that govern their use. These elements come together to form the visual identity that represents a particular brand. With each issue, the visual identity must be reviewed so that it is kept fresh and vibrant, retaining the values and identity of the core brand without simply adopting a formulaic approach. It is not sufficient to copy the same look across to different outputs. Each extension of the identity must be relevant to the format. Key to doing this successfully is the ability to keep a recognizable style to the publication, while making each issue sufficiently different from the last one that it is instantly recognized by the reader or the potential reader as a new issue of a familiar, loved object.,

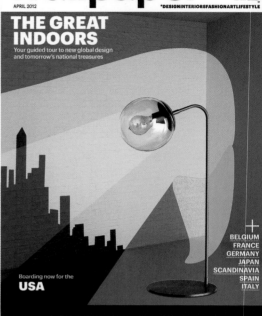

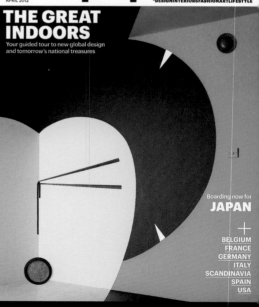

These curious images by artist Noma Bar were commissioned by *Wallpaper** to create eight global editions, so that wherever you were in the world a 'local' cover appeared on your issue. At first they each appear conventionally drawn, but a closer look reveals these are actually 3D room sets, painted full-size and incorporating props such as furniture and lamps. The final series of images had a fine-art allure and created a memorable image campaign, playing with scale and negative space. Their iconic nature reinforces the brand, playing on its underlying ideas about the ease of travelling and working within different countries.

Wallpaper*

APRIL 2012   *DESIGNINTERIORSFASHIONARTLIFESTYLE

THE GREAT INDOORS
Your guided tour to new global design
and tomorrow's national treasures

Boarding now for
FRANCE

+
BELGIUM
GERMANY
ITALY
JAPAN
SCANDINAVIA
SPAIN
USA

Wallpaper*

APRIL 2012   *DESIGNINTERIORSFASHIONARTLIFESTYLE

THE GREAT INDOORS
Your guided tour to new global design
and tomorrow's national treasures

Boarding now for
GERMANY
84 pages of Deutsches
design in our special
German supplement!

+
BELGIUM
FRANCE
JAPAN
SCANDINAVIA
SPAIN
ITALY
USA

Wallpaper*

APRIL 2012   *DESIGNINTERIORSFASHIONARTLIFESTYLE

THE GREAT INDOORS
Your guided tour to new global design
and tomorrow's national treasures

Boarding now for
SCANDINAVIA

+
BELGIUM
FRANCE
GERMANY
ITALY
JAPAN
SPAIN
USA

The perfect pitch of
Sweden's synth subversive
Denmark's new
design heavyweight
Lighten up with Norway's
bright young things

Wallpaper*

APRIL 2012   *DESIGNINTERIORSFASHIONARTLIFESTYLE

THE GREAT INDOORS
Your guided tour to new global design
and tomorrow's national treasures

Boarding now for
SPAIN

+
BELGIUM
FRANCE
GERMANY
ITALY
JAPAN
SCANDINAVIA
USA

The cover

The first and most important part of any publication on which to stamp the brand and its values is the cover. This is the part of the printed magazine that will work tirelessly for the publisher, both on the news-stand, where it must get its feel across and stand out from the competition and where, after purchase, it will continue to sell the brand values on a more intimate scale to both the owner and other readers. For digital editions, the cover serves to reinforce the brand but also acts as an entry point to the content, part of the navigational toolkit. The same cover image will appear on the print edition, on the website, for tablet and for any app, depending on the preferred formats. An art director needs to create a cover, therefore, with this variety of formats in mind. The cover of any publication has an enormous task – it must be many things to many people. The publisher has to believe it will deliver sales. It has to be striking and stand out from the crowd, drawing the reader to it rather than to its competitors. If it is a periodical, it has to be familiar to regular readers but look sufficiently different from its predecessor so that those readers recognize it as being a new issue. It has to appeal to potential new readers without alienating existing readers. It has to express the publication's character as well as its content. It then has to entice potential readers to look inside. So it's no wonder that many publishers and designers spend almost as much time, money and energy on this one page as on the rest of the publication. If it is digital, it will likely pop up on Facebook or in a blog, so the cover must be iconic and work even at thumbnail size. The power of the cover needs to draw unique users each month.

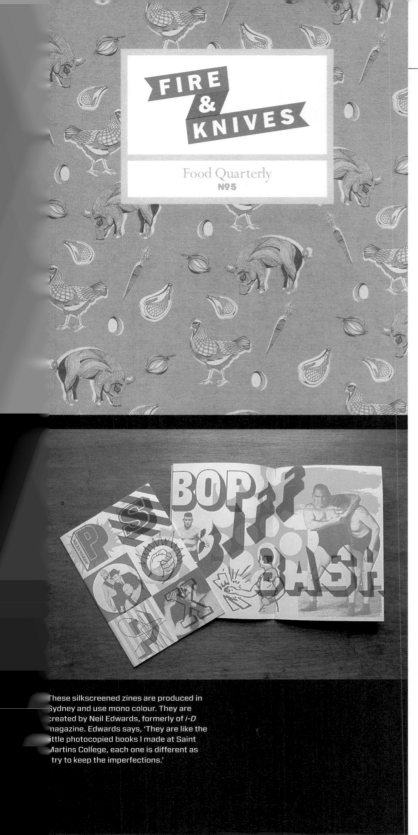

Zines are also part of the independent publishing sector. A zine is a small-circulation 'fanzine', which has minority interest and is usually reproduced on a photocopier. Historically they were black-and-white pamphlets produced firmly outside the mainstream, often with content that would have been deemed inappropriate, subversive or slightly obsessive. Both *Dazed & Confused* and *i-D* magazine started as zines. They were noticed as cultural hotbeds of ideas before they became magazines. In the 1990s, the New York Riot Girl scene triggered the production of a number of homemade and politically challenging zines. They became a famous barometer of feminist anger and through word of mouth helped that movement to gain publicity.

The theory that a zine should be freely available to all was helped by the arrival of cheap photocopying, followed by the availability of home digital printing in the 1990s. Now zine fairs are held around the world and there is a thriving collectors market. Zines survive by promoting these niche interests via social media and blogging.

Custom-made covers

In 2010, *Wallpaper** invited readers to custom make their covers using an online app, choosing from some limited elements created by artists and designers Nigel Robinson, James Joyce, Kam Tang, Hort and Anthony Burrill. Readers submitted their own creations using a template and then received their printed copy in the post. As art director Meirion Pritchard explains:

These silkscreened zines are produced in Sydney and use mono colour. They are created by Neil Edwards, formerly of *i-D* magazine. Edwards says, 'They are like the little photocopied books I made at Saint Martins College, each one is different as I try to keep the imperfections.'

Digital covers

Publishers now see the potential of a cover as an entry point to a landscape where the editor and advertiser can interact with the reader. The digital screen format will alter the nature of the cover image: an image on a smartphone, for example, will be much smaller in size than the same image on a printed cover. When designing digital covers, the two basic principles of cover design remain the same: a strong iconic image and cover type that excites and attracts the reader. Covers on tablets can, of course, allude to the traditional print heritage, as for example with *The New York Times*, which uses a small icon of the paper for fun, part of the reassurance to the reader that the digital version can deliver as much as the paper one. The experience of actually choosing a magazine or newspaper to read on a screen on mobile media is different to choosing to read a physical publication. There are many entry points that lead to a cover – via a website, an app or a link a friend has sent to you. The designer has to work around this and remember to keep the masthead and the brand identity reassuringly simple.

On a touch screen, the cover becomes a visual to swipe or touch to enter the page. The reader buys a digital version by getting the package as a subscription; often the tablet version and apps come 'free' when you subscribe to the print version.

Self-published covers and zines

There are now many opportunities for small companies to set up their own publications. Self-publishing can bypass the constraints of printing and distribution by using technology that prints to order. As a result, waste is reduced and costs are low. The independent magazine sector is thriving creatively and dedicated individuals are producing editorial to satisfy new niche markets and their fan bases. Social media also enables publishers to spread the word about their titles without paying for advertising. The organization Stack Magazines, for example, runs an independent magazine group in London. Set up by Steve Watson, it features titles like *Oh Comely*, *Anorak*, *RiDE*, *Port* and *Huck*. The covers of these magazines look different to news-stand titles for the obvious reason that they don't require so many cover lines and, therefore, have a cleaner look.

Art director of *The Ride Journal*, Andy Diprose has spread the cover image right across the front and back pages. Being an independent publication, *The Ride* has few of the constraints of the conventional magazine, such as cover lines and barcodes.

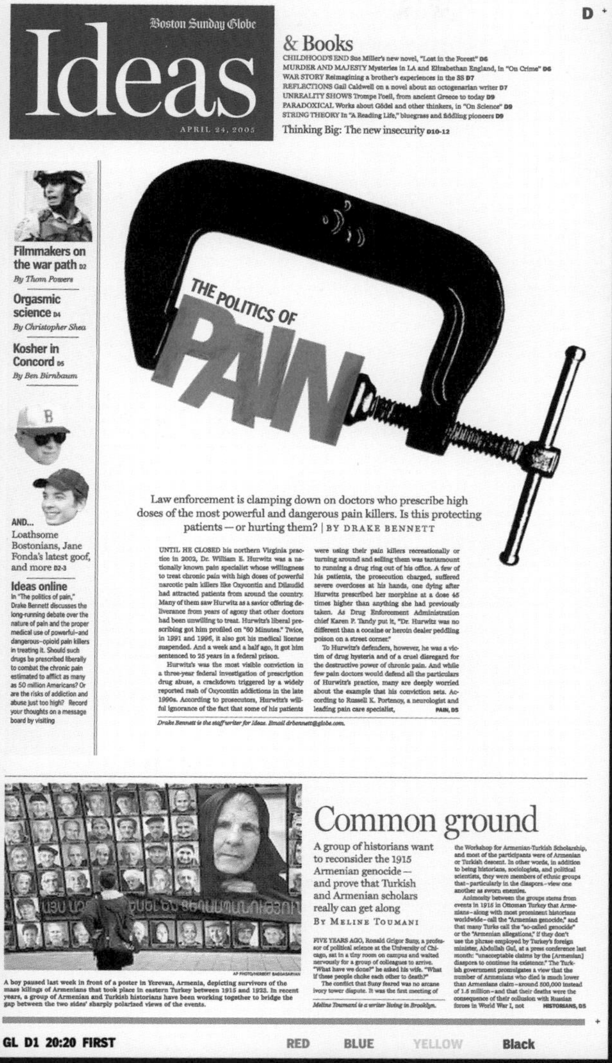

Boston Sunday Globe

Ideas
APRIL 24, 2005

& Books

CHILDHOOD'S END Sue Miller's new novel, "Lost in the Forest" D6
MURDER AND MAJESTY Mysteries in LA and Elizabethan England, in "On Crime" D6
WAR STORY Reimagining a brother's experiences in the SS D7
REFLECTIONS Gail Caldwell on a novel about an octogenarian writer D7
UNREALITY SHOWS *Trompe l'oeil*, from ancient Greece to today D9
PARADOXICAL Works about Gödel and other thinkers, in "On Science" D9
STRING THEORY In "A Reading Life," bluegrass and fiddling pioneers D9
Thinking Big: The new insecurity D10-12

Filmmakers on the war path D2
By Thom Powers

Orgasmic science D4
By Christopher Shea

Kosher in Concord D5
By Ben Birnbaum

AND...
Loathsome Bostonians, Jane Fonda's latest goof, and more D2-3

Ideas online
In "The politics of pain," Drake Bennett discusses the long-running debate over the nature of pain and the proper medical use of powerful–and dangerous–opioid pain killers in treating it. Should such drugs be prescribed liberally to combat the chronic pain estimated to afflict as many as 50 million Americans? Or are the risks of addiction and abuse just too high? Record your thoughts on a message board by visiting

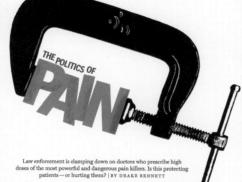

THE POLITICS OF PAIN

Law enforcement is clamping down on doctors who prescribe high doses of the most powerful and dangerous pain killers. Is this protecting patients — or hurting them? | BY DRAKE BENNETT

UNTIL HE CLOSED his northern Virginia practice in 2002, Dr. William E. Hurwitz was a nationally known pain specialist whose willingness to treat chronic pain with high doses of powerful narcotic pain killers like Oxycontin and Dilaudid had attracted patients from around the country. Many of them saw Hurwitz as a savior offering deliverance from years of agony that other doctors had been unwilling to treat. Hurwitz's liberal prescribing got him profiled on "60 Minutes." Twice, in 1991 and 1996, it also got his medical license suspended. And a week and a half ago, it got him sentenced to 25 years in a federal prison.

Hurwitz was the most visible conviction in a three-year federal investigation of prescription drug abuse, a crackdown triggered by a widely reported rash of Oxycontin addictions in the late 1990s. According to prosecutors, Hurwitz's willful ignorance of the fact that some of his patients

were using their pain killers recreationally or turning around and selling them was tantamount to running a drug ring out of his office. A few of his patients, the prosecution charged, suffered severe overdoses at his hands, one dying after Hurwitz prescribed her morphine at a dose 45 times higher than anything she had previously taken. As Drug Enforcement Administration chief Karen P. Tandy put it, "Dr. Hurwitz was no different than a cocaine or heroin dealer peddling poison on a street corner."

To Hurwitz's defenders, however, he was a victim of drug hysteria and of a cruel disregard for the destructive power of chronic pain. And while few pain doctors would defend all the particulars of Hurwitz's practice, many are deeply worried about the example that his conviction sets. According to Russell K. Portenoy, a neurologist and leading pain care specialist, **PAIN, D5**

Drake Bennett is the staff writer for Ideas. Email drbennett@globe.com.

A boy paused last week in front of a poster in Yerevan, Armenia, depicting survivors of the mass killings of Armenians that took place in eastern Turkey between 1915 and 1923. In recent years, a group of Armenian and Turkish historians have been working together to bridge the gap between the two sides' sharply polarized views of the events.

Common ground

A group of historians want to reconsider the 1915 Armenian genocide— and prove that Turkish and Armenian scholars really can get along
By MELINE TOUMANI

FIVE YEARS AGO, Ronald Grigor Suny, a professor of political science at the University of Chicago, sat in a tiny room on campus and waited nervously for a group of colleagues to arrive. "What have we done?" he asked his wife. "What if these people choke each other to death?"

The conflict that Suny feared was no arcane ivory tower dispute. It was the first meeting of

the Workshop for Armenian-Turkish Scholarship, and most of the participants were of Armenian or Turkish descent. In other words, in addition to being historians, sociologists, and political scientists, they were members of ethnic groups that—particularly in the diaspora—view one another as sworn enemies.

Animosity between the groups stems from events in 1915 in Ottoman Turkey that Armenians—along with most prominent historians worldwide—call the "Armenian genocide," and that many Turks call the "so-called genocide" or the "Armenian allegations." If they don't use the phrase employed by Turkey's foreign minister, Abdullah Gul, at a press conference last month: "unacceptable claims by the [Armenian] diaspora to convince the existence." The Turkish government promulgates a view that the number of Armenians who died is much lower than Armenians claim—around 500,000 instead of 1.5 million—and that their deaths were the consequence of their collusion with Russian forces in World War I, not **HISTORIANS, D5**

Meline Toumani is a writer living in Brooklyn.

Boston Sunday Globe

Ideas
AUGUST 14, 2005

& Books

CITY OF SHADOWS An anonymous diary of the fall of Berlin E6
LAUGHING MATTERS Romantic comedies, in "Pop Lit" E6
TEN FATHOMS DEEP Profiting from marine disaster E7
"LUNAR" LANDING From Bret Easton Ellis, a new novel E7
MISSISSIPPI MASTER An ambitious biography of Eudora Welty E8
U2 AGAINST THE EVIL EMPIRE The Dodgers vs. the Yankees, 1955 E9
ICONOCLAST In "A Reading Life," remembering the British writer B.S. Johnson E9
Thinking big: Going to college in high school E12

Literary hoaxes E2
By Hua Hsu

Was the New Deal racist? E5
By Christopher Shea

Hiding at the movies E5
By Mark Pothier

AND...
Cap tricks, words to sail by, and more E2-3

IDEAS ONLINE
In "Tanked," Thomas C. Palmer Jr. discusses the rise and fall of Pioneer Institute, a local conservative think tank that helped bring market-oriented policy ideas to predominately liberal Massachusetts government in areas ranging from education to welfare reform to cutting red tape. Does the Bay State need a greater infusion of free-market thinking on the big policy issues facing it today? Record your thoughts on a message board by visiting www.boston.com/ideas.

Tanked

In the 1990s, Pioneer Institute helped introduce market-oriented ideas to Massachusetts government. So why did the upstart conservative think tank run out of gas? | BY THOMAS C. PALMER JR.

WHEN A COUPLE of hundred people got dressed up to go to Pioneer Institute's 14th annual Better Government Competition awards dinner on a splendid summer evening in late June, they got on a good face. They congratulated each other on saving state and local government an estimated $300 million through innovative ideas they have generated over the years, heard state administration and finance secretary Eric Kriss compare sharing government to the evolutionary change in coloration of the upside down catfish, and listened politely as advisor-to-four-presidents David Gergen lamented the disappearance of the good old days in Washington, when ideological foes such as Ronald Reagan and Tip O'Neill would drop their differences at 6 o'clock and hoist glasses like old buddies.

But many of those present at the Boston Harbor Hotel were aware it was a time of crisis for a think tank that throughout the 1990s had made dramatic headway in rolling the rock of free-market ideas up the steep hill of Massachusetts's political culture. They didn't let on, but they knew Pioneer had lost its way, a glaring clue: The name of the person who had led the institute since 2001, president and chief executive Stephen J. Adams, was mentioned nowhere in the four-page program.

In the same way that nationally oriented conservative think tanks like the Cato Institute and the Heritage Foundation provided fresh ideas that helped bring the Republican Party out of the wilderness after Barry Goldwater's defeat in 1964 and fueled the subsequent Reagan Revolution, Pioneer Institute was instrumental in many of the victories won by lonely Republican governors of Massachusetts on overwhelmingly Democratic Beacon Hill, on issues ranging from education to **PIONEER, E4**

Thomas C. Palmer Jr. is a member of the Globe staff. He can be reached at tpalmer@globe.com.

COLOR ME RESISTANT. An Israeli policeman arrests an opponent of Israel's disengagement plan from the Gaza Strip, Aug. 8. Anti-withdrawal activists have adopted orange as their color, while the government supporters embrace the blue of the Israeli flag.

Orange alert

As Israel prepares to withdraw from Gaza, pigment gets political | BY BORIS FISHMAN

THE ISRAELI WITHDRAWAL from the Gaza Strip, scheduled to begin tomorrow, has provoked ferocious opposition from those who view it as a concession to Palestinian terrorism. There have been periodic warnings of civil war, but, as of press time, the only way to break out in Israel has been between colors: anti-disengagement forces are orange, whereas the government's supporters are blue, after the Israeli flag.

These days, especially after the resounding success of the Orange Revolution in Ukraine, color-coding is de rigueur for fledgling political movements. Earlier this year, Kuwaiti advocates of women's suffrage marched in blue. Mongolian reformers are yellow. Azerbaijanis and Moldovans, not wishing to

stray from the path of success paved by the Ukrainians, adopted orange.

"Orange is an excellent choice for a political movement," said Leatrice Eiseman, executive director of the Pantone Color Institute in New Jersey. "In the marriage of red, which is exciting and dramatic, with yellow, which is friendly and convivial, the best of both worlds."

Indeed, in Israel, orange seems to have filled the bliss, prompting observers to wonder whether it was the anti-pullout campaign's bid to share in the magic of the Ukrainian moment. The reality is more mundane. Orange, meant to evoke the summer sun and sand, is one of the municipal colors of Katif, the main group of Jewish settlements.

Earlier this year, the Israeli fashion establishment had anointed it as the "in" color of the season. If someone doesn't choose orange, **COLOR, E4**

Boris Fishman is the editor of "Wild East: Stories from the Last Frontier." He lives in New York.

Newspaper designers, who lack luxuries such as huge images, colour or glossy stock, have to make a title appealing in a very different way to magazine designers, as these examples from the *Boston Sunday Globe* show. 'Typography is the key to look and feel – what readers perceive in the first ten seconds when their eyes land on a page. It is through the feel of typography that one conveys seriousness, youthfulness, playfulness and so on. The colour palette is the second important criterion. We react instantly to the combination of type and colour on a page, and, as a result, white space and its allocation within the architecture of the page play the third most important role,' says Mario Garcia.

Newspaper covers

News no longer sells newspapers. The internet and mobile media have made newspapers redundant as the preferred media for breaking news, and newspapers have had to reposition themselves accordingly. 'The old definition was: news is what I find out today that I did not know about yesterday. My definition of news today, which I share with my clients, is this: news is what I understood today, which I found out about yesterday,' explains Mario Garcia, design consultant on a global range of newspapers. Consequently, the early years of the twenty-first century have seen a great number of newspaper redesigns, and this is apparent, above all, on the front page where, for publications across the board, the desire for impact has become all-consuming. As Mario Garcia says, newspapers have to offer readers 'good stories that surprise, with photos that have not been shown on television and the net for the last 24 hours. It's all about redefining news, offering surprises and not just reaffirmation.'

Newspaper covers still rely on eye-catching images and gut-clenching headlines as here in *The Guardian*. However, the modern newspaper selling on the news-stand has to show a spread of its stories so as to attract attention. In *El País* we see there are many teasers for articles which continue on the inside in the coloured horizontal banner and also in the vertical column. Even the main story about Syria only runs for 17 lines, so as to squeeze in an advertisement too.

Similarly *The Guardian* strips four or five 'turns' across the bottom of the page. The designer must find a balance, which should be predicated on the brand: a quality newspaper, in particular, will always want to present a number of stories on its cover. As Mark Porter says, 'Turns enable us to get a presence for a wide range of stories on the front page, which is essential for a newspaper that aims to give a broad and balanced view of the day's news.'

'The first time we did The Handmade Issue it was to get manufacturers and designers together and to get our readers involved as well. We made an app that allowed readers to combine some elements that our designers had created. We printed every different unique design. We had to find a printer who could produce a good print product. We wanted to push the print quality. Each reader received a unique cover of his or her own design. We printed 21,000, each one different.'

Alistair Hall at We Made This designed a cover and posted the image on their blog. *http://wemadethis.typepad.com/we_madethis/2010/06/we-made-this-wallpaper-cover.html*

The design awards judges at the Design and Art Direction association awarded this a Yellow Pencil in 2011. *http://www.dandad.org/awards/professional/2011/categories/mags/magazine-newspaper-design/18602/wallpaper-custom-covers*

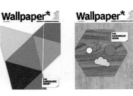

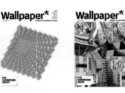

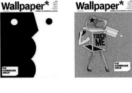

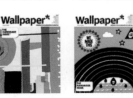

The development of covers from 1940 to the present day

1940 – 1950

During the 1940s, magazines in the UK were usually printed in black-and-white with perhaps colour covers. Some still resembled 1930s listing magazines, typeset by hand in metal type. This process restricted the use of fonts and what advertisers could do. Film magazines were early examples of specialist titles responding to the popularity of the cinema. They were cheap, although during the World War II there was a paper shortage in the UK and some magazines had to stall production.

In the US, *Esquire* magazine (launched in 1933) introduced features written by prominent authors such as F. Scott Fitzgerald and Ernest Hemingway. Magazines began using colour on their covers to stand out on the news-stand. The war also had an impact as creative talent fled Europe and headed for America, such as Austrian émigré Henry Wolf (*see* p.211). Post-war some of these talented designers, such as Alexey Brodovitch (*see* p.208) at *Harper's Bazaar,* introduced European artists like Salvador Dalí and A.M. Cassandre to the American public. Alexander Liebermann became art director at American *Vogue* in 1943, and went on to inspire art directors all over the US, and in the UK and Europe, with his flair for art direction and his modern attitude towards photography, art and the medium of print.

As women returned to the home after the war effort, women's magazines, such as *Good Housekeeping* and *Better Homes and Gardens* appeared. The cover images were important to attract the reader's attention.

1950 – 1960

The 1950s heralded the birth of modern advertising – magazines carried adverts for products and services with a readymade audience of women who stayed at home after the war effort. Women's fashion magazines benefitted from the influx of emigrant talent to the US, designers escaping from the aftermath of the World War II. Alexander Leiberman worked at Condé Nast and brought a whiff of European glamour.

George Lois at *Esquire* used simple iconic photographs and collage to communicate stories. The beauty of his style is that the text and image spark off one another. This style has been an inspiration to many art directors looking for an eye-catching idea to attract the reader.

A great example of visual confidence in the brand that might be misplaced if the brand was not well known. *Harper's Bazaar* or *Vogue* would still be recognized with barely any of its logo showing; a less well-known magazine would not be.

HARPER'S

BAZAAR

rch 1959   60 cents

Eyes
on
Paris
and
America

The seventh issue of *Oz* magazine is one of the publication's most famous, thanks to its iconic Bob Dylan cover by Martin Sharp. Sharp exploited new printing techniques to create an image that expressed the experimental, druggy mood, music and culture of the time.

Collaborators included Man Ray and Lee Miller. *Esquire* magazine started to print in colour and soon attracted advertisers. Britain's recovery after the war was slower than that of the US, but there was a crossing over of talent between London and New York. Magazine covers during this period featured news items, and reportage photography exposed the shocking images of war.

1960 - 1970

The use of composition and double-page spreads in *The Sunday Times Magazine* set the tone in the UK, with David King heading a team of young designers and talent spotting photographers like David Bailey. Magazine covers of the 1960s reflected the radical changes taking place in society. Covers dealt with political issues such as the Vietnam War and the sexual revolution. The stalwart work at *Life* magazine brought news photos into the home of the average American even before televisions became widely available. *Illustrated News* did the same in the UK. The magazine cover became an important visual window onto the outside world. Colour printing became more widely available and advertisements in the US and UK reflected changes in lifestyle. The 1960s also gave us the pop icon as a cover image. Celebrity photographers, such as David Bailey, Richard Avedon and Norman Parkinson, contributed to memorable covers that still look striking today.

Andy Warhol's
Interview
aug 72
50¢

INTER/VIEW 10th floor
33 Union Square West
New York, N.Y. 10003

BULK RATE
U.S. POSTAGE
PAID
NEW YORK, N.Y.
PERMIT 10245

Bianca
Blondell
Zsa Zsa
Marjoe

1970 – 1980

The 1970s was a decade of burgeoning cultural change, reflected in editorial design, with magazines like *Rolling Stone* and *Nova* setting exciting new standards. In the US, *Rolling Stone* began making its mark with its political coverage and focus on music and popular culture. The British magazine *Nova* was a woman's magazine with a politically liberal bias. As the German magazine *Twen* had achieved a decade earlier, these magazines reflected the society around them with bold cover photography aimed at a restless, enquiring and youthful readership. In Europe, political unrest gave rise to perfect opportunities for photojournalism and in Germany *Der Speigel* brought political issues onto their graphic covers.

Designers explored the double-page spread format with gusto. *Elle* magazine developed a strong use of the diagonal, reflecting a departure from the upright fashion photograph of the 1960s glossies. Magazines were suddenly a dynamic format, with *Interview*

RollingStone

ICD 08675 · JANUARY 22ND, 1981 · $1.50 UK80p

magazine using scale to full advantage on its celebrity cover models. Italian *Vogue* used Fabien Baron's strong sense of art direction, and Neville Brody (*see* p.216) brought a typographic flair to his magazines and gave other designers confidence to explore the grid and push it further. The specification of type was a skill that moved from specialist typesetters in type shops to the in-house Apple Mac (introduced in 1984), giving birth to the designer being the producer as well.

In the early 1970s, in production terms, magazines used black-and-white sections and restricted colour to certain sections, such as covers and features. As print technology advanced during the decade, colour printing on four-colour presses became cheaper and the use of colour became more widespread. Publications also began to print on gloss papers and experiment with different sizes and formats.

1980 – 1990

At the beginning of the 1980s, there were a few great fashion magazines and a handful of men's titles. The magazines published by newspapers (supplements) were an experimental place for fashion and almost the last bastion of proper reportage photography in print. Their covers basked in the glory of iconic photography with few cover lines. In the UK, style magazines like *i-D* and *The Face* really captured the fashion mood. In the US, interest in technology was triggered as people became computer owners. There was an interest in computer-related magazines, such as *MacUser* which launched in 1984. In magazine publishing, designers could play with early digital fonts and designed entire publications on a screen for the first time. In California, *Emigre* designers were experimenting typographically as they played with the pixel as a design element. David Carson applied his deconstructed approach to

This Annie Leibovitz cover photo of John Lennon and Yoko Ono helped establish *Rolling Stone* as one of the must-have magazines of its time. A beautiful cover image, full of symbolism, it captured the spirit of the time perfectly. Published by *Rolling Stone* as a tribute to the former Beatle, this picture was taken only five hours before John Lennon was shot dead outside the Dakota building in Manhattan in December 1980.

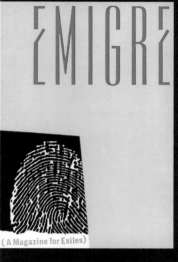

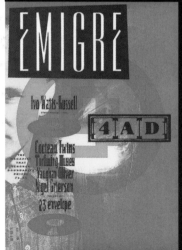

In 1984 *Emigre* captured the changing mood in San Francisco as Dutch designer Rudy VanderLans and his Czech-born wife Zuzana Licko created an innovative magazine using Zuzana's fonts and Macintosh computers. They used their magazine to experiment with digitized type and layout forms. Looking back it was a real turning point, as desktop publishing enabled designers to create their own fonts out of mere pixels and bend the established rules.

DENMARK DKR37 GERMANY DM10 GREECE DRA470 HOLLAND DFL8.25 ITALY L4700 SPAIN PTAS420 SINGAPORE M$8.90 USA $4.50

BLITZ

INTO THE FUTURE...

JANUARY 1989 No. 73 £1.65

And so to bed...

review 88
preview 89

*What to expect
in media,
film, music and print*

plus
herb ritts
pj o'rourke
peter o'toole
siobhan fahey
mike leigh

★ LONDON'S POLITICS ★ ART ★ BOOKS ★ CINEM

CLASSIFIEDS · SPORT · NEWS

CITY LIMITS

MARCH 12 TO 18 1982. NO.23 50P

16 PAGE PHOTO SPECIAL!
LIFE AND DEATH IN APARTHEID SOUTH AF

Dave King's bold covers for *City Limits*, the London listings magazine, used some of the techniques of political posters. Here the crowd scene is repeated in three different tones while the magazine's title is featured as a cut-out. King often used the *City Limits* name in different sizes and in a different position in each issue but kept to the same font, thus ensuring maximum flexibility while maintaining a strong identity.

Clever placement of the photograph in this Blitz cover from 1989 makes it appear as though the singer Madonna is looking fondly at the magazine's title, creating dynamic interplay between image and text.

Beach Culture and RayGun. In the UK, Neville Brody, Vaughan Oliver and Vince Frost showed a bold approach to the medium.

Fashion publications benefitted from the rise of fashion designer superstars and showcased their collections every season, producing fat issues in spring and autumn. These issues were beloved by advertisers, who in turn employed the same photographers to produce their advertising pages. The fashion industry boomed along with the economy, and luxury goods become more available to ordinary people. By the end of the 1980s in the US and the UK, magazines were enjoying a golden age of inspired collaborations and a respect for the specialist skills of designing editorial and visual journalism.

1990 – 2000

The rise of the celebrity cover seemed to dominate the style of this decade. Appearing on the front of a magazine launched the career of some celebrities, actors and musicians, and also helped to keep the medium fresh and vibrant. Magazine covers reflected the cultural appetite of their audiences. Consumer magazines were joined in the marketplace by customer magazines, which became more interesting with the development of brand building and innovations in cheaper digital print technology. Instead of customer magazines having to be printed on large-scale litho print presses, designers were able to go to smaller digital printers and produce shorter runs. Digital printing used simpler technologies, including inkjet, and there was no need for pre-press processes such as plate making, thus saving time and proving more cost effective.

Newspapers also had to rethink their traditional dominance of the news market and saw advertising sales fall. As the publishing arena became more crowded, competition increased. News websites were launched for free at first, but paywalls were soon introduced. The arrival of digital print technology and the improvement in its quality also changed the way newspapers were produced. Old presses were abandoned and broadsheets downsized. The lower cost of sending digital pages straight to the print press without the need for plates or colour proofs, meant that

Below, metallic embossing adds an unusual dimension to this *Dazed & Confused* cover. *Sleazenation*'s attention-grabbing typographic cover (bottom) is actually very simple and appears to state the obvious, but also plays on the ironic, knowing personality of the magazine's brand.

VOGUE

PARIS

SHOPPING

Héroïne Fifties

© Lachlan Bailey

SPÉCIAL ENFANTS ‹ MODE DÉFILÉS LOOK BOOKS BEAUTÉ BIJOUX CULTURE PHOTO SOIRÉES VIDÉOS THEVOGUELIST ASTRO LIVE ›

26
AVR
2013

PARTAGEZ

SHOPPING
Vernis parade

A effet velours, thermoactifs ou endiamantés…
Les vernis font leur grand show pour les fêtes de fin d'année.

Lire la suite

digital print became more widely available to all companies – not just to designers.

Fashion publications used celebrities on their covers as the trend for featuring supermodels waned due to cost. Editors tried introducing variety to increase their audiences. Lifestyle magazines appeared and the news-stand became crowded with titles. Some closed as the dot-com bubble burst in March 2000 and advertisers and publishers pulled in their belts.

2000 – 2010

In the 'noughties', before the iPad launched and other tablets arrived, magazines were in a strong position. Large publishing companies took their print titles onto the internet, designing web and mobile versions of them. Apps were soon to emerge for familiar titles such as *The New Yorker* and *Wired* in 2009 and *The Guardian* in 2011. The internet became the biggest threat to the advertising model and news organizations were forced to rethink. The integrity of the press was challenged by the WikiLeaks case and in the UK by the phone hacking scandal. Respect for the established press proprietors was in decline. In the US, jobs were lost as age-old newspapers reshaped their staff, for example at the *Boston Globe* when it shifted from print to digital in 2009. Print-trained designers had to retrain, learning to code and adapt their skills to interactive digital. Younger 'digital natives' found no problem designing across different platforms.

Literary culture magazine Zembla was designed by Vince Frost, who adopted a frenetic, in-your-face approach to typography and a bold, structural format.

Vogue is a good example of a publisher who covers all bases, with different editions being created for different platforms. The magazine enlisted the help of a website to expand its readership and give its advertisers a platform ▒▒ach readers in another way.

2010 to present day

The arrival of the iPad in 2010 meant that publishers and designers could include interactivity in their box of design tools. The lightweight, touch-screen tablet design made the iPad accessible to fans of the iPhone and other Apple technology. It appeared as a class above the other developing tablets, which had to adapt fast to catch up. Other tablet devices followed featuring new operating systems, such as the Android one by Google, which was developed on an open source model. Designers developed a visual navigational format to take advantage of the touch-sensitive screens and enhanced moving-image content of tablets and phones. Covers for the tablet editions of many consumer titles looked grown up, and became interactive for the first time. The design elements on the cover became entry points, allowing readers to move through the pages using a simple finger swipe.

Aggregated content was designed to flow into the reader's choice of format, whether tablet or mobile. The idea was that the reader's history of internet searches and data profile generated content pulled from various sources that was just right for him or her. The absence of an actual editor was daunting for some and liberating for others. The very nature of the editor/art director/publisher role changed to include developers as well. The idea that an individual could have his or her own version of a magazine flowing into a personal device also became a reality. Content publishers, such as Flipboard, emerged as publishers strived to bring targeted content to subscribers. Through a downloadable app, Flipboard are able to transform content from social feeds, websites and blogs into beautiful digital magazines for millions of readers to flip through.

Navigating through magazines is no longer linear. As this example from *The Guardian* iPad version shows, the designer's task is to guide the reader using the visual identity, and avoid putting any hurdles in the way.

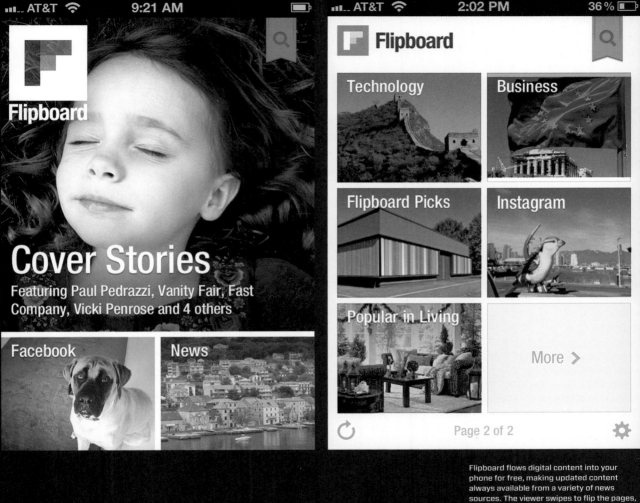

Flipboard flows digital content into your phone for free, making updated content always available from a variety of news sources. The viewer swipes to flip the pages, and can share pages instantly using social media. Inspired by the beauty and ease of print media, Flipboard describes itself as 'the world's first social magazine'.

The different ways of designing covers

There are many different approaches to cover design, but broadly speaking, covers can be categorized under three headings: figurative, abstract and text-based. The latter are rare now as editors shy away from text-dominated covers and graphic puns, but the very fact that they are rare creates its own impact.

Figurative covers

The traditional face or figure shot can be made more engaging by approaching it with some element of originality. For example, the smiling face shot can be replaced with a face displaying an emotion such as anger, fear or elation. The degree to which this kind of treatment can be attempted depends on the conformity of the publication's readership: readers of anti-consumerist magazine *Adbusters*, for instance, are unlikely to be repelled by a negative figure image, while the readers of a weekly women's magazine probably would be. Wit and humour can often attract readers, and an action shot with a sense of adventure invites us to join in the fun. Even a regular face shot can be made interesting: style magazine *i-D* has always shown its cover faces winking, aping the 'winking face' created by its logo. With full-figure shots there is a greater flexibility, a fact that *Dazed & Confused* plays with inventively. *Carlos* magazine uses illustration to depict cover figures, enhanced by a striking splash of metallic ink.

Fashion magazines can use illustration effectively, too; an illustration of a garment can convey an emotional sense of the material, rather than the literal representation of photography. And illustration has the advantage of enabling words to be incorporated in a way that is different from photography's clear boundaries, which make it distinct from any surrounding or superimposed text. Montage is an old device that can bring another dimension – that of metaphor – to figurative covers, and can be used most effectively to make incisive comments.

Quaterly Canadian magazine *Adbusters* (above) – subtitled 'the magazine of the culture-jamming revolution' – is an excellent example of the relationship that a special-interest publications can develop with its target audience. Each issue deals with one theme and is treated as a mini-book, enabling a compeltely different look each quarter.

Two very different interpretations of the usual close-up head shot. On *M-real* (above), creative director Jeremy Leslie playfully undermined the idea of the close-up female head shot making eye contact. *Pop* (right) did the same thing with a Jennifer Lopez cover, using a very different technique. Again, there is no eye contact with the viewer and Lopez's emotive and expressive state, as opposed to a passive, non-specific one, marks the image out from its competitors.

There is a simple guiding rule to cover design: appeal to the reader's interest. The image is the first point at which design does this, but it is by no means the only element of the cover that does so. Covers are, in fact, made up of four elements:

- format – size, shape and design characteristics;
- logo or title and other regular page furniture (tag-line, date and barcode);
- image(s);
- cover lines and headlines.

In the 1990s, 'lad mag' *Loaded* used all of these to great effect. Targeting its readership with a tag-line that read 'for men who should know better', its design and editorial approach was an exuberant 'we're off our heads' one that was completely in tune with the sex-, lager- and drug-fuelled, frenzied lifestyles its readers were – or wanted to be – living. Editor James Brown said at the time that it was 'for the man who believes he can do anything, if only he wasn't hung-over'. In design terms this attitude was successfully interpreted through art director Steve Read's clever devising of a style that looked undesigned but was full of energy and motion, with its excellent use of colour, typefaces, images and layout construction. Cover lines and headlines were big, bold, active and funny.

Concept covers can be particularly arresting. Pearce Marchbank at *Time Out* (above right) in the 1970s used such covers to great effect, skilfully employing photography, illustration, collage and typography to 'sell' difficult concepts such as Dadaism and 'Envy'. Vince Frost achieved equally striking results with his covers for *The Independent on Saturday* newspaper magazine supplement (right). These used abstract cut-out photography on white backgrounds with wit and elegance to intrigue readers and suggest a broad concept of a story, rather than explaining it literally. Both these designers knew that the key issue in designing a cover is to approach it as a poster, as that is, in effect, what it is. First and foremost, it has to be striking and draw in the viewer.

02/09/95

Independent
Magazine

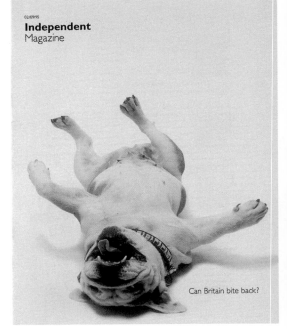

Can Britain bite back?

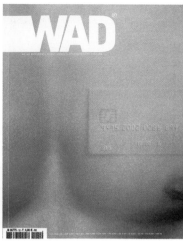

A figurative cover can be inventive and original if a publication's designer, editor and publisher have the courage to counteract the perceived notion of what is acceptable, popular or sellable, as seen in these examples from *Adbusters* (far left) and French magazine *WAD* (left). *Adbusters*, in particular, slyly undermines traditional notions of a cover's saleability by showing a traditional head shot of an attractive blonde woman in a very confrontational and unconventional way.

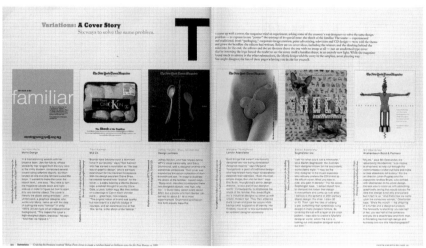

'This was our first "design special" issue, and we treated it as a primer, an advance-guard explanation to our readers of all the places where they would find good design. We decided to involve them slightly in the process, and made the cover into a graphic-design competition in which we invited six great graphic designers from varied backgrounds to create a concept. We printed all six solutions (above right). When we opened Jennifer Morla's contribution (above), we knew right away it was the winner – it was so simple.

"The Shock of the Familiar" was in bold, simple Helvetica, like signage, on a plain silver background. But *The New York Times Magazine* logo was upside down and at the bottom. It made you turn the cover upside down, and [be] aware of the cover as an object. And the shock factor was there as well. Its absolute clarity was riveting. It was also fun to read about the other five solutions inside, and begin to understand the way designers think and how they go about solving problems.' – Janet Froelich, former art director, *The New York Times Magazine*.

Abstract covers

Abstract covers are rare in publications that rely heavily on news-stand sales, but feature regularly in special-interest and subscription-only publications, news weeklies or newspaper supplements. These often have the luxury of minimal or no cover lines, and the freedom to place the logo wherever it best suits the design, since shelf visibility isn't an issue. This can result in highly original designs, but it is important to remember that the brand and its message must be maintained through a clear design direction and approach. *Wired* has always been particularly skilful at doing this (*see* p.68). From the magazine's inception, its designers John Plunkett and Barbara Kuhr made frequent use of abstract cover illustrations in order to communicate complex concepts in simple ways. *Adbusters* also uses this method, while *Tentaciones*,

The directness of text has an appeal and impact that sometimes simply cannot be conveyed by an image, as in this *Esquire* cover (below left) by George Lois. It can also work well as a conceptual tool, as in this *New York Times Magazine* cover (below right) for the 'Ideas' issue, the annual end-of-year compendium of the year's best. 'Our approach was to present the best ideas, inventions and schemes in an encyclopaedic fashion, using the alphabet as a construction device. To that end, we created a template that resembled both a dictionary and an encyclopaedia, in its use of thumb index, the illusion of thick pages, the wide columns, the little drawings in the margins and the somewhat stuffy, dictionary-style typographic conventions. The cover was designed as an old-fashioned book cover, with the texture of fabric and embossed gold lettering. It was then photographed in three dimensions, with the depth of the pages on the right forcing the image into a slightly narrower format,' says Janet Froelich. Scott King's use of words on youth-culture magazine *Sleazenation* (opposite) took its cue from a T-shirt design and was a direct, witty joke, slyly poking fun at its readers, magazines and fashion.

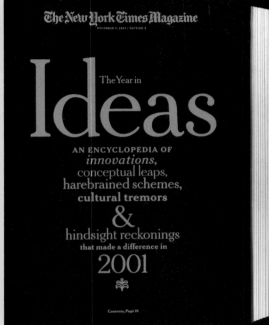

the *El País* supplement designed by Fernando Gutiérrez (*see* p.220), moves the logo around the white space of the cover at will, unrestrained by anything other than the fact that, because the magazine is printed on newspaper presses, it cannot use full-bleed photos, so instead floats images on white backgrounds to give the illusion of bleeds.

Text-based covers

Text-based covers are rare in contemporary periodicals, but many designers, including George Lois on *Esquire*, Herb Lubalin on *Fact*, and Scott King on *Sleazenation*, have used text-based covers to brilliant effect. Pearce Marchbank often took this option for his *Time Out* covers in the 1970s, for instance eschewing photography for an issue on Japanese movies,

choosing instead a graphic treatment of a bleeding Japanese flag with a single, pithy cover line. A more recent issue, featuring an Amsterdam guide, opted for a typographic approach because, as its art director at the time Jeremy Leslie explains, 'Amsterdam lacks an iconic location, building or event, so a typographic solution was used to express the buzz of the city.'

There is no doubt that text-based covers work, but in a culture that is now so visually orientated their use is minimal – which, of course, can be useful for the editor and designer who are looking to make an impact or stand out: hence their use when tragedy strikes or a famous person dies.

SLEAZENATION

AN IDEAL FOR LIVING THROUGH HONEST FASHION, ART, MUSIC AND DESIGN

I'M WITH STUPID

JARVIS COCKER & BARRY 7 • ARAKI FASHION EXCLUSIVE • BIBA • THE HIVES
DJ BIRD • KILLED BY DEATH • CHARLIE LUXTON • RAPING STEVEN SPIELBERG

Time Out
London

LONDON'S WEEKLY LISTINGS BIBLE
DECEMBER 14 – 21 2005
No.1.843 £2.50

North
South

vs

vs

London

Time Out

London's weekly listings bible
December 14 – 21 2005
No.1.843 £2.50

A weekly magazine has to look very different from issue to issue – the reader needs to be aware that the one on the news-stand is new. Moreover, it is possible for two issues to be on the news-stand at the same time (as was the case with *Time Out*, which overlapped by a day). Consequently, *Time Out* made the most of the ability of text to stand out in a way that a succession of images can't. For this cover (above), it's hard to imagine anything working as well as the type does. Micha Weidmann's solution to an issue on whether North or South London is better was innovative and original; rather than simply show a photo or illustration of the Thames River, he devised two covers: depending on which side of the river you bought your copy, either 'North' was the right way up or 'South' was – an ingenious and simple solution to a difficult concept.

…magazine, launched in San Francisco in 1993, is that rare thing in print publishing: a magazine whose design is perfectly attuned to its times and subject matter. As a general-interest magazine that specialized in the rise of technology as a cultural force, it replaced traditional, technology-related severity in design and visual expression with a layout, structure and aesthetic that challenged readers with their frenetic pace, and an inventive and web-inspired content and design format. It made eye-popping use of colour, which, through the placement of tinted text on a background of the same colour, often frustrated as much as it excited. In giving readers a very real sense of how amazing this emerging medium and technology were, and of their potentiality, it demanded much of them. An intelligent, knowledgeable readership understood, however, the connections immediately and responded enthusiastically as circulation soared. When the internet bust came, most magazines folded, but *WIRED* slimmed down and survived. Overall creative direction, design and typography for *WIRED's* first five years were by John Plunkett, and his partner Barbara Kuhr of Plunkett+Kuhr. Then designers included Tricia McGillis, Thomas Schneider and Eric Courtemanche.

In 2010, *WIRED* led the way forward when Scott Dadich presented a video to the Society of Publication Designers in New York about redesigning the magazine for the iPad. He demonstrated the new features of *WIRED* designed for the iPad and the choices that readers could expect from the magazine in the future. Speaking in 2010, Dadich explained they wanted 'to offer more choice to our readers and advertisers and move beyond the static notion of a magazine.'

In 2012, the Nieman Journalism Lab asked Dadich about reinventing magazines for the iPad. Justin Ellis wrote that 'there are some things, old-school things, that don't change whether you're dealing with print or tablet.' Dadich, then Condé Nast's vice president of digital magazine development, said, "The cover. As magazine makers, we see the cover as the one and only ad we have for your purchase and your time. It's an inducement to pick it up and give us your time.'

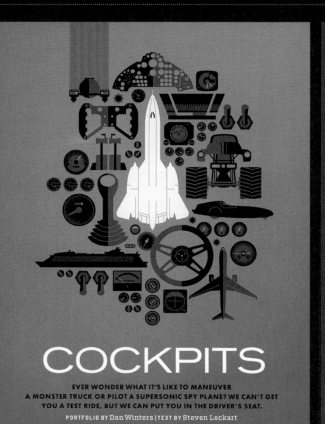

COCKPITS

EVER WONDER WHAT IT'S LIKE TO MANEUVER A MONSTER TRUCK OR PILOT A SUPERSONIC SPY PLANE? WE CAN'T GET YOU A TEST RIDE, BUT WE CAN PUT YOU IN THE DRIVER'S SEAT.

PORTFOLIO BY Dan Winters | TEXT BY Steven Leckart

The skipper of this massive cruise liner sits atop a cushy leather throne, naturally. Just don't expect the seat to get much use: "When we're going into port, we typically push the chairs out of the way and stand up. It makes us more agile," says Bill Wright, who was the first captain of Royal Caribbean's $1.4 billion *Oasis of the Seas*. Situated on the center line of the ship, the captain's station has two trackball-controlled 27-inch LCDs (foreground) that are used to display the electronic chart and the ship information system, which aggregates mission-critical data like radar, GPS, and sonar. Nineteen additional screens are positioned less than 10 feet away, so the captain can quickly access, say, the machinery automation system, which tracks everything from the 5.5-megawatt bow thrusters to the fore and aft ballast tanks. So how does the captain steer? "The port and starboard command chairs have built-in joysticks for controlling the ship," Wright says. But those are typically operated by other officers. "Captains should be mentoring and teaching."

Oasis of the Seas

LENGTH	CRUISING SPEED
1,187 FEET	22.6 KNOTS

CAPACITY	
8,690 PEOPLE	

WORLD'S LONGEST CRUISE SHIP

 PHOTO TEXT 360°

The components
of a cover

The term 'cover' comprises the outside front cover (or OFC), the inside front cover (IFC), the outside back cover (OBC) and the inside back cover (IBC). In most periodicals all but the OFC will be given over to lucrative advertising, but if they are not, it's worth remembering that these pages are infinitely more valuable than any other available pages, apart from the main cover. The publication's logo – the graphical representation of its title (sometimes referred to as a 'masthead') – is the first and often most important element of its cover. Cover lines, which indicate content, are also a vital component of any periodical cover.

The logo

While the publication's title may be as important as the way it looks, for the majority of designers this is something that will already have been decided. A logo is intended to capture and impart the publication's character, subject, stance and attitude to its intended readership, often in a subliminal way. While its primary function is to appear on the cover of the publication, it also needs to work on all of the brand's representations. Thus, it will appear in print and on digital editions for various platforms, and on promotional and marketing material, including the

Style magazine *Flaunt*'s covers are always highly original in both production and design terms, and always include an inside and outside front cover. This one features a teasing two-part cover that has an unrecognizable colour-by-numbers front (top). Only when readers turn the page do they see that it's Reese Witherspoon (bottom). 'Where other magazines would use a simple card cover, Flaunt always goes the extra distance. Cover ideas are discussed with the photographers many times prior to shooting the inside cover, but the majority of the time we find a particular artist who has a gallery show opening, or recently opened, or just someone whose work we like, and let him or her run with it. It's also great when you find an art director/designer/illustrator group all-in-one situation to work on the cover – that's only happened a couple of times.' – Jim Turner, creative director, *Flaunt*.

website. All these uses need to be considered when designing a logo. If a publication is successful, then its logo will be around for a very long time and its treatment, manipulation and positioning, along with any obscuring it, become significant.

Playing with the logo

A logo is a publication's calling card and should therefore be visible. Publishers are not happy with the logo of their title being obscured (by a photo or an illustration), but there have been many examples of a title being covered or partially covered and still selling very well; the trick is to show just enough of the title to make it instantly recognizable. There are many instances when obscuring a logo strengthens a concept that would otherwise be weakened if the logo had to be visible in its entirety: Henry Wolf's cover for the March 1959 issue of *Harper's Bazaar* (see p.51) interwove gloves with the magazine's title to create a riveting cover that looked three-dimensional and offered a seamless, completely integrated image.

Nest, the American interior design magazine, changed both the design and position of its logo for a while, as did David Carson for *RayGun*. This conceit was copied by sister title *Blah Blah Blah*, designed by Substance UK. *FT The Business* magazine (*see* p.101) also played decorative and visual tricks with its logo each week, treating it as a moveable graphic element that was an integrated and witty part of the image and stood out boldly from it. Other publications stuck with a good thing. *Nova*, with its elegant logo set in an old wood type, Windsor, worked brilliantly with just the logo and an expressive single theme on each cover, using just one cover line to sell it (*see* p.214). *Interview*, too, with its hand-drawn logo by illustrator Mats Gustafson, rarely played around with the logo or cover lines, which remained minimal. It played to its strengths – a large format, a unique logo and a visual style of tight, harsh crops of celebrities that was all its own.

Fox News... AND OTHER FASHIONABLE EPHEMERA.

T DESIGNED BY FENDI. PHOTOGRAPH BY STEPHEN LEWIS.

Easy as Cherry Pie

RECIPES FOR LIVING THE GOOD LIFE.

PHOTOGRAPH BY JAMES WOJCIK

Colour

The choice of colour or colours on a cover is important. Green logos and blue backgrounds don't sell. Red sells. Blondes on a cover sell better than brunettes. Yellow is often seen as an unpopular cover colour choice. All these are accepted conventions in magazine design, but hard evidence for these beliefs is hard to come by, and designers and editors would do well to follow their gut instinct, which will often be based on colour and its emotional impact. Remember, any colour can be used to emphasize and highlight, and specific colours can be used symbolically or to trigger emotions and memories, but trying to use colour to sell a publication is unlikely to work, largely because colour is so personal, and associations with it are dependent on so many different factors.

Colour use

While there is little hard evidence for many conventions that have grown around colour use in publications, there is one area in which colour use does follow hard-and-fast rules: cultural colour psychology. The high visibility of red might make it appealing in the West, but in South Africa, where it is associated with mourning, it would be seen on a cover about as often as black would be in the West. Blue is generally appealing to all of us irrespective of culture because of its calming influence, but is a turn-off when used for food. It's all about context. So while it is simply useless to tell you how to use colour, here's a helpful guide on how NOT to use it.

Black is complex; it can be sexy, authoritative, powerful, menacing, intriguing, rich, depressing, dull, glossy, textural, timeless ... on many occasions it will be at least two of these at the same time. Avoid using black on the cover, where it is too widely associated

with death and tragedy, but on the inside pages of a magazine its use can be striking. In colour psychology, many people think that it implies submission.

White is almost as complex as black: innocence, cleanliness, wealth and purity are some of the associations we make with white, but it can also be sterile and neutral to the point of blandness.

Red The extreme vibrancy of red has both good and bad points: it is confrontational and can render other elements on a page almost invisible. But it will definitely attract the eye and has been proved to create a strong emotional response in a viewer, stimulating faster heartbeats and breathing.

Blue Peaceful and tranquil, blue causes the body to produce calming chemicals, but choose it carefully – it can also be cold and depressing.

Green is the easiest colour on the eye and is calming and refreshing. As the colour of nature, most associations viewers make are positive ones. Additionally, dark green implies wealth and power.

Yellow is the most difficult colour for the eye to take in, thus is potentially overpowering – possibly why it's seen as an unpopular colour choice for covers.

Purple Used in the right way, purple has associations of luxury, wealth, romance and sophistication, but it can also appear overly feminine or gauche.

Orange Our associations with orange are good ones: exciting, vibrant and joyous. But it can be a difficult colour to use – too red and it can overpower; too yellow and it can appear washed out.

Brown Another 'nature' colour with good associations: light brown implies genuineness, while dark brown suggests wood or leather. The combination of these makes them appealing for men's subjects.

Cover lines

These apply exclusively to periodicals. News-stand titles will usually display a mass of these in a bid to show they have more and better content than the competition. The largest cover line, if the publication is using size to distinguish order of 'importance', is nearly always related to the cover image. The content, use and placement of cover lines in such titles as *Vogue*, *GQ*, *Vanity Fair* and *Marie Claire* are generally decided by the editor and art director, but marketing and competition considerations drive this process (they often appear on the left third of the cover, as this is most likely to be visible on the newsagents' shelves). But the look and tone of the cover lines – their colour, how they stand out against competitors and each other, what their number, length and words say about the magazine and its personality – are very much the responsibility of the designer. In newspapers, too, designers have started to use the space above the banner for cover lines that highlight featured articles inside the paper and its supplements.

Spines

While book designers know the value of spines as a design area, this little band of space is generally ignored by periodical publishers, beyond using it to show the title and publication date. This is a shame for two reasons: first, the spine has excellent sales value as, when stacked, it is more visible than the cover, and, second, because this strip is an excellent place in which to reinforce the brand and style of the title, a fact not lost on the designers of titles such as *Arena*, *Loaded*, *Vanidad* and *Wallpaper**. Rather than simply list title information, the first two of these use the spines to build up arresting narratives that make readers feel they are buying part of a series and not just a single issue, thereby encouraging loyalty and the desire to build up a whole set. *Wallpaper** uses it to carry a list of key contents, an excellent indexing feature. Separating what's important from what's not can be achieved by using different weights and sizes of fonts: the title logo and date should attract from a distance, drawing the potential reader closer to finding further, more detailed information.

The separate spines of Fernando Gutiérrez's design for *Vanidad* combine to form the crossed-through 'V' of the title, or upside down (as here) forms a perfect 'A'.

Brief Two
Masthead and covers

AIM

To design a masthead and three covers for an imaginary pitch of your magazine concept.

THE BRIEF

Take your magazine mood board from Brief One (see p.38) and use it to develop three covers. Use the typography of your masthead (logo) to reflect the visual philosophy of your magazine. Find a suitable font or draw your own. Decide whether the masthead should dominate the page or be more demure. Who is your magazine aimed at? Think about the clarity of communication in the visual language that you are using.

Now create visual layouts for your covers using a digital page template. Choose a format for your magazine. Avoid A4 if you can as the page will be a little bit too tall and not quite right for page turning. Magazines tend to be slightly wider than A4 and slightly shorter. To start, scan images in or, better still, shoot or create your own imagery. Think about how the typography you use on the cover will reflect the visual identity of the whole magazine. Should it be serif or sans serif? Light or bold?

Imagine that your first cover is for the launch issue and the other two for following monthly or quarterly editions. If you imagine your publication to be A5 size then produce your covers at 100%. If your publication is tabloid size, however, you may need to tile your layouts using the tiling settings in the printout menu and tape them together on the back. It is very important to get each cover off the screen and output it in actual size. Trim your covers to actual page size if necessary.

Repositories for random thoughts

Sketch
March 2012

Fashion Photographer
Gary Wallis

Fashion

Repositories for random thoughts

Sketch
March 2012

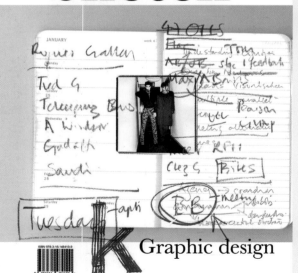

Graphic design

Pictured here are layouts for an imaginary student project. The first is *Sketch,* a magazine about sketchbooks by Central Saint Martins College BA graphics student Jetmire Dvorani. The masthead is strong and becomes an icon in itself. Shown here are pages from the sketchbooks for the development of the masthead. First the name is simple and used in a satisfying thick black font, with an underline, a bit like an extended doodle. If you use another photographer's image, make sure you get permission.

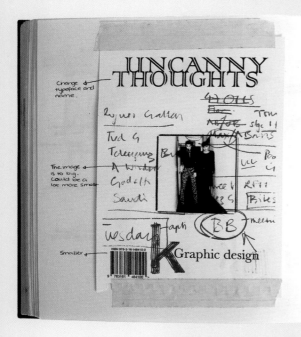

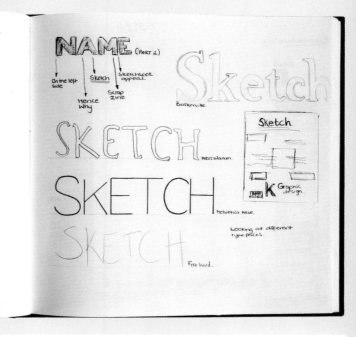

Photography: Gary Wallis

Photography:Gary Wallis

"magical, treasuring a special moment"

Onseri conseque volum repel est, solum saectae enda voloreh enianis essi volo beatur molupicipis animo quo is repratus experitat dolestia velluptae repratincte illabo. Et odi to corisquam, quatia nosanime molupta tionseribus nis con provid quia poratia nones exerepe llendisquia serferchil et, conseque officitiate quasitiae quia nis ressinia sitaqui veliqui cusdae sum eat omniend usamet elest ma nonsequi del id eum rest imo tem aute perum quia voloribusa dolut es doloria quianih iliqui corit laboreperum eum dit et lanihilicius quibus.
Turest opta quatem nonsequia cum hit aliam verist, que necabor epudant omnihil ipient ommodit atempor roviti nimi, si simincil maion consenimenis nonseriae volenis doluptatem. Nam, te parum eatur?
Alicte num iditi as es accusam, nus is commolo rehendae rempor alique etur,

nonsecepuda precea dolut aut officiureped utas everum entotatus dolupta tempor reium ipienti te ped quam quae. Itaecaes repe vollit idelitam re consequi ipid unt autaqui doluptatur?

VOGUE

JUNE
£2.90

SPECIAL
ISSUE

BEST
OF
BRITISH
HOT, HAPPENING AND HERE

Chapter 4 : Inside the publication

Having a proper understanding of editorial design is just the first ingredient in a complex mix. Another essential element is a real understanding of the publication and the ability to apply this to the constituent parts of the magazine or newspaper. It's not simply about design decisions, but a deep knowledge and fascination with what underpins and motivates these design decisions.

Anatomy of a publication

A publication is broken down into areas that largely follow an established format for its particular type. Thus, a magazine breaks down into three areas: the news-led first third (called the front of the book), a middle third housing the features (called the feature well), and a back third (called the back of the book), which is usually where information-based content – reviews, listings, directories and so on – is located. A newspaper can be similarly broken down into areas of content: hard news (the unpredictable, including international news and business); analysis and opinion of the news; expected content (television, stock-market information, reviews, weather, sport reports, etc.); and irregular features.

A flick through any newspaper or magazine will reveal that the different areas are often signposted by varying layouts or grids: column widths, headlines, fonts and their weights, images and so on are all likely to differ subtly from each other, identifying departments and making navigation easier for the reader. There is, of course, no reason why designers should not deviate from these formats, but, if they do, they should use consistency in flow and navigation to compensate for the reader's lack of familiarity with the structure. This is particularly true for popular and predictable content – TV listings, weather forecasts, letters, crosswords, horoscopes and so on.

Contents page

What does the contents page of a magazine do? Contemporary readers use the contents page in a number of different ways: to find the cover story, browse the entire content of the publication, find favourite sections or find a story they vaguely remember reading years earlier. Some people don't use the contents page at all; others read or flip from back to front, making the contents page at the front fairly redundant. But the contents page remains very important because, after the cover, it is the only device that can literally guide the reader deeper into the publication and signpost a way through and around its content. Because of this status, contents pages are

Zembla magazine >contents

#1

BEGINNING

09>Contributors

11>Editor's Letter

12>Letters

14>VIP Letter
By Dame Edna

15>Notebook
Words in the World, including Where is Zembla?; Microsoft Jargon; Ancient Insults; Avocados: The Manhattan Monkey; Notes from the Woman's Suburban Democratic Club; and Brian Eno on jargon in Washington, D.C.

MIDDLE – Fact

24>The New Celebrity Interview: Tilda Swinton on John Byrne
The star of *Orlando* and *Young Adam* talks to h favourite writer, who happens to be her lover

30>Photo Finished
Robert Mactarlane on whether writers should be read and not seen

46>The Ten Commandments – in Klingon
An art project by Simon Patterson

64>Writing Is Easy!
Steve Martin thinks he can do it

68>Pistol Whipped
The original manifesto that launched the Sex Pistols

72>Close-up Stand-off
Bug books from 1663 and 2002

88>The Dead Celebrity Interview
Michel Faber interviews Marcel Duchamp
Illustration by Manolo Blahnik

Contents pages have to list everything in the publication, but there is no reason why their design cannot be handled inventively, as these examples from *Zembla* (below) and *The New York Times Magazine* (below right) demonstrate. For the latter's November 2003 annual issue on 'Inspiration', former art director Janet Froelich found inspiration at the Cooper-Hewitt Design Museum's biennial. 'I saw the wonderful "Alphabits", which designer and writer Paul Elliman constructs from scrap materials, found objects and bits of industrial waste, including bottle tops, computer components, engine parts and so on. As such, they are a perfect embodiment of the question of where inspiration comes from. His letterforms are powerful graphic objects and they made our pages look fresh and inspirational. They were so much fun to work with,' says Froelich.

END

92>Writer's Shock
Toby Litt remembers the writer and educator Malcolm Bradbury

95>Global Literary Calendar
Upcoming events around the world

96>Reviews
Authors on their own books; real kids on kids' books; and Zemblans on what to read now, damn it

102>Big Philosophy, Big Talk
By Alexander Bard and Jan Söderqvist

112>Cartoon
By R. Crumb and Gavarni

115>Crossword: Crass Words
By Francis Heaney

116>Competition: Sex and Death
Who is the best-qualified person to write on sex and death? Tell Zembla publisher Simon Finch and win a first-edition classic novel

120>Lost Page
Never-before published pictures

MIDDLE – Fiction

38>Sanchakou
By Matthew Kneale

54>Under the Weather
By James Hopkin

66>The Marcus Van Heller Legend
An exclusive excerpt by John Stevenson

81>Sometimes the Daughter Says the Things Her Mother Thinks
By Donna Daley-Clarke

87>Dr Mortimer's Observations
The problem with 'nice' people

september_two thousand and three zembla magazine **[05]**

often located on the right-hand side, since this is the page most easily read. However, precisely because of this, right-hand pages – and particularly those near the front of a magazine – are more appealing to advertisers and therefore may be sold, forcing contents pages onto the left-hand side of a spread.

Designing the contents page

First and foremost, the contents page – and particularly the essential information it contains – should be clear to read, simple to follow and easy to find. While traditionally it is placed as close to the cover as possible, its position isn't as important as consistency of positioning. Every issue of the same magazine will put the contents page in the same place. Regularity leads to familiarity. This, in turn, fosters the sense of a publication being a friend. The arrangement and organization of a contents page should be

4   Geht die Kultur der Liebe
    kaputt?
    **Ein Mädchen beklagt sich:
    Die Männer sind wie Kaninchen**

8   Die Lust, ein Polizist zu sein
    **Polizeibeamte schreiben in
    twen über ihre Erfahrungen
    mit Demonstranten**

15 Feliciano. Die neue twen-Platte
    **Die aufregendste Stimme, die
    in den letzten Jahren entdeckt
    wurde**

22 Werden Gehirne manipuliert?
    **Gehirn mit elektronischer
    Ladung. Wissenschaftler bauen
    den mechanisierten Menschen**

26 Witze

28 Machen Sie Ihr schönstes
    Farbfoto
    **Startschuß zum zweiten großen
    Farbfotowettbewerb**

30 Die Jungen machen das
    Geschäft
    **Vier Rezepte, wie man einen
    eigenen Laden auf die Beine
    stellt**

41 Wenn ich ein junger Deutscher
    wäre
    **William Saroyan schreibt für
    twen**

45 Auch an der Garderobe
    abzugeben: Citybikes
    **Die kleinsten Motorflitzer auf
    zwei Rädern**

51 Leserbriefe

53 Die Verfolgung
    **Kurzgeschichte
    von Henry Miller**

60 Sex und Schule
    **Die Klasse der
    schwangeren Mädchen**

78 Steve McQueen ist nicht
    zu fassen
    **Hollywoods erfolgreichster
    Außenseiter**

85 Warum malt Hockney
    am liebsten Knaben?

88 Dieser Sommer
    wird noch heißer!
    **Werden die Studenten
    den politischen Kampf auf die
    Spitze treiben?**

100 twen fordert einen deutschen
    Pop-Sender

102 Morgen bin ich ein anderer
    Mensch
    **Wie ein Mädchen mehr aus sich
    machte**

108 Fiesta der Zigeuner
    **Fahrendes Volk trifft sich in
    Saintes-Maries-de-la-Mer**

121 Supermann in Unterhosen
    **Gordon Mitchell in den neuen
    Geblümten**

131 Das heiße Lied
    **Georg Stefan Troller schreibt
    über französische Chansons**

138 twen-Magazin
    **Neue Bücher, neue Filme,
    neue Platten**

166 Sterne und Zitronen

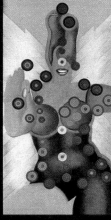

80 Kopf. Herz oder Bauch?
    **Das twen-Testspiel verrät alles
    über Ihr Temperament**

70 Bikinis in Israel
    **twen flog mit EL AL ans
    Rote Meer**

90 Touching ist schöner als Sex
    **Die Kunst, zu berühren und
    zu fühlen**

Contents pages can be designed well as lists, as illustrated by these examples from *Twen* (this page), *Sleazenation* (opposite below) and *About Town* (opposite top left), which use strict underlying grids and a Swiss formalism to make the text matter-of-fact and informative while retaining a graphic elegance. But there are many different ways of representing the navigation of the magazine. In *Metropolis* (opposite top right), 'The map on the table of contents is a graphic device that was created by Paula Scher when she redesigned the magazine in 1999. It provides a framework to show the reader where the stories appear in relation to each other. Although the table of contents has gone through many design variants over the last five years, the map has remained, and has actually become a more significant element in the design of the page,' says former *Metropolis* art director Criswell Lappin.

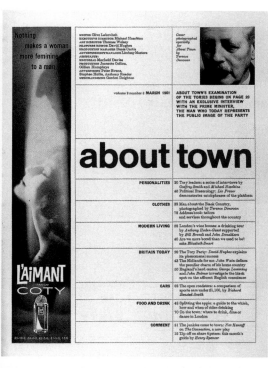

attractive, lucid and quick to absorb and navigate – to find the cover story, for example, or a favourite regular section. It should highlight individual features and important section stories through the use of type, imagery and graphic devices such as rules and icons, and it should summarize main stories to tempt the reader to them. After all, someone reading the contents page may not have bought the magazine as yet. Finally, it should echo the arrangement of the contents that come after it; so, if there's a news section followed by a feature well (*see* p.83) and a directory, this should be reflected in the contents page.

Some publications don't bother with a contents page at all. Chris Dixon, former art editor at *Adbusters*, did away with the contents page because he and the editor, Kalle Lasn, agreed that it segmented the magazine too much and dictated the approach. Instead, navigational tools, including colour bars and colour stock, were used, the former signifying the length and variety of the section's contents by their width, colour selection and length. This is an extreme solution to a design problem and one that, in any case, can only be applied to certain types and sizes of publications; a news weekly or listings magazine with no contents page would quickly annoy its readers, while a publication with 300-plus pages simply has to be navigable in a practical way.

IT WAS a game at first. A publisher had been stonewalling my proposal for a new magazine so I started to toy with the idea of publishing it myself. Independence – now there's a thought to set any journalist's pulse racing. But I never honestly thought I'd go through with it. On the other hand, what if I *could* actually escape the frustrations and constrictions imposed by having to conform to somebody else's notions of how a magazine should be run and what it should be? So I started to check it out, juggled a few figures using some £4,500 of savings, and calculated that – yes – I could just about cover the costs in the event of total public rejection. Then there arrived the day when I telephoned an order for £7,500 of Finnish paper, literally feeling queasy in my stomach as I replaced the receiver and contemplated the commitment. I had the same feeling at 5am one April 1980 morning in South Wales when the first issue came off the presses. The initial idea was, in a sense, self-indulgent. To hell with market research! This would be the magazine that I would enjoy reading – visually attractive, surprising, diverse, colourful, stimulating. Wind it up and let it go! Profits (sic) would be spent improving the product; behind-the-scenes costs cut to the bone. To survive during the first year I was the only full-time staffer, working first from a corner of a room in somebody else's office, then in a musty one-roomed basement. In that period there were at least two occasions when disaster was imminent. The fact is that it's relatively easy to start a magazine, a major act of endurance and faith to keep it going when things don't immediately click. But there has always been enormous goodwill towards THE FACE and it was this, with equal measures of stubbornness, pride and my wife's support, that kept us afloat. Today we have a rising circulation and an international reputation. On top of UK sales, every month we export 24,000 magazines to some 36 countries. Quality of content improves with every issue; there's no room for complacency. Last year we were elected Magazine Of The Year in two polls. This year (so far) we've put out two 96-page issues, expanded the scope of coverage, tried to stick our necks even further out. Profits are still being reinvested. Not just me, but all of us at THE FACE would like to thank the readers, contributors, advertisers, associates and friends of the magazine for their generous and continuing support. *And* we're still independent!
NICK LOGAN

THE FACE

25 YEARS: THE PIGOS RISE AGAIN AND GARY FAGIN

The World's Best Dressed Magazine

AMERICA ● AUSTRALIA ● CANADA ● DENMARK FRANCE ● GERMANY ● GREECE ● HOLLAND HONG KONG ● ITALY ● JAPAN ● NEW ZEALAND

I N T R O

8   "Chaka Khan meets Eurythmics" **Helen Terry**
11   **Sara Sugarman**/Olympic shirts/Sunday Best
15   The Black Theatre Coop/Richard 'Popcorn' Wylie
16   **Yellowman**/Grace Jones/**Was Not Was**
18   Alternative Country – High noon in NW1!
20   **Jermaine Jackson**/Intro's record selections
22   **Absolute Beginners**/Loose Ends/**Bronski Beat**

F E A T U R E S

24   Hippie as Capitalist – profile of **Richard Branson**
28   **Mods!** The Class of '84 hit the Trail of '64
38   The General Revisited – **Jerry Dammers**
44   **Gang Wars!** Sudden death in Olympic City
52   Photospread **The funeral of Marvin Gaye**
58   Saint **Joseph** the Tastemaker!
62   Exclusive! **Stevie Wonder has a dream**
67   EXPO **Night People** by Derek Ridgers
79   All for Art – **Gilbert & George**

S E C T I O N S

42   **Julie Burchill** How to get *It*! How to lose *it*!
50   **Music** for June reviewed by Geoff Dean
55   **Letters** The readers bite back!
66   **Back Issues** (going fast!)
74   **Films** New on the circuits
76   **Nightlife** THE FACE in Turin/Club selections
82   **Bodylicious!** 12 pages of **Style** start here. . .
94   **DisINFORMATION** for THE FACE's 50th
95   Subscriptions advice **THE FACE by post!**

The Face ● 4th Floor, 5/11 Mortimer Street, London W1, England

Publisher/Editor ● **Nick Logan**
Assistant Editor ● **Paul Rambali**
Designer ● **Neville Brody**

Features ● **Paul Rambali**
Intro/Features assistant ● **Lesley White**
Accounts/subs ● **Julie Logan**
Design assistant ● **Ben Murphy**

New York Editor ● **James Truman** (212 969 4579)
Ad Manager ● **Rod Sopp** (01-580 6758)

+ Peter Ashworth/Janette Beckman/Max Bell/Ian Birch/Chris Burkham/Julie Burchill/David Corio/Kevin Cummins/Giovanni Dadomo/Chalkie Davies/Anthony Denselow/Robert Elms/Anthony Fawcett/Jill Furmanovsky/Laura Hardy/David Johnson/Marek Kohn/Neil Matthews/John May/Joe McKenna/Jamie Morgan/Neil Norman/Steve Pyke/Derek Ridgers/Dave Rimmer/Helen Roberts/Sheila Rock/Fiona Russell Powell/Chris Salewicz/Jon Savage/Kate Simon/Carol Starr/Jay Strongman/Kevin Sutcliffe/Steve Taylor/David Thomas/Paul Tickell/Steve Tynan/Elissa Van Poznak/Jane Withers/Patrick Zerbib

THE FACE 7

On alternative style magazine *The Face*, editor Nick Logan and designer and typographer Neville Brody recorded a post-punk era by taking typography, layout and design in new directions, which drew on the politics and visual aesthetic of Russian Constructivism. However, the layout of the contents page was still clear, and remained fairly traditional in its design.

The front sections

Magazine editorial-department pages – pages into which all the editorial departments on the publication will feed, whether culture, fashion, sport, music, travel or interiors and so on – will generally have well-structured style sheets and templates that are based on a selected range of fonts (size and weights), colours and page furniture (including graphic icons, rules and keylines), all laid out across a well-defined grid. Design has a part to play in the masthead and editorial comment, too, where the way in which information is laid out sends strong clues as to the style and tone of the publication. This is particularly true of the editorial comment, which should deliver the editorial tone of the publication very clearly.

Contemporary news pages (and the writing for them) have learnt much from web design, which uses boxes, colours and a variety of font weights and sizes to make pages lively and energetic. *Wired* and *Business 2.0*, in particular, pioneered this approach, which was picked up by Gary Cook at *FT The Business*. In an effort to make the *Wired* news pages busy and energetic, designers use an abundance of overlapping boxes, shades, tints and colours, fonts, photos and shapes. White space, which would add an unwelcome sense of calm to the layout, is completely obliterated.

A newspaper's front section shares certain aspects with magazines in that it contains the most up-to-the-minute content laid out across flexible templates on a well-structured grid. The bulk of unpredictable content – breaking news stories, developments in current news stories and so on –is contained here.

water sports story by **TIM SOUTHWELL** photos by **NEALE HAYNES**

hawaii
FIVE-OH!

When the world's swashbuckliest pro windsurfer invites you for a weekend of free lessons, shark baiting and pina colladas thrown over you by beautiful women in bikinis, you can hardly say no can you?

It's 6.30AM, (that's AM!!) and I'm standing (that's upright!) on Kanaha beach on the Hawaiian island of Maui with Nik Baker, one of the best windsurfing wave riders in the world. It's his 24th birthday and he should be in bed getting rid of last night's party hangover under the soothing guidance of his fine lady or be out at Hookipa beach ripping the shit out of big waves. Whichever way you look at it, he's suffered a

The feature well

Features are the most important textual element of a magazine's branding. Whether it be the handling of a celebrity interview that every other publication is running that month, an in-depth analysis of an event, situation or topic that is currently hot, or a scoop that no one else has, the style, content and tone of the writing and layout are what will make it stand out from competitors.

Many publications use a standardized house style or 'look' for features, and employ design to distinguish them from other editorial content through elements such as wider columns, more white space, different typefaces, larger headlines and longer stand-firsts or 'sells' beneath them. If the feature begins on a spread, it will often open with a full-bleed image – a head shot, figure or illustration – facing the feature opener, which will usually consist of the text (a headline, stand-first

In becoming the first 'lad mag', *Loaded* in the 1990s identified a new market, but it remained successful because the features and how they were written both tuned in perfectly to that market. Here were great writers expressing all the things their readers wanted to be doing, thinking, seeing, having and being. Its design also brilliantly conveyed and illustrated the energy, mayhem and anarchy expressed in the writing. Art director Steve Read achieved this by developing an 'undesigned' style that suggested features had been thrown together. The combination of vibrant colour, big, full-bleed action shots, huge headlines that were manipulated to convey movement and depth, and body copy printed out of the image created an effect of sheer *joie de vivre*.

Elle a choisi l'Hôtel, rue des Beaux Arts, QG d'Oscar Wilde, à quelques pas du Café de Flore où elle se régale de croque-monsieur avec les doigts, tout contre l'immense appartement dépouillé qu'elle occupe le temps d'un film. Le clin d'œil du réceptionniste, son «bonjour mademoiselle» connivent, laissent à penser que Sofia Coppola a ici quelques habitudes. Peut-être vient-elle, dans ce cadre «rococo-Art déco-bordelo» rêver à Marie-Antoinette, tête d'affiche de l'Histoire, couronnée reine de son troisième long métrage? Silhouette frêle parfumée à la fleur d'oranger, teint transparent semblable à celui de ses jeunes héroïnes indécises, lèvres pleines, comme un rideau de chair tendre sur un émail éblouissant, nez de caractère, phrasé sucré, hérissé de «you know what I mean», Sofia Coppola, interrogée sur sa devise, répond du tac au tac «tais-toi et agis». Une ligne de conduite talonnée par la réalisatrice qui, en l'espace de deux films, a su tracer sa route très personnelle, se soustraire à l'ombre d'un père dont le nom charrie à lui seul le mythe Hollywood. Avec *Virgin Suicides* (adaptation du livre de Jeffrey Eugenides) puis *Lost in Translation* (Oscar du meilleur scénario, trente millions de dollars de recette), Miss Coppola s'est imposée fascinante «fée-ciné» du cool et de l'innocence dont les films, comme des albums intimes, des collages photos, recèlent une sensibilité visuelle chic et moderne. Un halo soyeux qui prend dans la toile de sa langueur diaphane, de ses couleurs crème glacée, de ses ralentissements abyssaux, de ses lumières tamisées, de ses mélodies planantes, les supplices et les délices d'un âge impossible, d'une passion platonique, l'essence de l'essentiel comme la substance des petits riens. «C'est drôle, dit Sofia Coppola, quand j'étais jeune, ma mère s'inquiétait parce qu'avec mes copines, on avait un avis sur tout. Aujourd'hui, j'ai un boulot où tout ce qu'on me demande c'est justement d'avoir une opinion. Un cinéaste doit être curieux de toutes sortes d'images et de sons. Je suis une généraliste, sensible à la mode, au design, à la photo, à la musique et je jette dans mes films tout ce que j'aime, sans la moindre restriction. Je rends les choses le plus personnel possible avec tout ce que ça comporte d'effrayant.»

D'où l'irrépressible tentation de cerner l'autobiographie, de démêler les fils du soi de Sofia sur le tapis de la fiction, ceux-là mêmes qui suturent le huis clos moiré avec un quinquagénaire au sommet d'un cinq étoiles tokyoïte ou l'odyssée laconique d'une fratrie de blondes évanescentes qui se soustraient au monde des vivants. «J'ai adoré le livre d'Eugenides, au point de m'angoisser quand j'ai appris qu'un réalisateur avait l'intention de l'adapter, dit-elle. Je me sentais comme investie de la mission de protéger ce bouquin. À la plupart des films américains qui abordent l'adolescence sont affligeants de caricature et de niaiserie. Ce qui m'intéressait, moi, dans cette étape cruciale de la vie, c'est la collision entre l'obsession des grandes questions, la mort, l'amour, et l'infatuation du futile, Gio, alors que j'avais une quinzaine d'années. Mon adolescence, qui aurait dû être la période la plus insouciante de mon existence, a été la plus triste. Un poison dont on ne se débarrasse jamais.»

Sofia Coppola est née à New York, le 14 mai 1971, en plein tournage du *Parrain*, «moment où, pour la première fois, mes parents ont gagné beaucoup d'argent».
L'enfance est vécue entre la grande demeure victorienne de San Francisco – décorée de néons et de canapés en forme de lèvres par Eleanor, la mère éprise d'art conceptuel, où défile le tout-cinéma, de George Lucas à Wim Wenders en passant par Marlon Brando, et les différents plateaux de tournage aux quatre coins du globe où Francis Ford, alias «le Sultan», débarque invariablement avec son clan. Pour *Apocalypse Now*, Sofia est exilée trois ans à Manille, elle s'éveille sur les bancs d'une école chinoise, s'amuse de tours en hélicoptère sur les genoux du patriarche, de pâtés de boue au bord de la rivière, et croise avec la même fascination mandarins de Hollywood et serpents venimeux de deux mètres de long. «Mon père nous voulait toujours autour de lui, dit-elle. J'étais constamment entourée d'adultes ce qui, du coup, m'a rapprochée de mon second frère, Roman. Et de mes parents, bien entendu. Je ne crois pas qu'il y ait beaucoup de pères qui donnent des conseils de réalisation ou de scénario à une petite fille. Le mien n'arrêtait pas. Je crois que j'ai hérité de son caractère obstiné, tenace, de sa motivation. Et de la discrétion de ma mère. Elle a toujours préféré être observatrice plutôt que centre d'attention.»
L'adolescence de Sofia a eu pour cadre Napa Valley, ses somptueux jardins, ses vignes vallonnées, le dernier refuge de l'ogre Coppola qui prend le large, se protège d'un Los Angeles sous perfusion d'un «cinéma business» dans lequel il se sent à l'étroit. Études d'art, premiers flirts sur fond d'Elvis Costello, de Siouxsie and the Banshees, des Clash, escapades à répétition en grosse américaine, direction San Francisco ou Seattle, pour se frotter en live aux prémisses du grunge... composent le «moodboard teenager» d'une jeune boudeuse aux yeux noirs qu'aurait pu imaginer Salinger, vie capitonnée, destin en suspens. «J'ai été torturée par l'idée de ne pas savoir ce que j'allais faire, dit-elle. De n'être géniale en rien.» Sans avoir l'air d'y toucher, elle s'essaiera à la comédie (sur injection du père, qui l'impose sur le *Parrain III*), à la photo, à la peinture   *(Suite page 295)*

"J'ai le caractère *obstiné, tenace*, la *motivation* de mon *père*. De ma mère, j'ai hérité la *discrétion*. Elle *préfère* être *observatrice plutôt* que le *centre d'attention*."

"Cela m'a sans doute *arrangée* qu'au *départ*, on m'ait pas prise au *sérieux*. Ça m'a laissé la *latitude* de *surprendre*."

On *Vogue Paris*, former art director Fabien Baron used both black and white space to construct spreads that reference, the underlying grid and accentuated display text. Willy Fleckhaus's bold use of white space in this issue of *Twen* (opposite top) from 1968 is an unexpected treatment for the subject matter, and is therefore an elegant surprise, both visually and conceptually.

or sell, body copy and pull quotes) and perhaps further images that will tie the full-bleed image to the feature (if no such imagery is used, the headline usually does this instead). If the feature begins on a single page facing a full-colour ad, a bleed image in black-and-white to contrast with the ad next to it, or judicious use of white space, can create a distinction between the two pages and draw the eye away from the ad towards the editorial. Using white space formed part of a move away from the excessive over-design of the 1990s towards a clean simplicity, a move whose popularity has, unsurprisingly, continued well into the new century. One way of ensuring consistent use of white space is by incorporating it into the grid or templates: for example, in top or bottom margins or in the relationship between headline and stand-first, in 'blank' columns and in space around pull quotes.

Back sections: reviews, listings, commentary

As with the front of the publication, elements that come after the feature well (for instance, reviews, listings, letters and horoscopes) are often laid out by junior designers and have a fairly well-determined structure and grid. A colour palette is usually in place, as are font selections, weights and styles. Imagery is all-important in these pages: good use of illustration and photography will determine whether the pages are lively, and, indeed, which individual story on the page is read. Equally, layout is crucial: using cut-outs on white backgrounds will make an image stand out and allow the page breathing space, something that can be difficult to achieve on editorial department pages, which are often crammed with stories and imagery. Very few people will read all the stories, but they may be tempted to do so if faced with a page that surprises and excites

This section opener for *The New York Times 'T:Travel' Magazine* reinforces the brand through the use of the hand-drawn Fraktur font of *The New York Times*, and the concept of the content through lettering in sand, while also presenting an image that is both original and inviting.

Sand Blast MAYBE AN ENGLISH BEACH SHACK IS YOUR IDEA OF PARADISE, OR A *PALAZZO* ON THE GRAND CANAL. THE TRICK IS TO LOWER THE THERMOSTAT AND CHILL. Photograph by James Wojcik them, a fact that is true for all editorial design, even listings pages, where the intelligent use of typefaces and rules is crucial if the page is not to look an overall grey. Of the back section, the most valuable page is that facing the inside back cover; readers flicking from back to front will see this page first, which is why some titles use it for high-volume or popular content such as horoscopes, letters or the masthead.

Section openers

Section openers are often an indulgence in a periodical publication, but a welcome one for the reader. In content terms, they are generally unnecessary spreads with an eye-catching image and a minimal amount of text, but they do allow breathing space and, if used as a spread, offer a rare opportunity for a landscape, image-led layout, which can be used to create a much greater design impact than a portrait (though ensuring that you have an image of good-enough quality and impact to repeat this regularly can be tricky). Because they generally stand out in a memorable way, such openers can act as a useful 'marker' for the reader looking for an article in a particular section. If this is their primary use, it can be helpful to create a distinct format that the regular reader can recognize and use to navigate the publication.

The role of typography

Type design is the backbone of editorial design and every designer has to know the basics. In digital formats the same typographic principles still apply as in print, but with a few additional adjustments. Any designer with a keen knowledge of type and an ability to handle complex typographic material will find they can work on any number of different publishing systems.

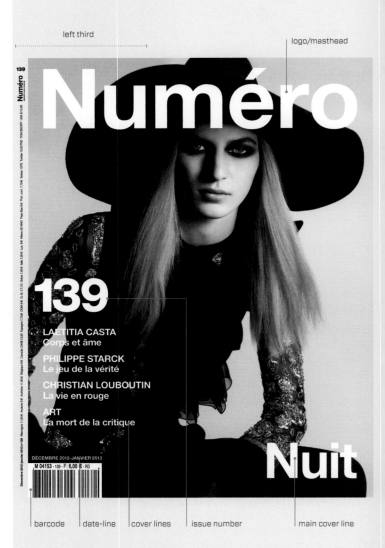

left third

logo/masthead

barcode   date-line   cover lines   issue number   main cover line

Copy

The terminology for copy can be confusing to a designer unused to the array of terms used in editorial design. It doesn't help that many of them have different names for the same thing (*see* illustration p.88), but it is important for the designer to know four things when it comes to copy:

- the different terms for copy;
- what these different forms of copy are;
- how writing for editorial generally, and these types of copy specifically, differs from other types of writing;
- how this affects the designer.

Tag-lines

Tag-lines or slogans under a logo can add enormous value to a publication. A well-worded tag-line not only tells the reader what a title is, but also indicates tone and target audience. For regular readers, it reinforces the feeling that they are 'the men who should know better' (*Loaded*), the people who care about 'the stuff that surrounds you' (*Wallpaper**) and the fashionistas that form part of the unusually styled 'we'ar different' cognoscenti (*WAD*). For newcomers, it's a handy instant clue to content that they may not otherwise get.

Headlines

A sub-editor will argue that the headline is just as important in persuading a reader to read a story as the layout. A headline creates a strong bond between the publication and the reader; it says, 'We know you, we're like you, we share the same sense of humour/interests/ cultural references and we know you're intelligent enough to understand this headline and story'. Therefore, appropriate size, positioning and treatment are vital. This is particularly true on a text-driven newspaper, which may not have the luxury of images with which to entice the reader into a purchase.

Stand-first

he content of the stand-first (aka sell, deck or intro t) is textually more important than the headline, for it sets the tone, after the headline, in informing the reader of the story's intention, and acts as the bridge or link, both textually and visually, between the headline and the body copy. As such, it must contextualize the headline, but also summarize and sell the story to the reader in a pithy, arresting way.

Pull quotes

Pull quotes are another very useful tool at the designer's disposal when it comes to orientating the reader and breaking up copy to make readability easier and the feature more enticing. The content for pull quotes is pulled directly out of the copy, or is a summarized excerpt.

Subheads (aka cross-heads)

Subheads can break up dense columns of copy and are most usefully employed in lengthy news items, where continuous copy can be off-putting or a reader may be looking for a particular aspect of a story. Subheads are also useful for denoting a new section, chapter subdivision or a subject change, and they will help readers find their place if not reading the article in one sitting.

Bylines and credits

The treatment and positioning of bylines and credits should be determined largely by the publication and the importance of these elements to it: a magazine will generally want to flag contributors and staff, particularly if they are using a well-known writer, photographer or illustrator; newspapers (which used not to have bylines at all) focus on the news, not who is reporting it, so bylines will be smaller on news pages than on feature pages.

 'A designer should have a willingness to read the material, to discuss it thoughtfully and passionately, and to develop visual components that expand the read while still working within the publication's architecture.'
Martin Venezky, art director, *Speak*

headline   byline   body copy   running head   sell/stand-first   folio

panel/box copy

caption/cutline

pull quote   credit

Body copy

On many titles, a publication's design will draw a readership in, but if the textual content or body copy does not match expectations, sales will fall, advertisers will stop advertising and the publication could fold. Of course, a publication's content will change to meet trends and remain relevant to its readership, but key to such change is the ability to remain true to the brand and the brand's message, and essential to this is the strength of content, its writers and its entire staff. The designer's involvement in body copy is, therefore, twofold: he or she must deal with its main requirements and characteristics, using column and font selection to reflect and deliver the brand and the individual content of the story to the reader; but they should also contribute ideas and knowledge of cultural trends to the editorial mix, as this can lead to dynamic content.

Panels, box copy, sidebars and infographics

Panels function as short news items or adjuncts to lengthy articles, where they are used to impart data such as facts and statistics, a case study or another element that is separate from but still relevant to the main article. Because of this, panel and box copy is

Black shirt by **Tom Ford** for **Yves Saint Laurent Rive Gauche Homme**.

NOT HALF BRAD

by **Jim Turner** *photographed by* **Tony Duran**

The *Flaunt* headline (above) is more traditional, but is still strong, clever and insightful, suggesting as it does a self-effacing attitude to (and on the part of?) superstar actor Brad Pitt, but also promising real insight rather than half a story.

More and more newspapers are using pull quotes, a device borrowed from consumer magazines, to catch the reader's eye and also to break up dense columns of body copy, as seen here in Spanish newspaper *El País* (left).

Two differing approaches to body copy from two very different publications: *The New York Times Magazine* (above) fills the page with body copy yet retains a sense of space, light and accessibility through its selection of fonts (Cheltenham redesigned by Jonathan Hoefler, Stymie redesigned by Cyrus Highsmith and Matthew Carter, Garamond and Helvetica). In *Speak* (opposite), Martin Venezky shapes the body copy to create space, but also to create a sense of cohesion across the spread, unifying the various elements.

usually snappier than the more discursive or in-depth approach of feature writing. This is reflected in shorter sentences, a more factual tone, lots of snippets of information and elements that break down continuous text into lists, points and the like. The design should, of course, visualize this snappiness.

Captions

Just as stand-firsts act as the bridge between headline and body copy, captions bridge the image and the text, and are therefore an important design element that requires a well-thought-out design solution. There are different approaches to designing captions and their placement (as outlined in Chapter 5), but their design will be dependent on the designer knowing what the role and tone of the caption is in the publication.

Folios

Consisting of a page number, the publication's title and, in some cases, a section or chapter title, folios are an indispensable part of the page furniture, helping to orientate the reader in the publication and strengthening

george segal

by Amanda Nowinski George Segal's sculptural environments allow the viewer a voyeuristic glimpse into the muted, introspective moments of everyday life. Augmented by a realistic backdrop—sitting in a restaurant, talking on the phone, operating a dry cleaning store, riding the bus, driving the bus—the narrative is seemingly clear and straight-forward. But upon further inspection, it becomes evident that the tableaus represent more than just a fleeting snippet of tedium; many of Segal's characters, who appear unwittingly tied to urban life and capitalist drudgery, are caught in the only form of escape they know—daydreaming. Conversationless, the characters impel viewers to fill the silence with their own psychological interpretations, which are infinite and remain unresolved. Unlike an isolated video frame, *with all the* Segal's narratives are heavily organic, weighed down in their environments with layers of hospital bandaging and white plaster. Here the temporally mundane is transformed into a complex, unsettling permanence.

Born in 1924 in New York City, Segal is the son of Jewish immigrant intellectuals who made their living on a chicken farm in New Jersey. Although he pursued a degree in arts education at Cooper Union after graduating high school, his escape from the fourteen-hour workday was cut short when his older brother was drafted. It was through his life on the farm that Segal developed his views on the hardships of the labor class.

Beginning as a painter in the late 1950s, Segal's early canvases evoke the grand simplicity of Matisse, but are rendered less playfully through his use of muddied primary colors and non-figurative lines. Segal was an artist emerging from the tail end of Abstract Expressionism and he and his New York peers were faced with the daunting task of creating something entirely new. To rebel against the anti-figural and material gestures of the Abstract Expressionists, however, meant that the new art must not only provide the antithesis to the previous movement, but that it must also avoid the Renaissance perspective that the Abstract Expressionist school worked to destroy. Robert Rauschenberg and Jasper Johns, leaders of the New York school, provided the link between pure abstraction

I wanted to deal with reality, with psychology, interior stuff plus the vivid reality of the world.

and the advent of Pop with their Dadaist-inspired Assemblages—the use of real objects was the logical divergence from the splatters of Jackson Pollock.

Inspired by the three-dimensionality of Rauschenberg and Johns, Segal expanded his vision to plaster casting—a move which would change the direction of his career forever. Beginning with sparse tableaus, normally of people sitting, Segal soon embraced more complex backdrops, including the quintessential Gas Station (1963-1964) and Times Square at Night (1970), a neon-lit setting for two disengaged pedestrians. His later work transgresses the quiet narratives, depicting more politically engaged scenarios, including the controversial In Memory of May 4, 1970: Kent State—Abraham and Isaac (1978),

2 5

---

the structure of the format and therefore the brand. On a title where the content is straightforward and direct, folios will not usually be made into a design feature, but a publication whose readers are visually literate will use fonts, weights and positioning to make folios stand out as design elements in their own right. David Carson, Martin Venezky and Rudy VanderLans often did this on *RayGun*, *Speak* and *Emigre* magazines. Many magazines will drop folios on pages featuring full-bleed images. There is nothing intrinsically wrong with this, but too many folio-free pages together might make production difficult for the design team and printer, and make navigation difficult and irritating for the reader. If choosing a left- or right-hand page for a folio, the right is the more visible page.

Screen fonts versus print fonts

There is one big difference between the way the human eye reads text printed on paper and text on a screen: the human eye is actually reading backlit letterforms on a screen. Depending on the brightness and calibration of the screen, letterforms can appear slightly bleached out if the contrast is too high.

Compare this to paper where the eye is seeing black letters printed on a natural white background. The quality of the reading experience depends on the light reflecting off the paper stock. The traditional 'dot gain' effect is also a factor when text is printed on newsprint or recycled paper, where letters appear slightly softer or blurry under a magnifying glass.

These factors mean that the designer must choose fonts carefully and know the difference between a font designed for screen and a font designed for print. Digital fonts are design products in their own right and commercially available from manufacturer companies, which are aptly named foundries. There is a bewildering array of digital fonts available to download from the internet and a little background knowledge of type history will certainly help the beginner. There exists a thriving community of typography fans who are only too willing to engage via blogging, type societies and lectures. For the more experienced designer, learning about typography is a life-long special interest. Learning new software and staying informed about technological advances is an essential part of continuing professional development as a designer.

News organizations, such as *The Times* newspaper, are able to draw on their vast archive of material, and use this content in both print and digital formats to make reference to a current story. In this way publications can bring forward some of their heritage into the present. Readers of *The Times* still want a reliable and trusted journalistic product. If they now have to pay to read content on the website, then they want a polished product, not the aggregated content they could get from free news sites. The digital product needs, therefore, to be of a high standard.

Jon Hill is Design Editor at *The Times* in London and oversaw redesigns of the paper, *The Times* website and the iPad edition. He also oversaw the launch of the *Eureka* supplement. In the interview which follows he explains his views on typography and the impact of the digital environment on design.

How do you take the *The Times* brand and keep it looking fresh?
It is a bit like setting up a kit or palette: not so much setting up templates as setting up a toolbox that all the designers can use. That goes all the way down to the font. We use Times Modern, which was created as part of the Neville Brody redesign in 2006/'7.

We worked very hard to make sure that the font worked across all the platforms from print to digital. Times Modern is our DNA; it is our brand if you like, because, of course, a big part of *The Times* is its headline font. It appears on everything we do.

You are known as a strict typographic designer who knows the deep structure of editorial pages and the visual language of page architecture. Do you still use these typography skills when working on the screen versions of *The Times*?
The biggest challenge for me is working with developers and the people that work with and build our content management systems. When you work with these people, you realize that their idea of a successful publication is one that is published automatically: it takes the journalism then automatically flows it into the web or the tablet edition. Meanwhile, art directors want to retain control and craft every page of the edition and this can be an area of conflict. The editing team want to have the last word on the way it looks, for example to make the headline better or adjust the picture crop for the iPad edition. The truth is somewhere in the middle. Where possible, the systems will automate much of our digital editions, but we have a level of control that allows for typographic and editorial adjustments.

Who has the last word when setting up these digital editions?
One of the things that we have learned is that, because of the paywall at *The Times*, we aim to give our readers an elegant and considered product if they are paying for it. Therefore it is important to get specifics like drop caps right and paragraph spacing. Polishing these details also shows that we care and

makes the product stand out from all the free news sites. We discussed this with the developers and made sure they knew this was important to the integrity of *The Times* when they were prioritizing their work.

Do you feel like the quality of digital fonts has improved to match the print version?
We are happier. We are still working with Monotype to try and improve the website fonts because there are still different browsers to consider and each browser displays the type differently. On the tablets you are in control because you know the resolution and quality of the device. Now in 2012 on some of the retina screens it is as good as it is in print. I am confident that we are now in control of our brand and the colour palettes across our digital editions in a way that we weren't, say, five years ago.

Can you explain how the new digital environment has had an impact on your work?
No publisher has really cracked what it means to publish editorial on the iPad and how you make that a rich experience. It hasn't quite happened yet but I am sure it will. It is important that our designers know about interactive graphics, motion

THE TIMES   Saturday June 27 2009

MICHAEL JACKSON
1958 — 2009

THE JACKSON FAMILY TREE

Kendall Brown (great-great-grandfather)

Mary Etta (great-great-grandmother) b circa 1860 – 1920

Prince Screws (great-grandfather) b circa 1860

Julia Belle Jordan (great-grandmother) b circa 1860

Crystal Lee King (grandmother) b circa 1900

Samuel Jackson (grandfather)

Prince Albert Screws (grandfather)

Martha "Mattie" Upshaw (grandmother)

Joseph Walter Jackson (father) b July 26, 1929

Katherine Esther Screws (mother) b May 4, 1930

MICHAEL JOSEPH JACKSON
August 29, 1958 – June 25, 2009

Wife	Lisa Marie Presley, married 1994, divorced 1996
Wife No 2	Deborah Jeanne Rowe, married 1996, divorced 1999
Son	Prince Michael Joseph Jackson Jr b 1997
Daughter	Paris Katherine Jackson, b 1998
Unidentified mother	
Son	Prince Michael Joseph Jackson II "Blanket" b 2002

Maureen Reillette "Rebbie" Jackson (sister) b May 29, 1950

Sigmund Esco "Jackie" Jackson (brother) b May 4, 1951

Toriano Adaryll "Tito" Jackson (brother) b Oct 15, 1953

Jermaine LaJaune Jackson (brother) b Dec 11, 1954

Joh'Vonnie Jackson b Aug 30, 1974

Janet Damita Jo Jackson (sister) b May 16, 1966

La Toya Yvonne Jackson (sister) b May 29, 1956

Steve Randall "Randy" Jackson (brother) b Oct 29, 1961

Marlon David Jackson (brother) b March 12, 1957

Brandon Jackson (brother) b March 12, 1957

A LONELY LIFE IN REVERSE

Michael Jackson lived his childhood as an adult, then, when he grew up, retreated into infantilism and a dangerous fascination with children

WILL PAVIA

Michael Jackson...

End of the road for Jacko caravan

CAITLIN MORAN

THE EARLY YEARS

August 25, 1958 Born Michael Joseph in Gary, Indiana to Joseph and Katherine. Lives with his five brothers Marlon, Tito, Jermaine, Marlon, Randall and three sisters Rebbie, La Toya, Janet in a two-bedroom clapboard house at 2300 Jackson Street.

1963 His mother Katherine becomes a Jehovah's Witness. Enrols at Garnett Elementary School. Also becomes the 'lead guy' in the Jackson singing group

1964 They make their first professional debut at a Big Top supermarket.

1968 The Jackson Five release their first single, Big Boy, on Steeltown Records. Later that year they sign a contract with Motown Records.

October 1969 They make their first Motown single, I Want You Back

October 18, 1969 The album The Jackson 5 on The Hollywood Palace

December 1969 The album Diana Ross Presents the Jackson 5.

January 31, 1970 I Want You Back reaches No 1 in the Billboard chart, and goes on to sell more than six million copies worldwide.

GOING SOLO

October 1971 I Want You Back is his solo single, Got To Be There is released but sells with OWERBRO copies

Roger Daltrey had been expelled for smoking [from Acton County Grammar School in 1963], but was still impudently showing up on campus to visit his various cronies. I'd first met him after he won a playground fight with a Chinese boy. I'd witnessed the fight, and I'd thought Roger's tactics were dirty. When I shouted as much, he had come over and forced me to retract. Since then I'd seen Roger around at the foot of Acton Hill, carrying an exotic white electric guitar he'd made himself. He was usually with Reg, a friend I knew from infancy, who carried a 15-watt Vox amplifier. Serious stuff.

I was outside our classroom talking to the form teacher for the final year, the redoubtable Mr Hamlyn, when Roger swaggered up in his Teddy boy outfit, his hair combed into a grand quiff, trousers so tight they had zips in the seams. Mr Hamlyn welcomed Roger with the weary patience of one who knew there was little point inquiring why Roger had returned to an institution that wanted nothing to do with him. Until he was expelled Roger had been a good pupil, and I think Hamlyn begrudgingly respected him.

A few boys looked over at us with interest, curious to see whether Roger still bore me any ill will. He simply informed me that John [Entwistle] had told him I played guitar pretty well, and if an opportunity came up to join his band, was I interested? I was stunned. Roger's band, the Detours, was a party band. They played country and western songs, *Hava Nagila*, the hokey-cokey, the conga, Cliff Richard songs and whatever was high in the charts at the time. Roger ruled the Detours with a characteristically iron hand. Judging by the faces of those around me, just the fact of Roger speaking to me meant that my life could very well change.

As calmly as I could I told Roger I was interested. He nodded and walked away, but I wouldn't hear from him again until months later. By that time I had enrolled in Ealing Art College.

On May 17, 1963 the band played at the Carnival Ballroom at the Park Hotel in Hanwell, which was near Ealing, so all my college chums turned out. Some pretty girls from the fashion school stood at the front of the stage, pretending to scream at me like Beatles fans; they were teasing, but everyone was impressed, especially when we played the slightly funkier R&B tunes I'd managed to sneak into our otherwise catholic repertoire. This was a formative moment for me. My friends from college could see the band I had been so reluctant to talk about; John, Roger and Doug [Sandom, the drummer at the time] could see my art-school friends, and how →

'I KNEW THE WHO HAD A GREATER MISSION THAN JUST BEING RICH AND FAMOUS. I KNEW THAT WHAT WE WERE DOING WAS GOING TO BE ART'

Townshend with his Who bandmates (from left) John Entwistle, Roger Daltrey and Keith Moon, during the cover shoot for their 1967 album, The Who Sell Out

THE TIMES

MAGAZINE

29.09.12

I can explain.
Pete Townshend in his own words.
Exclusive extracts from his memoir

PLUS
KOFI ANNAN'S VERDICT ON TONY BLAIR
By James Harding

graphics and are able to handle large amounts of data. They need storytelling skills in a digital context. It is no longer a case of moving around text and images on a page layout. Designing for digital newspapers demands a whole new approach.

Tell us about the iPad. Is making the tablet version very different to making the website?

A bit of history: Rupert Murdoch made a promise to Steve Jobs, so the story goes, that we would be the first newspaper to publish on the iPad, within three months of its UK launch. From a standing start we created the app within three months. It is a daily edition as opposed to a constantly updated website, with the editorial mantra that it is 'like the newspaper but better'.

The idea behind the app is that it shouldn't be a 'live' product, like the website, but a daily edition with all the journalism you'd get in the paper plus interactive graphics, video and extra archive material to give background content to bigger articles.

The reader can have an edition-based linear experience. We think readers prefer this, they don't want an infinite, overwhelming product, which is sometimes what navigating a news website can be like.

Jon Hill's advice for getting into news design

Do you think that young designers still need to know typographic rules and basics or can they survive without this knowledge?
Yes, they need to have a passion for design and typography and show some evidence of working with complex information and large amounts of text.

Graduates need to have a basic knowledge of typography and information design, but now they must also have the ability to teach themselves new software. Designers in the workplace update their knowledge all the time by using online tutorials. They need some knowledge of coding, so that they can appreciate what website developers do and be able to speak their language.

In terms of specialist publishing software, that is learned on the job. Many large publishers have custom-built systems that are not publicly available and so training is done in-house. This means that an aptitude for learning quickly is the most important attribute. If an applicant can demonstrate an ability to learn, this would be a good thing.

Once they are at work, can students pick up typographic rules as they go along?
The temptation is to bring people in who have a technical set of skills, but you can spend longer explaining rules of typography. We take students with technical skills, but we spend time training them to work with type. We can train them on our own system, called Methode. I like to see portfolios that show the person has a real interest in typography so you can have a deep conversation with them about that.

We look for people who have done some heavyweight typography before, or who show some sort of passion, even if it's for wooden type, so you know you can have a conversation with them about details. After all, crafting type is common to everything we do at The Times, from print to digital, information design to animation.

everything we do at The Times, from print to digital, information design to animation.

What specialist skills would you look for?
An understanding or appreciation of how websites and basic coding works is an advantage. Currently that includes HTML5 and CSS. We wouldn't expect a designer to code everything by hand, but they have to appreciate how it is done. Knowledge of how to handle stories with a lot of data, visuals and graphics is important. The rising popularity of storytelling using infographics has come about because of the trend towards organizations and governments sharing more of their data and this is good for designers. Designers need to interrogate the journalism, and be able to tell complex stories simply, especially when designing for the tablet, perhaps by using maps or moving graphics. It is not just about pure typography now; we need to tell stories in a number of different formats. Moving image, handling data and coding is all part of a designer's skill set now, on top of the more traditional skills of page layout, typography and how to crop an image. I want designers who can do all those things.

Myths about type

True or false? All mastheads need to appear at the top of the cover.

This principle came from the days when magazines were only sold in shops or kiosks and covers were stacked for display purposes, so the masthead had to appear at the top of the cover. Now, with many customers subscribing, this is no longer the case. However for hierarchy and a sense of authority the top is an ideal place.

True or false? Never run small x-height body copy across long line lengths to create wide columns.

This is a question of legibility and there are many books you can read about legibility. See *Better Type* by Betty Binns (Roundtable Press, Watson-Guptill Publications, 1989). Once the eye reads too far down a line it can't find its way back again. As a general rule, keep lines of moderate lengths. (The x-height is the height of a lowercase 'x' of a given typeface measured from the baseline to the mean-line. Different fonts can be the same point size but have a different x-height.)

True or false? Headlines should never be placed over a beautiful/reportage picture or any image if it can be avoided.

When reportage pictures were as precious as pieces of art, then this was the maxim. Any fine artist will be irritated by a headline placed over his or her work reproduced in a magazine. However, there is nothing wrong with text on pictures. The 'pop' of a headline on an image can be amazing and the design can make brilliant combinations. See George Lois's book *Covering the Sixties* (The Monacelli Press, Inc, 1996).

True or false? Don't reverse white text out of a black background. People won't read it.

In a printed glossy magazine, the 'black' of an image is made up from at least black plus blue; sometimes magenta and yellow as well. This is part of the four-colour printing process: the colours are known as CMYK. Once on the press the registration can vary. Tiny reversed-out type will not hold its shape and the reader will be unable to read pieces of the letters. (In colour printing, registration is the system that print machines use to ensure colours are lined up and print clearly and crisply.)

True or false? Headlines should run across the top of the page but never across the gutter.

This statement came from the days when type hierarchy existed to help the reader digest the content step-by-step. In our multi-channel world there is no reason why a more unconventional publication should adhere to this. When tablets can flip a page from portrait to landscape, a headline might move or even appear as a navigational link. Headlines along the bottom of a page can use scale to dominate. Because of the way magazines are bound, the gutter in thick glossy magazines is a 12mm (half-inch) no-go area. Most magazines use a binding technique known as perfect binding, which uses hot-melt adhesive to glue folded sections together. For those thick publications, headlines should be kept out of the gutter to avoid losing a letter. In a digital or saddle-stitched magazine, you can place headlines across the gutter. Think about your reader.

REF

Type resources

Website references:
For a description of fonts for print and fonts for screen:
Opinionated Font Facts, Research and writing, Alissa Faden with Ellen Lupton. This site is linked to Ellen's book and Princeton Architectural Press.
http://www.thinkingwithtype.com

To find out more on the psychology of reading:
The Science of Word Recognition, Kevin Larson, Advanced Reading Technology, Microsoft Corporation

July 2004, *http://www.microsoft.com/ typography*

Book references:
While You Are Reading, Gerard Unger, Mark Batty Publisher, 2007

Detail in Typography, Jost Hochuli, Hyphen Press, 2008

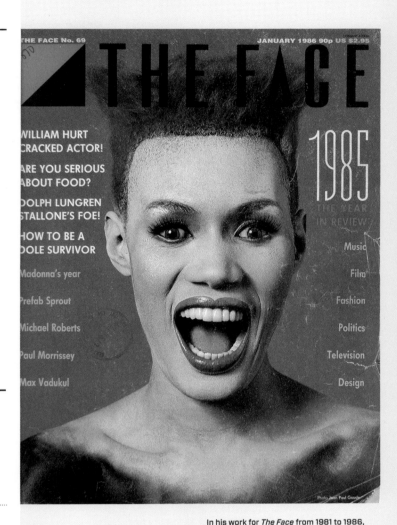

In his work for *The Face* from 1981 to 1986, Neville Brody made radical experiments with typography and layout. Influenced by Constructivism and Dada he broke many of the conventions of typography, highlighting individual words and phrases and changing the size of letters within the same word. The cover above from January 1986 features a portrait of the singer Grace Jones by Jean-Paul Goude.

Image treatment

Imagery and what the designer does with it have an enormous impact on a publication's feel. Newspapers are increasingly relying on pictures as storytelling. As more newspapers move from text-driven to image-driven content, their use of all kinds of images – graphs, illustrations and graphic devices – is growing. But there is a key difference between the use of pictures in newspapers and magazines. As Mario Garcia puts it, 'The nature of the content is different; newspapers need imagery that imparts immediacy in contrast to the more relaxing environment for the images that you'd find in a magazine.' Production and budget issues are also factors, as time and money spent on images for a newspaper will be minute compared to that of magazines.

Myths about art direction

True or false? The cover is the most important page in any magazine.

Increasingly true. If the cover doesn't attract the reader's attention then all the work inside is wasted. For digital magazines, the cover is an entry point and a home page that reinforces the brand. On the web, magazines are represented as thumbnail icons and covers have to work hard, therefore, to be memorable even at tiny size.

True or false? Designers only exist to do what editors say.

Designers are partners and equals in the creative process. They add spark to the fire and can make dull editorial content look good. The best editor/designer team is one of mutual respect and partnership.

True or false? Every picture needs a caption.

If you want readers to follow the meaning of a picture story then every picture does need a caption. If pictures are used as decorative elements then it is not necessary. Pictures always need to be credited to the photographer or to the stock agency that supplied them. Copyright infringement is not good design practice and must be avoided.

True or false? Money spent on original photography or illustration is worth every penny.

Creating something original is what designers get out of bed for. If the budget allows for new material then it is worth creating something unique to the magazine. In addition, the rights to use that image again can be included in the original fee. A publisher can, therefore, start to build a library of images that can be reused. Fashion and lifestyle magazines have profited by syndicating images in this way.

True or false? Using images for free from the internet is the way of the future.

Aiming for a unique product should be the top priority. Producing original images cannot be beaten but this can be expensive. Remember that images available for free on the internet can turn up anywhere. If using

These fashion photographs from *Wallpaper** for a story in their 'Reborn In India' edition explode with colour and movement. The fashion shoot was created during the Hindu festival of Holi and can be seen on the *Wallpaper** website as a video clip. The use of full-bleed colour shows how photographs can underpin the identity of a magazine – in this case a curiosity for different cultures and locations.

Observations
Margaret Howell

Duffle Coat

The clothing designer Margaret Howell pays homage to a classic British coat that's popular with schoolgirls and Naval officers alike

Monty duffle coat
GLOVERALL

STYLE BRIEFING

PHOTOGRAPHY THOMAS BROWN

When shooting for the iPad, still-life photos can make good use of the single-page format. In this *Port* fashion shoot, the bench provides a strong diagonal emphasis within the composition. Instead of a cut-out garment shot, this lovely photographic set-up helps to define the thick texture of the coat, and in so doing tells the story of the garment.

images from the web, credit must be given to sources and care taken to check permission for usage.

True or false? White space does not sell magazines.
If white space adds to the atmosphere and visual storytelling (tension/absence) then it has value. If it exists simply to stretch out copy and fill up pages then it has no editorial value. See *Emigre* magazine (*see* p.179) and *RayGun* as examples of magazines that use white space to create dynamic and graphic visual elements.

Using photography

Photography functions as visual reporting or storytelling, and the huge range of contemporary photographic techniques and styles available offers the editorial designer a vast choice of reporters and storytellers. Even if photography cannot be commissioned for financial reasons, the photos that are supplied by a PR agency, or by the subject of the story, can be edited just as text is. Commissioning a visual story or style is just the beginning (*see* p.190 for successful commissioning), for although photographs are taken in a rectangular format, the designer then has the option to crop the image or change the shape, as well as alter tonal values and employ other photo-manipulation techniques. All of this is visual editing; just as the editor makes selections and decisions about the copy, so art directors work with the image content of a publication.

But they can go further than that: if an art editor wants a different perspective on a story, he or she has the luxury of not giving the photographer any information about it, possibly resulting in two very different interpretations (image and text), which can add up to much more than the sum of their parts. Just as editing can shape a viewpoint, so can editorial design. The selection, juxtaposition, combination and positioning of images and text with captions that 'tell' viewers what they are seeing can strongly suggest a 'truth' that may not be there at all. Added to this is the growing sophistication in photo manipulation (both in and out of camera), which literally changes truth to lies. Hence the intervention of art editor, editor, picture editor and photographer can result in myriad representations of a story. Michael Watts, editor of many newspaper

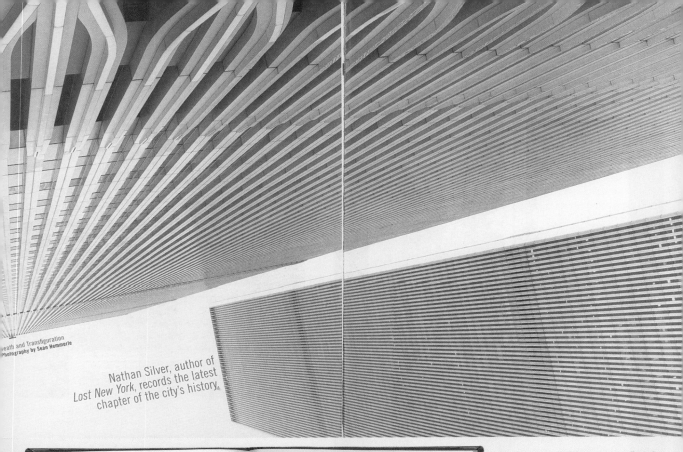

Death and Transfiguration
Photography by Sean Hemmerle

Nathan Silver, author of *Lost New York*, records the latest chapter of the city's history.

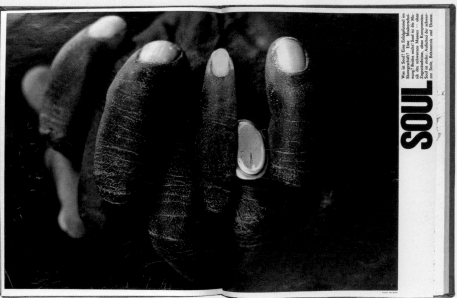

'The December 2001 issue was our first after 9/11. Because of our two- to three-month lead time, the world had been saturated with images of the Twin Towers being destroyed by the time this issue was printed. We decided not to show any images of destruction but use the space to celebrate the past and look towards the future,' says Criswell Lappin, former art director of *Metropolis*. This photograph by Sean Hemmerle did just that.

A great photo is the basic requirement for a great image, but equally important are sympathetic and appropriate cropping, scaling, positioning, format and stock. This image from *Twen* (left) is a brilliant image, brilliantly cropped.

The Guardian
A declaration of war

2 2001
London
tor
JA

supplements, recalls experiences on the *FT The Business* magazine for the *Financial Times*:

> '*Sometimes there were difficulties between myself and Julia Cuthbertson, who ran the weekend paper. She wanted conventional magazine items like food and restaurant reviews, while we wanted something that was visually dynamic and new, reflecting the dot-com boom and the new, cool status of business. The trick was to subvert the genre. On the food pages we photographed food in its raw state, when everyone else was showing cooked dishes. Our picture editor, Caroline Metcalfe, came up with some great food photographers, notably Rob White. Then we illustrated the restaurant reviews – by the very witty Marion McGilvary – with a mixture of maps showing where the restaurant was located, and bills that we reproduced. The combination of all these elements made the mag highly idiosyncratic, which irritated some but pleased many more. It gave it character. And sales of the weekend* Financial Times *rose to over the 250,000 mark in my time there – a 20 per cent leap. People who never read the* Financial Times *in the week would get it at the weekend.*'

Whereas photography in magazines is as much about image as text, in newspapers imagery is very much used to support text. But aspects of magazine design are creeping in, so that a front page will ofen use one striking image to attract the eye immediately and communicate something that no words

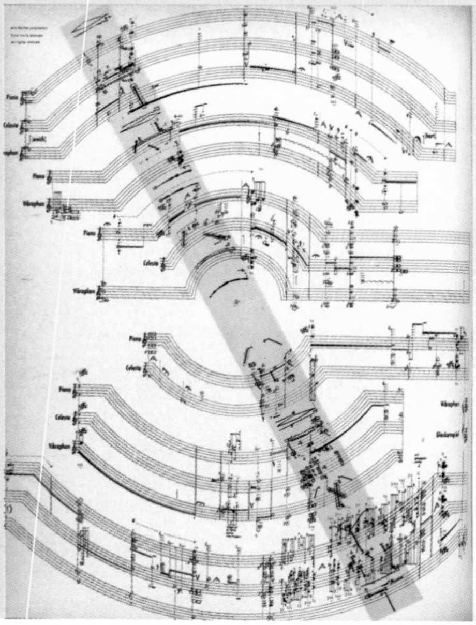

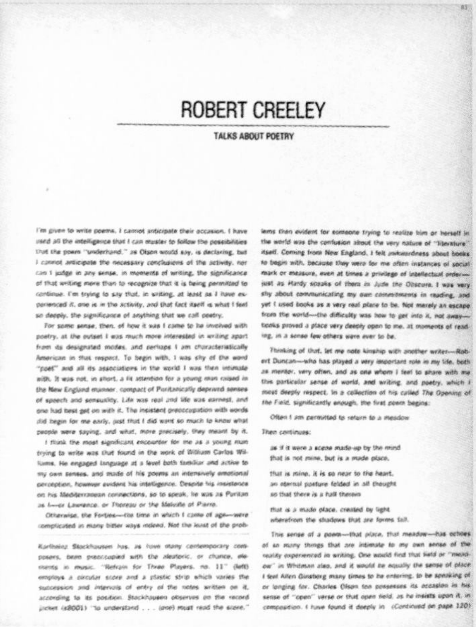

ROBERT CREELEY

TALKS ABOUT POETRY

I'm given to write poems. I cannot anticipate their occasion. I have used all the intelligence that I can muster to follow the possibilities that the poem "underhand," as Olson would say, is declaring, but I cannot anticipate the necessary conclusions of the activity, nor can I judge in any sense, in moments of writing, the significance of that writing more than to recognize that it is being permitted to continue. I'm trying to say that, in writing, at least as I have experienced it, one is in the activity, and that fact itself is what I feel so deeply, the significance of anything that we call poetry.

For some sense, then, of how it was I came to be involved with poetry, at the outset I was much more interested in writing apart from its designated modes, and perhaps I am characteristically American in that respect. To begin with, I was shy of the word "poet" and all its associations in the world I was then intimate with. It was not, in short, a fit attention for a young man raised in the New England manner, compact of Puritanically deprived senses of speech and sensuality. Life was real and life was earnest, and one had best get on with it. The insistent preoccupation with words did begin for me early, just that I did want so much to know what people were saying, and what, more precisely, they meant by it.

I think the most significant encounter for me as a young man trying to write was that found in the work of William Carlos Williams. He engaged language at a level both familiar and active to my own senses, and made of his poems an intensively emotional perception, however evident his intelligence. Despite his insistence on his Mediterranean connections, so to speak, he was as Puritan as I—or Lawrence, or Thoreau or the Melville of Pierre.

Otherwise, the Forties—the time in which I came of age—were complicated in many bitter ways indeed. Not the least of the problems then evident for someone trying to realize him or herself in the world was the confusion about the very nature of "literature" itself. Coming from New England, I felt awkwardness about books to begin with, because they were for me often instances of social mark or measure, even at times a privilege of intellectual order—just as Hardy speaks of them in *Jude the Obscure*. I was very shy about communicating my own commitments in reading, and yet I used books as a very real place to be. Not merely an escape from the world—the difficulty was how to get into it, not away—books proved a place very deeply open to me, at moments of reading, in a sense few others were ever to be.

Thinking of that, let me note kinship with another writer—Robert Duncan—who has played a very important role in my life, both as mentor, very often, and as one whom I feel to share with me this particular sense of world, and writing, and poetry, which I most deeply respect. In a collection of his called *The Opening of the Field*, significantly enough, the first poem begins:

Often I am permitted to return to a meadow

Then continues:

as if it were a scene made-up by the mind
that is not mine, but is a made place,

that is mine, it is so near to the heart,
an eternal pasture folded in all thought
so that there is a hall therein

that is a made place, created by light
wherefrom the shadows that are forms fall.

This sense of a poem—that place, that meadow—has echoes of so many things that are intimate to my own sense of the reality experienced in writing. One would find that field or "meadow" in Whitman also, and it would be equally the sense of place I feel Allen Ginsberg many times to be entering, to be speaking of or longing for. Charles Olson too possesses its occasion in his sense of "open" verse or that open field, as he insists upon it, in composition. I have found it deeply in (Continued on page 120)

Karlheinz Stockhausen has, as have many contemporary composers, been preoccupied with the aleatoric, or chance, elements in music. "Refrain for Three Players, no. 11" (left) employs a circular score and a plastic strip which varies the succession and intervals of entry of the notes written on it, according to its position. Stockhausen observes on the record jacket (s8001) "to understand . . . (one) must read the score."

In this July 1967 issue of *Harper's Bazaar* (left), a piece on poetry is illustrated with a picture of the score for Karlheinz Stockhausen's 'Refrain for the Players, no.11'. Art directors Ruth Ansel and Bea Feitler were making the conceptual link between the elegant intricacy and visual lyricism of the score (and the music it represents) and the nature and concept of poetry. It is a brilliant visual metaphor for the article. Newspapers are also increasingly using illustration to give readers a less literal interpretation of a story, as illustrations will offer a different dynamic to a page. Below, Marion Deuchars' illustration for *The Guardian* gives breath and life to the page. Its composition and colour contrast well with the blocks of text beneath it, while its obvious hand-craftedness gives the story something a photo would struggle to do. Below left, in this page for iPad, the brushstrokes of the illustration by Dan Williams contrast with the crisp typography.

Secret City
Lorin Stein

The Tailor
New York

"Wearing clothes is a pleasure," wrote the photographer Edouard Levé, "buying them a trial." My feelings exactly, until a friend sent me to Kirk Miller of Miller's Oath. Wearing Kirk's clothes is indeed a pleasure. His suits, shirts and coats are beautifully cut, and the place is fun too. Kirk takes a sort of editorial joy in solving unusual problems in the most elegantly simple way. Last month I asked him for a suit that I could wear over a two-week train journey. The result, a light two-button corduroy, had strangers stopping me on the street from New York to San Francisco, and yet there is nothing dandified about it. It is the most comfortable thing I own – and was, from the moment I put it on.

INITIATIONS [Map] [Miller's Oath] ILLUSTRATIONS BY DAN WILLIAMS

The Guardian | Saturday September 17 2005 23

Saturday

Marina Hyde Lost in Showbiz 25 | Marian Salzman, doyenne of trends 27 | Mark Lawson on scriptwriters 28 | Norman Johnson joins the Guardian 29

An American on Exmoor grapples with an eccentric British tradition

Goodwill hunting

Essay by PJ O'Rourke Illustrations by Marion Deuchars

A stag flanked by two female red deer, or "hinds," trotted down a steep moorland pasture toward a wood. Two mounted hunters were behind them, and staghounds were in between. The deer's trot was faster than the hunters' canter and as fast as the all-out run of the hounds. A horn was blown. We were off – over a soaked, slippery sheep meadow, between the stone posts of a narrow gate, down a muddy track perilous with ruts, into a country lane barely an arm's length wide, through the tiny streets of an old village with tourists hopping out of our way, and then making a hairpin turn on to a paved road, speeding uphill around blind curves, and narrowly avoiding several head-on collisions with trucks. It was a thrilling ride, even if it was in a Suzuki SUV driven by a retired grocer – an enthusiast of stag hunting who had volunteered to show me the Devon and Somerset Staghounds hunt on Exmoor.

We arrived at a hilltop above the woods. From there I could look across a valley at ... not much. On the crest of the far slope several dozen members of the hunt were sitting on their horses. They watched two dogs sniffing the underbrush below. Two men in scarlet coats were with the dogs, more closely watching them sniff.

The idea of a stag hunt evokes chivalry – knights in jerkins and hose, ladies on sidesaddles with wimples and billowing dresses, a white stag symbolising something-or-other, and Robin Hood getting in the way. An actual stag hunt is more like a horseback meeting of a county planning commission. The equestrian committee is responding to deer-population-growth issues. Red deer are noble animals – big, anyway. But red deer are also pests. A farmer may find a hundred deer in his pasture, each eating as much grass as three sheep.

Each stag hunt has a "harbourer", a specialist whose job is to watch the herds and select a specific quarry, chosen for its lack of Darwinian promise ... the herd. It was this singling-out that I was watching. Although it wasn't working perfectly. As unpromising as that young stag may have been from the harbourer's point of view, the two hinds thought he was worth running away with.

Once the stag is solitary, the huntsman's assistant, the "whipper-in," is supposed to bring up the full pack, and the hunt's members and guests fall in behind the hounds. Miles and miles of furious cross-country galloping ensues.

Unless it doesn't. As it seemed not to be doing from my vantage point across the valley.

When the chase does happen, the usual outcome is that the stag, at last, turns and "stands at bay", facing the hounds. Then (rather disappointingly for those whose imaginations run to tenderhearted indignation or to bloodlust) the hounds do not tear the stag to shreds. They bark. There's probably not much else they could do with an irked and antler-waving stag. Staghounds are not giant Scottish deerhounds or hulking, red-eyed mastiffs. They're just foxhounds, happy and hound-doggy and friendly if you aren't prey. "You can set your baby down in the middle of a pack," a hunter told me, "and they'll lick him silly."

What happens to the stag is that the huntsman walks over to it and prosaically shoots it in the head with a special short-barrelled, folding-stock shotgun. This is an illegal weapon in Britain. But on stag hunts it's legally required. Speaking of Britain's laws, killing wild mammals with the aid of dogs, as the Exmoor hunt was trying to do, is forbidden. Except when – as I understand the Hunting Act of 2004 – it is mandatory. The act contains certain conditions for "exempt hunting" that allow the killing of wild mammals with the aid of dogs – if "as soon as possible after being found or flushed out the wild mammal is shot dead by a competent person". No letting it go, even if it's Bambi's mother.

The Hunting Act came into effect on February 18 2005, a few weeks before this Exmoor meet. I got in touch with Adrian Dangar, the hunting correspondent for the Field magazine. He said that I shouldn't write about foxhunting, which is the most notable activity banned under the act. He said that the stag hunters were a doughty and resolute lot, and stag hunting was more of a way of life.

I went to Exmoor with Adrian. We stayed with the chairman of the stag hunt, Tom Yandle. He was doughty and resolute, the owner of a family sheep farm of centuries' standing. I went to the meet expecting a scene of American seething, full of the half-suppressed violence that Americans thwarted in their beliefs or their hobbies half-suppress so well. What I found was a cheerful, natty crowd on horseback listening to a talk from the hunt secretary about strict adherence to the Hunting Act, especially in the matter of using just two dogs.

Having just two dogs in the field was exactly the problem. So I was told by the retired grocer and other hunt followers gathered on the hilltop vantage point. Two hounds were not enough to break the stag away from the hinds. Or two hounds were not enough to make the stag stand at bay. Two hounds were certainly not enough to make what I was told was the music of a pack in full cry.

The hunt was moving. Horses were trotting over the far hill. The two hounds did their best in the music department. There was a spate of elderly, excited driving as hunt followers hurried to find a better view. We parked by a tributary of the Exe. ... from a van. There was a tense murmuring, as from a golf gallery.

The staghounds and stag hunters trotted through a farmyard, and I followed on foot. Some local farmers are not hospitable to the traffic through their property – not hospitable, specifically, to the traffic of me. I was trying to take notes and make haste and avoid deep puddles and horse droppings, and I wasn't wearing a necktie. "Is he all right?" I heard a farmer ask. "He thought you were an 'anti'," the retired grocer explained later. "They come around bothering the hunts."

Wind, rain, and temperature grew worse. The hunt descended into a precipitous dell where I'd have thought the riders would have to walk their mounts. They didn't. The stag and every trace of it had vanished, and the hunters decided to "pack it in, to spare the horses".

Tom, Adrian, and I headed back to Tom's farm in his horse van, a bit disappointed. And then came that music I'd been told about: the full cry of a pack. It is a bouillabaisse of a noise, with something in it of happy kids on a playground, honking geese headed for your decoys, and the "wheeee" of a deep-sea fishing reel when you've hooked something huge.

A beagle pack, 30-some strong, was bounding across a pasture. Beagling is like foxhunting or stag hunting except that the quarry is hare, and it's done without horses. Beaglers follow the pack at a very brisk pace – on foot. Hunting hares with beagles is banned by the Hunting Act. But rabbits can still be hunted. "Because they're considered pests," Tom said. "Because a lot of Labour voters hunt rabbits," Adrian said. Also, for some reason, "the hunting of a hare which has been shot" is permitted.

The pack arced away from us across a broad field. "The hare went that way!" Tom shouted to the ...

RED DEER ARE NOBLE ANIMALS – BIG, ANYWAY. BUT RED DEER

By choosing to use illustration in place of photography, which is only used for high-gloss, full-colour ads confined to two or three spreads in the centre of the magazine, first-class Virgin Atlantic fanzine *Carlos* (right) 'set out to avoid the clichéd world of celebrity-led magazine content, both editorially and visually. Or, in the words of the then art director, *Carlos* is "post-photography"!' – Jeremy Leslie.

'If we didn't incorporate the textiles into an illustration [right], then we would be left showing carpet swatches, which would be pretty dull. By having Christopher Neal incorporate the textiles into his one-colour line drawings, we accomplished two things. First, we made carpet samples interesting to look at without taking away from the product. Second, the illustrations give the viewer information about the product. The environments, while somewhat tongue-in-cheek, indicate the locations that the different textiles are designed for – schools, offices, airports and so on. I gave Christopher a rough page layout, the approximate size for each illustration and told him which environment went with each textile. Christopher came up with the content of each illustration with little direction. Once he sent me the finished illustrations, I decided to hand-letter the word 'edges' in the headline to reflect what he did.' – Criswell Lappin, former art director, *Metropolis*.

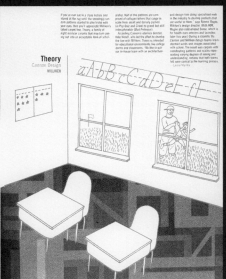

Using illustration

When at *The Guardian* newspaper, Mark Porter used illustration because 'it has always been an important part of *The Guardian* visual mix, and, by introducing more contemporary illustrators, we have ensured that the paper feels fresh and modern'. Other art editors use illustration when a story demands a conceptual or oblique interpretation, or there are no good photographic images to be used, or simply to create an interesting and constantly varying dialogue between visuals and text. Illustration can express a concept or feeling more than photography can, because readers often cannot help but attach a narrative to a photograph, particularly if it's figurative. This is because they 'read' the photograph literally: 'This image is made up of this figure wearing these clothes in this setting doing this thing, therefore I am being told this.' But illustration is not read in this way, allowing the story, art editor and reader to create other, often more expressive and abstract associations. Illustration can also illustrate the zeitgeist in a more obvious way than photography can, and it can be used

Many editorial publications incorporate illustrations into their design, but none besides *The Illustrated Ape* (above), edited by Christian Patterson and Michael Sims, designed by Darren Ellis at See Studio and illustrated by top illustrators such as Paul Davis, builds its whole *raison d'être* around it. Created by using open submissions from writers, artists and illustrators, this cultural quarterly of poetry and fiction uses only illustration as its imagery – and more often than not its text, too. The resulting large-scale spreads are rich and textural, and form an intelligent, cohesive whole that always looks fresh.

to support a brand. *The Illustrated Ape* magazine in the UK is famed for only using illustration, as is *Carlos*, which retains colour photography solely for the ads.

Cropping an image

Cropping, magnifying, repeating or shooting an image from unusual approaches can have a huge impact on a layout and create original and unexpected perspectives. Techniques such as cropping and magnifying can also concentrate the eye on the portion of an image that contains its essence, or create a meaningful dialogue with the text, and, ultimately, a dynamic rapport with the text and layout. If more than one image is used, this rapport becomes more complex, with the need to create a narrative interaction both between the images and between the images and text. American industrial design magazine *I.D.* uses these tools to great effect: by blowing up a product to massive proportions on a page, an everyday item such as a toothbrush becomes a surreal object of beauty whose sculptural qualities are revealed, making for a visually arresting page. Tight close-ups can be equally effective, as can using images to create abstract patterns and focusing on or bringing out an unusual curve, shape or aspect in an object.

scary monsters

Trailblazers

Balancing comfortable economics with functional innovation, Copenhagen bicycle-maker Biomega taps high-profile designers for new concepts.

By David Pescovitz

On the spread from Japanese magazine *Eat* (top), the close-up photograph of the scales of an upside-down artichoke turn what could have been a mundane image into a sculptural, striking graphic. In *I.D.* magazine, the image of a bicycle (left) works hard to pull two spreads literally and boldly together while also suggesting movement and continuity; in another issue, toothbrushes become abstract translucent objects (above).

Brief Three
Typographic style sheets

AIM

To create typographic worksheets for your magazine.

THE BRIEF

Work on a visual typographic identity for your magazine and think about how the fonts will relate to the philosophy of your magazine's content. Start with two or three fonts that relate to each other and work together visually as a headline font, subhead font and text font. Other design elements tend to be sisters and brothers of these main three fonts. As you progress, you might cut this number down to one font or two, but be open to ideas at the start. Remember that if your magazine is bold and powerful then use fonts that have a dynamic page presence. If your magazine is contemplative, however, choose fonts that reflect a softer visual sensibility.

- Write some headlines and stand-firsts. Explore scale by looking at what would work for drop caps. Which font reads smoothly for pull quotes? Print them out and pin them to a wall to view them from a different perspective. Collage your elements together in your sketchbook for reference later on.
- Consider the letter kerning. Almost all digital fonts will need adjusting. Don't accept the output from the computer. It does not have your human eye and cannot 'see' type. You are learning to feel type and really see it in use. Look at the letters off screen and absorb the shapes they make.
- Be confident in your ability. You are aiming for a typographic style sheet that reflects and enhances the idea of your magazine.

This magazine is an example of a student project that utilizes and explores a largely typographic format. It uses graphic language to reflect the opinionated content of the editorial, which is a slightly cynical take on the art-school experience and a critique of the lifestyle. The creator Jordan Harrison-Twist has chosen sharp Futura Italic as his headline font and made provocative covers that challenge the reader.

I'M AN ART STUDENT; I'M SO FUCKING UNIQUE.

PROJECTS ON COFFEE AND SMOKING.

PIONEER/ INNOVATER/ GODHEAD/ CREATOR.

Mind-blowing bubbles

The Guardian space

interiors/property/design January 23 1998

"IT'S AMAZING, APPARENTLY ALL HOMELESS PEOPLE LIKE TO BE PHOTO-GRAPHED."

Weirdly sparse page gives eyes less daunting task of actually reading something as opposed to nodding sycophantically at pictures.

It contrasts to every other grid system previously used which makes the publicist seem either rebellious, or consciously aware of his/her choice of breaking convention, which makes the page seem even more important.

Even though it is only a few paragraphs and it is probably the least visually impressive page on display, you can't help keep reading as it shows you are interested, and everybody can see you're interested and hey it ain't too long, so it's not tiresome and you can move on fairly swiftly after finishing.

This section may even be tilted slightly to one side which is utterly mental. Though there is a fairly simple uniform grid-system used, it is used in a dynamic way to sustain interest, regardless of the content.

written by Jorgen Harrison-Twist

"You see, it's all about thought. Art can't be anything that's been done before. And, you know, not everything is, like, beautiful. It's about capturing a moment that inspires or... or excites. Like, I did a project on homeless people last year and I think it kinda, really opened everyone's eyes to, to the plight of these people."

"Like, sometimes you just don't notice homeless people, but if you take a photograph of them, it kinda forces people to think about it. It's like Live Aid or Children in Need."

"You know, it's all about perspective. What we thought was ugly years ago, now isn't necessarily ugly. It's just different. You put your personal philosophies into what you make, and that's beautiful."

-24/02/12 - anonymous

"I FIND YOU CAN OFTEN GET TOO *TIED DOWN* WITH WHAT THE WORK ACTUALLY MEANS."

Lorem ipsum dolor sit amet, consectetur adipiscing elit. Fusce suscipit, nibh id fermentum tincidunt, orci velit convallis nibh, at tincidunt nulla nisl quis odio. Cum sociis natoque penatibus et magnis dis parturient montes, nascetur ridiculus mus. Sed lobortis molestie sapien non convallis. Phasellus dictum ultricies ullamcorper. Praesent elit libero, rhoncus nec tempus id, accumsan a libero. Nunc lacinia volutpat tellus vitae mollis. Duis ullamcorper laoreet dictum. Praesent ultricies ligula a diam lacinia tempus. Mauris eget molestie velit. Cras congue, elit a porttitor congue, arcu arcu sollicitudin magna, a suscipit nisl diam nec leo. Aenean eu lorem at ipsum tempor luctus. Cras id augue a ante interdum fringilla. Suspendisse ligula lectus, posuere quis aliquam laoreet, vehicula eget enim. In hac habitasse platea dictumst. Morbi nunc massa, tempor eu pretium in, ornare cursus erat. Sed leo risus, volutpat et malesuada et, elementum sed nibh.

Duis aliquet accumsan egestas. Pellentesque id velit orci. Phasellus pulvinar ornare semper. Nunc consequat lorem quis odio accumsan eget interdum nisl vestibulum. Maecenas et eleifend lectus. Vivamus a leo elit, sed condimentum ligula. Morbi nec ultricies sapien. Nam fermentum blandit viverra. Cras vestibulum cursus metus. Duis tincidunt fringilla dui sed porta. Nulla ut iaculis quam. Duis libero ante, elementum vitae aliquet a, bibendum a enim. Phasellus cursus molestie massa, eu sollicitudin enim sagittis non.

Nunc ac tellus tortor, vitae lacinia velit. Nulla facilisi. Etiam ut fringilla ante. In ut nulla lacus, quis cursus turpis. Mauris a dui in mi condimentum suscipit. Nulla facilisi. Donec ipsum nisl, vulputate non mattis id, dapibus quis lorem.

A practical illustration to show the fragmented nature of today's society and that there's unworthy everywhere.

"I FIND MY WORK IS OFTEN FAR TOO CONCEPTUAL AND OFTEN FAR TOO DEEP FOR MY CRITICS TO UNDERSTAND. I'M A DARK, BROODING INDIVIDUAL AND I FEEL THAT COMES THROUGH."

Pellentesque semper euismod sapien, vel dictum urna viverra ut. Cras ipiscit taciti sociosqu ad litora torquent per conubia nostra, per inceptos himenaeos. Pellentesque diam diam, tincidunt eget ultrices vel, pulvinar sit amet augue. Sed vestibulum ultricies consectetur. Ut eu nulla magna.

Aliquam sollicitudin gravida volutpit. Aenean rutrum adipiscing risus, vel bibendum eros cursus suscipit. Nunc metus lacus, adipiscing sed gravida et, imperdiet nec mi. Maecenas nec mauris non eros gravida aliquam. Suspendisse potenti. Integer est

cpit condimentum ante, id aliquet nulla euismod sed. Quisque nec tortor a ipsum ultricies fringilla. Cum sociis natoque penatibus et magnis dis parturient montes, nascetur ridiculus mus. Sed scelerisque, nisl at hendrerit vestibulum, libero mauris tincidunt purus, ac iaculis sem nunc eu arcu. Aenean ornare aliquam mi id tempor. Fusce sit amet gravida orci. Proin blandit metus eget nulla ullamcorper eleifend. Aenean odio lacus, dapibus ac egestas et, ultricies at tellus. Vestibulum at varius mi.

Jorkson   Harrison-Twiko

Much of the content was written by Harrison-Twist, who is talented in that area, but the visual looks raw in its lack of respect for convention. The magazine evokes a fanzine feel in its use of two colours and line drawings, all of which serve to reinforce the concept of the editorial.

Chapter 5 : Creating layouts

Having established what editorial design is, and how an understanding of it and its components is essential to good design and art direction, we come to a key part of the design process itself: creating layouts. Although there is no magic formula for composing the perfect layout, there are certain considerations that condition the design of an editorial publication. Those dealing with roles, branding and the publication's identity and readership have already been discussed, but others, such as specific factors (space, amount of copy, time, purpose) and required elements (type styles, weights, symmetry, images) play an equally important part. All these elements combine to act as guiding principles for the design. The way in which a designer interprets, applies or sets aside these principles is fundamental to editorial design, as is the ability to look at content and make the constituent parts work within the proportions of a rectangular page on paper or on screen.

Principal components of a layout

The components of this layout are contained on two single pages, which, together, form a double-page spread (DPS). Some of these components have been defined from a branding and identity point of view in preceding chapters; here, they are examined from a visual and layout-composition perspective. The box opposite shows the component parts, but it also shows the grid substructure, which consists of columns, column gutter, spine gutter, margins, folio line, baseline and trim area (see Chapter 6 for more information on grids).

Templates

For newspapers and news pages of magazines, flexible templates will speed up the layout and production processes, and give the pages and overall design a cohesion that might otherwise be lost in the frantic days and hours before going to press. Templates simplify all aspects of page make-up, but they can also be restrictive in design terms, and care must be taken to ensure that they don't make pages look too alike. Imagery plays an important part here; subject, crop, scale and tension can all be used to distinguish pages from each other.

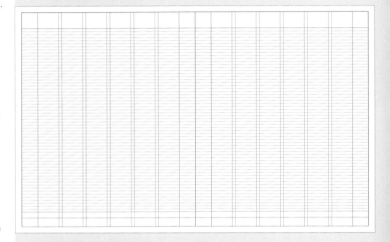

Template essentials

The essential elements of a template consist of margins (blue), columns and gutters (green), baseline grid (pink), folio (purple) and bleed area. This template uses a six-column grid, allowing the option of two-, three- or six-column layouts. The sizes of the margins are integral to creating white space on a page – their size is often influenced by advertising revenues as every extra centimetre can be sold. The baseline grid determines the variations in leading, and consequently type size, allowing the possibility for type of varying sizes to align. This baseline grid is founded on 9-point type on 11-point leading, meaning that all other type sizes need to fit on leadings that are multiples of 11. The folio is a guide line to mark the positioning of page numbers and sections.

The spread opposite top incorporates some of the principal components of a layout. The image, headline, stand-first and pull quotes help to grab attention and provide easy, instant access to the article. The drop cap and folio help guide the reader, while the caption and credit add interest to both image and article. These components, plus colour and graphic rules, create variety within the layout.

There are many other components that can be included in the design. The spread opposite bottom shows the added use of a subhead, a byline and sign-off. It also demonstrates the flexibility of the same template, using two columns instead of three, and a varying headline size and colour, all of which contribute to creating a different look and feel for this article.

The headline
of this story

This is a stand-first. Intended to be read but have no meaning. A simulation of actual copy, using ordinary words with normal letter frequencies, it cannot deceive the eye or brain.

Dummy settings which use other or even gibberish to approximate text have the inherent disadvantage they distract attention to themselves. Simultext is effective in any typeface, at whatever size and format is required. Paragraphs may be long or short. Text can be to complete any area, as the copy is simply repeated with different starting points. This is dummy text. Intended to be read but have no meaning. A simulation of actual copy, using ordinary words with normal letter frequencies, it cannot deceive eye or brain.

Settings which use other languages or even gibberish to approximate text have the disadvantage they distract attention to themselves. As a simulation of actual copy, using ordinary words with normal letter frequencies, it can't deceive eye or brain. Simultext is effective in any typeface, at what ever size and format is required. Paragraphs may be long or short. What you see is dummy text. It is intended to be read but have no real

meaning. As a simulation of actual copy, using ordinary words with normal letter frequencies, can't deceive eye or brain. Copy can be produced to complete any area, as the basic copy is repeated with different starting points. It is intended to be read but have no meaning.

Presentation copy uses languages or gibberish to approximate text have the disadvantage that they distract attention to themselves. Simultext is effective in any typeface, whatever size and format is required. Paragraphs may be long or short. This is dummy text. Intended to be read but have no meaning. As a simulation of actual copy, using words with normal letter frequencies, cannot deceive eye or brain. What you see here is dummy text.

Simultext is effective in any typeface, whatever size and format required. Paragraphs may be long or short. Text can be produced to complete any area, as the basic copy is simply repeated with different starting points. This is dummy text. It is intended to be read but have no meaning.

This is a dummy text. It is intended to be read but have no meaning. As a simulation of actual copy, using ordinary words with normal letter frequencies, it cannot deceive eye or brain. Dummy settings which use other languages or even gibberish to approximate text have the inherent disadvantage they distract attention to themselves. As a simulation of actual copy, using ordinary words with normal letter frequencies, it can't deceive eye or brain. Simultext is effective in any typeface, at whatever size and format is required. Paragraphs may be long or short. What you see here is dummy text. It is intended to complete any area, as the copy is simply repeated with different starting

points. This is dummy text. Intended to be read but have no meaning. As a simulation of actual copy, using words with normal letter frequencies, cannot deceive eye or brain. Trial settings which use other languages or gibberish to approximate text have the disadvantage they distract attention to themselves. A simulation of actual copy, using ordinary words with normal letter frequencies, it can't deceive eye or brain. Simultext is effective in any typeface, at whatever size and format is required. Paragraphs may be long or short. What you see is dummy text. It is intended to be read but have no meaning. As a simulation of actual copy.

A pull quote intended to be read but have no meaning. A simulation of actual copy, using ordinary words.

Using ordinary words with normal letter frequencies, it cannot deceive eye or brain. Copy is produced to complete any area, as the copy is simply repeated with different starting points. This is dummy text. Intended to be read but

have no meaning. The Presentation copy which uses languages or gibberish to approximate text have the inherent disadvantage that they distract attention to themselves. As a simulation of actual copy, using ordinary words with normal letter frequencies, can't deceive eye or brain. Simultext is effective in any typeface, at what ever size and format is required. Paragraphs may be long or

A pull quote intended to be read but have no meaning. A simulation of actual copy, using ordinary words.

short. What you see is dummy text. It is intended to be read but have no real meaning. As a simulation of actual copy, using ordinary words with normal letter frequencies, can't deceive eye or brain. Copy can be produced to complete any area, as the basic copy is repeated with different starting points. It is intended to be read but have no meaning.

Presentation copy uses languages or gibberish to approximate text have the inherent disadvantage that they distract attention to themselves. Simultext is effective in any typeface, whatever size and format is required. Paragraphs may be long or short. This is dummy text. Intended to be read but have no meaning. As a simulation of actual copy, using words with normal letter frequencies, cannot deceive eye or brain. What you see here is dummy text.

Simultext is effective in any typeface, whatever size and format required. Paragraphs may be long or short. Text can be produced to complete any area, as the copy is simply repeated with different starting points. This is dummy text. It is intended to be read but have no meaning. What you see here is dummy text. It is intended to be read.

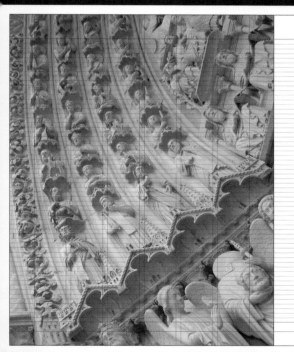

This is a caption. Intended to be read but has no meaning.

The headline

A stand-first is a short summary of the following article allowing quick and easy access for the reader. Often it includes the Author's and Photographer's Names as a byline

This is dummy text. It is intended to be read but have no meaning. As a simulation of actual copy, using ordinary words with normal letter frequencies, it cannot deceive eye or brain. Dummy settings which use other languages or even gibberish to approximate text have the inherent disadvantage they distract attention to themselves. Simultext is effective in any typeface, at whatever size and format is required. Paragraphs may be long or short. Text can be produced to complete any area, as the copy is simply repeated with different starting points. This is dummy text. Intended to be read but have no meaning. A simulation of actual copy, using ordinary words with normal letter frequencies, it cannot deceive eye or brain.

Trial settings which use other languages or even gibberish to approximate text have the disadvantage they distract attention to themselves. As a simulation of actual copy, using ordinary words with normal letter frequencies, can't deceive eye or brain. Simultext is effective in any typeface, at what ever size and format is required. Paragraphs may be long or short. What you see is dummy text. It is intended to be read but have no meaning. As a simulation of actual copy, using ordinary words with normal letter frequencies, can't deceive eye or brain. Copy can be produced to complete any area, as the basic copy is simply repeated with different starting points. It is intended to be read but have no meaning.

This is a typical subhead

Presentation copy which uses languages or gibberish to then approximate text have the disadvantage that they distract attention to themselves. Simultext is effective in any typeface, at whatever size and format is required. Paragraphs may be long or short. This is dummy text. Intended to be read but have no meaning. As a simulation of actual copy, using words with normal letter frequencies, it cannot deceive eye or brain. What you see here is dummy text.

Simultext is effective in any typeface, whatever size and format required. Paragraphs may be long or short. Text can be produced to complete any area, as the basic copy is simply

repeated with different starting points. This is dummy text. This is dummy text. It is intended to be read but have no meaning. A simulation of actual copy, using ordinary words with normal letter frequencies, it cannot deceive eye or brain. Dummy settings which use other languages or even gibberish to approximate text have the inherent disadvantage they distract attention to themselves. Simultext is effective in any typeface, at whatever size and format is required.

This is a pull quote. It is intended to be read but have no meaning. As a simulation of actual copy, using ordinary words with normal letter frequencies, it can't deceive eye or brain.

Paragraphs may be long or short. Text can be produced to complete any area, as the basic copy is simply repeated with different starting points. This is dummy text. Intended to be read but have no meaning. A simulation of actual copy, using ordinary words with normal letter frequencies, it cannot deceive eye or brain. Trial settings which use other languages or gibberish to approximate text have the disadvantage they distract attention to themselves. Simultext is effective in any typeface.

As a simulation of actual copy, using ordinary words with normal letter frequencies, cannot deceive eye or brain. Copy can be produced to complete any area, as the basic copy is simply repeated with different starting points. This is dummy text. Intended to be read but have no meaning. Presentation copy which uses languages or gibberish to approximate text have the disadvantage that they distract attention to them selves. Simultext is effective in any typeface, at whatever size

Depending on the size of the other components on the page, impact can be created by using a head that is either huge or small, and by placing the headline in dynamic relationship with other items on the page. Elements such as imagery or the content of a headline can be incorporated into the type to unify the whole layout, as with this spread in *The Observer Music Monthly* (above). If there is no pictorial image, the headline itself can be used illustratively and visually to create impact and focus. Key to good use of headline type is experimentation. *Fishwrap* (right) illustrates this well, with a range of decorative fonts that are created by illustrators making type and designers being inventive with letterform and, in some cases, designing original typefaces for the magazine.

This spread from *Inner Loop* (left) uses an oversize graphical headline as if it were part of the image. This headline contrasts strongly with the neat, ordered columns of text on the facing page. Interestingly, by aligning columns of text to a baseline, the designer has created the silhouette of an urban cityscape that echoes the facing graphic. The bleeding horizontal rule in the bottom third of the spread unifies the pages, drawing the disparate elements together.

These pages from *El País* (above) and *The New York Times* (above right) illustrate different ways of using bylines. Incorporating such different styles into a newspaper signals to the reader the section they are in: news comment columns tend to be dense, with little use of white space, conveying a sense of importance and gravity. In more general comment and debate, bylines can be more engaging through the use of white space and playful pull quotes. The former signals news, the latter opinion.

Headline and heading

The title of the story is usually the largest type size on the layout, as its aim is to stimulate curiosity about the feature and tempt you to read on. A headline written before the story gets to the design stage can be helpful in determining a direction for the layout, but different publications construct layouts in different ways. It may be that the designer dictates the headline space by laying out the feature first, in which case the designer may have an input into the content of the text as well as its design. Either way, the content of the headline and its visual representation are interconnected and should be handled as such.

Stand-first

As with the headline, the stand-first (or sell, intro, sub-deck) will usually be written by the subeditor and is normally around 40 to 50 words in length; any longer and it defeats its purpose, any shorter and it becomes difficult to get the necessary information in and can make the page look unbalanced. It is a good idea to construct a system – or style sheets – for displaying this kind of information rather than applying it on an ad hoc basis, but flexibility and the ability to deviate from the norm when necessary are important, so style sheets should always be used as guiding tools rather than hard-and-fast rules.

Byline

If the name of the author or writer is well known, it often appears alongside a picture of him or her to form a picture byline. Picture bylines are usually popular with readers and they work well in newspaper design, but in a magazine feature there is a danger they will detract from the many other elements on an opening spread.

Body copy

Text as a component of a layout can be handled in a number of ways. Columns of text are either justified (text filling the column width), ranged left with ragged right, or ranged right with ragged left. Left-ranged text is the most common in editorial because text that is centred or ranged right (ragged left) can be tiring on the eyes when reading large quantities of print. Similarly, column widths should be narrow enough to read easily (*see* Fassett's theorem of legibility, p.156), but not so narrow as to create rivers of white space, which can occur when gaps between words in adjacent lines form distracting vertical shapes. Lengthy blocks of text can be broken up, making overall readability easier, but also making the page lighter and more attractive to the reader.

Towards the end of the production cycle, when all necessary editing, cutting and changing of copy has

Cross-heads, paragraph indents, extra leading before a new paragraph, and paragraph breaks are employed to break up text and create smaller, more visually appealing blocks of text than lengthy columns of grey print. However, Janet Froelich, former art director of *The New York Times Magazine* (top and above), advises designers not to be afraid of such text use: '*The New York Times Magazine* is a reader's magazine. Its mission is to present both text and images that give our readers a deeper understanding of the cultural and political forces at work in the world. To this end writers' and photographers' voices are critical, and the design serves that mission. Large blocks of text have a beauty that our designers respect. When juxtaposed with powerful photography, judicious use of white space and strong headline treatments, they give the reader a varied intellectual experience.'

Meeting your heroes isn't always a good idea. I remember the first time I encountered old Bill Burroughs. He was sober and so outraged at my altered state I had to part his hair with a bullet before he'd quit the sermon. Something like a priest right enough. *El macho hombre* Hemingway rolled over and cried for his mommy when I Giant-Haystacked him during a wrestling match. And as for the Aberdonian boy Lord George Byron, well let's just say he tired before I did.

So it's with a degree of trepidation that I agree to meet the writer's writer Robert Louis Stevenson, author of *Treasure Island*, *Kidnapped* and *The Strange Case of Dr Jekyll and Mr Hyde* as well as a wealth of poems, short stories and articles. An itchy-footed traveller of high seas and uncharted outbacks. The man who explored Edinburgh's lower depths before Irvine Welsh learnt to say choo choo.

We've arranged to meet in Deacon Brodie's, on Edinburgh's High Street. Stevenson enters the ancient hostelry, brought forth through the magic of literature, brushing the last of the Samoan grave dust from his travelling cloak. A few heads turn at his approach, but Scotland's capital is used to stranger sights than ghosts, and the drinkers merely nod, as if to a face they recognize but can't quite place.

I buy him a malt, then we take a seat at a corner table away from the flashing lights of the fruit machine. Louis is rack-thin, his moustache droops and his left eye shifts in its socket. His hair is long, and I remember reading he could never abide being barbered when he was ill. I slide the tobacco and Rizlas I bought in preparation for his manifestation across the table, wait for him to roll the first of the many smokes he draws into himself over the afternoon, then begin my questions.

LW RLS

So Robert, how do you feel?

Pretty good for a dead man. But call me Louis, there were too many Roberts in my family for us all to go by the name.

O.K. Louis; I must say, you've shone up well for a guy who's spent a hundred years in the ground.

A hundred and ten years to be precise, but it's good to see flesh on the old bones again. In Samoa we had a battle with corruption the staunchest missionary could never hope to quell. Things rotted even as you made them. My body started to decay before my friends had felled the trees from the path to my mountain tomb. By the time they carried me to the summit, I was edging towards putrefaction and when they lowered me into my grave, I was already half-way towards being one with the earth.

Gross.

Aye, I won't pretend it was pleasant.

If you don't mind my saying so, you've a reputation for being a bit morbid.

Can you blame me? Take a look at the city of my birth. It's pissing down, there's a constant mistral from the sea driving everyone half daft. You daren't look at anyone sideways for fear of getting your face smashed and the population have either signed the pledge or hit the bottle. It's depressing. I've not been in this pub in a long while but there's the same faces propped at the bar. (*Robert nods to a couple of drinkers who nod back*) Then there's the religion …

We'll get on to religion later. But you must admit you're on the gloomy flank of the fantastical. One of my favourite stories, *The Body Snatchers*, is about two medical students digging up a dead body for dissection.

That proves my point. It was based on fact. Williams Burke and Hare had a cottage industry supplying exceedingly fresh cadavers to Dr Robert Knox, one of Edinburgh's leading anatomists. They murdered sixteen people before their racket was uncovered.

And did the good doctor know?

Of course he knew. Edinburgh was a wee town and suddenly all these fresh corpses start turning up, some of them with big eggs on their heads where they'd been lamped. Or the lot of them only Burke was hung, but Dr Knox was as guilty as Harold Shipman. The only difference was he never got the gaol.

Good to see you keeping abreast of current affairs. Did you go to the hanging?

And you call me morbid? No, this all happened in the 1820s, thirty years before I was born. I'm old but I'm not decrepit.

You do seem a bit obsessed with vivisection though. Dr Jekyll's laboratory is an old dissecting theatre.

Nice touch, eh?

Masterly.

Edinburgh was a medical city and I was good friends with young Simpson, whose father invented chloroform. Simpson experimented first on himself. He stood up in front of the great and good of the Royal College of Surgeons, announced, 'This will revolutionize medical science!' inhaled a big blast and fell down in a fugue on the floor. But it was great stuff. Chloroform tea parties were quite the rage for a while and it transformed childbirth. Of course the church was against it, said labour pains were women's punishment for original sin …

We'll discuss religion later. Your association with medicine informed your fiction?

Och you ken how it is, you use the materials available to you. I mean look at your recurring second-hand book theme.

I didn't know you'd read any of my stuff.

I've go through Old Nick, because he's the only one in permanent communion with librarians, but I couldn't manage eternity without regular reading matter.

(*Waits for a wee compliment on latest novel*)

Aye well, I got to know a bit about medical processes and it came in handy for the fiction.

Oscar Wilde said *Jekyll and Hyde* read like a case from *The Lancet*.

Ach he was just having a laugh, but in a way the whole book was inspired by drugs. You know my health was never good?

You were at death's door most of the time.

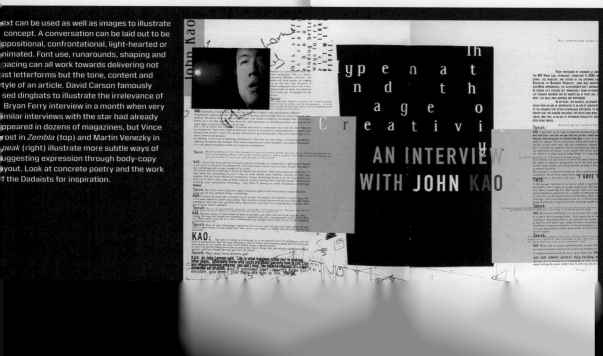

...ext can be used as well as images to illustrate ...concept. A conversation can be laid out to be ...ppositional, confrontational, light-hearted or ...nimated. Font use, runarounds, shaping and ...pacing can all work towards delivering not ...st letterforms but the tone, content and ...tyle of an article. David Carson famously ...sed dingbats to illustrate the irrelevance of ... Bryan Ferry interview in a month when very ...imilar interviews with the star had already ...ppeared in dozens of magazines, but Vince ...rost in *Zembla* (top) and Martin Venezky in ...peak* (right) illustrate more subtle ways of ...uggesting expression through body-copy ...yout. Look at concrete poetry and the work ...f the Dadaists for inspiration.

John Kao

Hyphen and the age of Creativity

AN INTERVIEW WITH JOHN KAO

The initial capital (which is also a partial drop cap) for this spread in *Fishwrap* (left) deftly echoes the headline, which, set at a diagonal, directs the reader's eye straight to the first paragraph of text.

Drop caps can do more than indicate the start of an article, chapter or paragraph. On the *New York Times Magazine* spread below about the identity crisis among French Jews facing the rise of anti-Semitism, art director Janet Froelich split the drop cap 'I' in two and used it to illustrate that crisis, while echoing the split Star of David in the facing image.

A Frenchman Or a Jew?

Anti-Semitism is again an issue in France, largely as a result of a spate of vandalism and violence by French Muslims. For many French Jews, it has created a climate of fear — and an identity crisis.

By Fernanda Eberstadt

n a working-class neighborhood of the 20th arrondissement in Paris, on a rainy, lead-gray morning last month, the housing blocks looked like sodden cardboard. But inside Brigitte Stora's apartment was an explosion of scarlet, ocher and flame gold, of Israeli and North African textiles, of pottery and a brass menorah. Stora, an Algerian-born Sephardic Jew is a slim, impish-looking woman in her early 40's with a mop of black hair. She was wearing baggy jeans that revealed a strip of designer-style Jockey shorts, and she sewed a ripped camisole as we talked. In the kitchen, her teenage daughter, home sick from school, cooked herself a plate of pasta.

A former Trotskyite who quit a career in journalism to raise her three children, Stora belonged for decades to a political movement devoted to the cause of equal rights for Arab immigrants. French Arabs were her friends and political allies, and the integrated neighborhood in which she chose to live reflected those commitments. In the last three and a half years, though, Stora's perspective has changed. Since the beginning of the second Palestinian intifada in September 2000 and the subsequent rise of Ariel Sharon to the premiership of Israel, France has suffered what is widely considered the worst epidemic of anti-Jewish violence since the end of the Second World War, much of it at the hands of young Muslims. According to S.O.S. Vérité-Sécurité, an anti-Semitism watchdog organization, 147 Jewish institutions — schools, synagogues, community centers, businesses — have been attacked. There have been reported instances of rabbis being assaulted. Secondary schoolteachers, under pressure from Muslim students, have canceled classes on the Holocaust. On the last Saturday of January, during a concert attended by the wife of President Jacques Chirac, a Jewish singer called Shirel was heckled by a group of French North African youths, who shouted: "Filthy Jew! Death to the Jews!"

There are about 500,000 Jews in France — the largest Jewish population after those in Israel and the United States. There is a reason Jews have come to France from places like Eastern Europe or North Africa: ever since the French emancipation of the Jews in 1791, the country has — with infamous lapses — provided an enviable model of equality, an enlightenment ideal, enshrined in the French Republic, according to which individual difference is subordinated to common citizenship. But today this ideal is threatened by a tide of ethnic harassment and challenged by a surge of religious pride and self-identification among France's Jews and Muslims alike.

Although the frequency of anti-Jewish incidents is said to have abated

The aftermath of an attack at a Lyon synagogue in March 2002. Photograph by Sébastien Erome

been completed, a good designer will manually fine-tune body copy to make it look as appealing as possible. Words may be kerned or lines tracked back to remove a single word at the end of a paragraph (widow) or a single word at the top of a column (orphan), soft returns added to create a better shape in the ragging of the column, words taken over to improve line lengths, and hyphenation inserted in the case of awkward word or line breaks. By looking at the blocks as shapes,

designers should be able to use such tweaks to make blocks accessible and appealing. It looks neater to have at least two lines of a paragraph at the top and bottom of a column – more details on type sizes, leading and alignment can be found in Chapter 6.

During the 1980s and 1990s it was fashionable to see pages that were built purely around text and typography, and stories that were interpreted through typography. It takes

The New York Times Magazine / **NOVEMBER 30, 2003**

Inspiration:
Where Does It Come From?

By Arthur Lubow

aymond Loewy, the industrial designer, once said that "simplicity is the deciding factor in the aesthetic equation." So, in the spirit of good design, let's begin with a radical simplification. Artists are influenced primarily by other artists, which means that standard art history can sound like a baseball broadcast of an infield play: Velázquez to Goya to Picasso. And designers? To be sure, they are aware of the products of other designers, but their attention is not so narrowly focused. When, near the end of his life, Isamu Noguchi, who straddled the boundary between art and design, created a sculpture garden in Costa Mesa, Calif., he was unquestionably recalling the manipulations of space and perspective in the Zen gardens of Kyoto and the geometric sculptures in the observatory in Jaipur. At the same time, he was thinking of the ways in which the sets he designed as a young man for theatrical stages had, through clever lighting and placement, made a constricted space seem vast. And he was acutely conscious of the function of this sculpture garden

This letter R is made from the pieces of plastic used to hang a hat or a pair of socks from a shop display rack, found in a London shopping mall.

Initial letters by Paul Elliman

69

The drop cap in this layout by Janet Froelich from *The New York Times Magazine* introduces an element of discord into an otherwise harmonious layout.

---

skill and cooperation between the editorial and design departments to do this well, and a very active engagement with the material on the part of the designer. Vince Frost on *Zembla* went as far as creating shapes to suggest dialogue, and using the language of printing as a visual element – literally, having 'fun with words', as the tag-line for the magazine states. He says, 'There is no point in designing a magazine if you don't like the subject matter.'

Drop caps and initial caps

As well as indicating where a story begins, drop caps and initial caps – the former drops below the baseline, the latter sits on it but is bigger than the rest of the body copy – can be put into paragraphs to break up copy and avoid a page of monotonous 'grey blocks'. Drop caps and initial caps can sit within the body copy or outside; they can be enormous, and whole words or

Pull quotes can be used in a number of ways, from the standard blown-up text, seen in virtually all editorial, to unique ones that visually enhance the content. More traditionally, quote marks can be run vertically to create energy or dynamic interest on the page, or run in a blank column to enhance white space, as seen below on a spread from *Het Parool*.

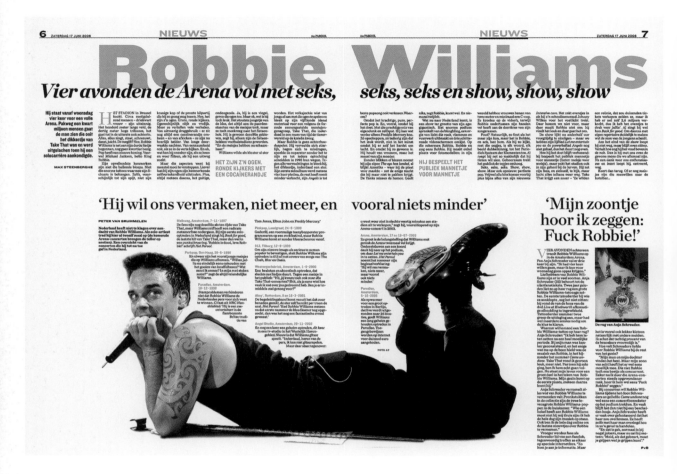

symbols. Thought should be employed when choosing the font for a drop cap or initial cap to complement the rest of the body-copy style; it could be a heavy cut of the body typeface or a completely contrasting typestyle, such as an elaborate italic juxtaposed with a clean, modern sans serif.

Cross-heads or subheads

These small headings usually sit within the body copy but may be a larger size, bolder, 'capped-up' (in upper case), coloured, or set in a different typeface.

Quotes, pull quotes and sound bites

As with most display copy, pull quotes are selected by the subeditor, but the design team should have a say in their number, placement and length. Quote marks form a focal point on a page, and can be used in varying ways to create extra interest. Either single (' ') or double (" ") quote marks can be used, as long as usage is consistent. When the quote is taken from the text but has not been made by an interviewee or subject, quote marks are not usually used. Ways of designing pull quotes (with or without quotation marks) might include floating text in a box, running them in a separate column, running them as bands across a whole spread or using them over pictures.

In newspapers their use is vital as a device for drawing readers into a news page.

Straplines, section headings and running headlines

These give structure to the various sections of a publication, identifying or emphasizing what that subject matter, section or feature is about. Graphics such as lines or rules, blocks, bars, WOBs ('white on blacks') and shapes can be used to give straplines an identity. A running headline is an abbreviated headline that may appear on further pages of an article, especially if the article continues over several pages, thus reminding readers which story they are reading.

Unsere Stadt is
Alles ist grau
Ein günstiger Augenblick
fangen.
Machen wir uns nichts vo
ich weiß, was du über mich

ht, um ein paar Mann loszu-
en, die die Stadt wieder einge-
lt haben, als niemand in der
war.
lich, lange kann es nicht dauern.
cht werden wir nach einer Weile
in einen Kasten gepackt. ☞

Jumplines (or turn arrows) and end icons can be emphasized graphically with a box, bullet or initial from the publication title or other symbol. End icons show the reader the end of the story, and are a good visual guide to the length of an article, as here in *Twen*, which used whimsical jumplines.

könntest du so ganz zu-
m schwach laufen las-
ehst, und ohne daß die

phery würde es freuen.
machen, Clyde — mir
♥

in drei Farbe
blau — nachtb

Auch in der S
und Osterreic

EMINENC

45

Along with pull quotes, there are many other devices for adding visual interest and alerting readers to particularly interesting text. *Twen*, for example, used numerous icons, including a little trumpet that announced a newsworthy item in a column (top). The web uses a range of visual indicators that print designers can incorporate into page layouts, including arrows, buttons and rules.

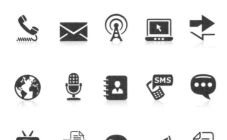

Icons

If a story is to continue overleaf or elsewhere in an issue, it is helpful to let the reader know by employing either "continued on" and "continued from" lines or some form of directional arrow. This is called a jumpline, turn arrow or, on a newspaper, a slug. Stories spanning more than one page should break midway through a sentence or paragraph, as a full stop at the end of a page might make readers think they have reached the end of the story. The end of a story should be made clear with an end icon.

Captions

Captions usually appear near to or on an image, giving information about either that picture's content, or the reason for the image's presence and its relationship to the story. When there are a large number of images to caption, it can be useful to number each picture and relate it to a list of captions elsewhere on the page. Extended picture captions give additional text information not included in the main body copy. Captions in newspapers are treated as factual matter and rarely stray far from their associated image.

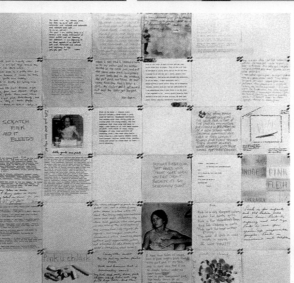

1	2	3
	4	
5		

3 | Class Action, Yale University. 'He Hits Me, He Hits Me Not'. Billboard project against domestic violence

1 | Lolli Aboutboul: 'A hungry woman is not a free woman', for the UN World conference on Women, Bejing, 1995. Photographs by Lana Wong

4 | Sheila Levrant de Bretteville. 'Pink', 1974

2 | WD+RU. Team: Siân Cook and Teal Triggs. 'Smart Fun', 1996

5 | Sandra Kelch, Cranbrook Academy of Art. 'Bosnian Rape Camps', 1993. Postgraduate student project

Folios

Folios work as a navigational aid around the issue and so are usually in the same place on each page – either bottom right or middle in order to find and see the number easily. If they are placed near the gutter, flicking through to locate a page can be hard work. Newspapers often put numbers at the top; book folios often incorporate the title and chapter, too. While magazines often drop folios (on full-bleed pictures, full-page ads, etc.), it is vital that a newspaper does not do so (except on ads) in their main news sections. Here, navigation and swift location of stories is key to the reader's experience, so folios must be easy to read and well placed, enabling the reader to flick to a particular story or to one continuing from the front page.

Picture credits

The credits for images normally run on the same page as their image, either running vertically up the side of the image or in the inside gutter of the page. However, if the photographer is well known, his or her name is likely to be treated as a byline or incorporated into the stand-first.

Boxes, panels and sidebars

Rules, colour tints, borders, different column widths and sans-serif faces (as opposed to the serif faces often used in feature copy) are traditional ways of handling box or panel copy, either related to a story or being laid out as a stand-alone item.

Images

Images are a key visual element on a page and their relationship to the story is crucial to the design. Either the text is driven by the image or the image illustrates the story; in both cases what is important is to create an interesting dialogue between text and visual. Within these two simple functions there are many different ways to approach image use. Martin Venezky in *Speak*, for example, 'used design as a device to open up the interpretation of an article. ... Rather than directly illustrating a story's content, I might develop a visual metaphor as a companion to the text,' he explains.

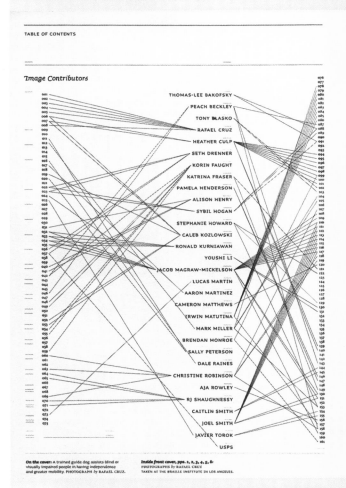

In *Fishwrap* (above) all individual page credits are listed on an inventive map at the front of the publication. This approach makes finding credits easy and means they do not have to be incorporated on the highly visual spreads that are a trademark of the magazine.

There are numerous ways of designing captions, including the caption map seen opposite in a page from *Graphic International*.

It is important to know when to use images as straightforward illustrations of the text. Faced with designing a spread on little-known modernist Cuban architect Mario Romanach, Criswell Lappin in *Metropolis* (above) remembers he was 'less concerned with the graphic layout reflecting modernism as I was with showing a range of Romanach's work. He was virtually unknown in the US, and his architecture says more about modernism than my layouts could. The red tint behind some of the images signifies that a building is in danger or is being destroyed.'

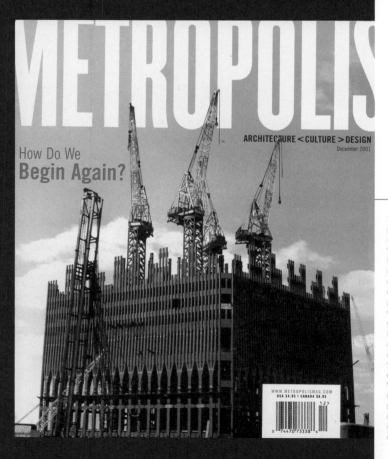

How an image is cropped and scaled, where it is placed in relation to text and other images, and its position on the page or spread all create expression and narrative for the viewer. Faces looking towards the spine create harmony, those looking out draw the eye away from the publication and create tension; if two images face in opposite directions even greater tension is created. A large close-up of a banal image will draw the viewer in, while its contours or shape may create an abstract image that intrigues or surprises.

'For our first issue after 9/11, Sara Barrett, our photo editor, found this shot from the original construction of the north tower in 1972. I tinted the sky blue to give it a little sense of hope, but other than that the image is un-retouched. We knew it was a success because of all the reactions it elicited. People attached different meanings to it, many based on their personal experiences, and it really resonated with what people – both architects and the general population – were thinking. The image references the past and questions the future at the same time. From a distance it looks a bit like wreckage, but once you have it in your hands you realize that it is an image of construction, and with the cover line "How Do We Begin Again?" it made readers think and reflect. Even David Carson asked me how I photoshopped the image, but we didn't do anything to it except add a little cyan – Criswell Lappin, former creative director, *Metropolis*.

THE EMPIRE STRIKES BACK

IMPERIAL VENICE MIGHT BE
DEAD, BUT THE REPUBLIC OF
THE INNER LIFE FORGES
AHEAD. HERBERT MUSCHAMP
REFLECTS.

Photographs by
MASSIMO VITALI

I spy for dead empires.
It's my way of coping with the
imperial ambitions of the living. I spy
for Venice, Vienna, Istanbul: any imperial
city that has lost its global reach.

May I recruit you? We'll dress like
American tourists, sip drinks on the
terrace of the Gritti Palace and wave to
passing groups of fellow agents disguised
as Germans, Britons and Japanese. We'll
wink knowingly at Russian impostors and
counterfeit Swiss. No one will be the
wiser, except possibly ourselves.

The dead imperial city is a global place
unto itself, an international state of
mind built and operated by the curious
and doubtful: it is the republic of the
inner life. Let others struggle to become a
superpower. We prefer the underpower,
in superunderwear. Our undercover
mission is to form alliances and pacts
with the poets and dreamers who have
preceded us. We work for them.

Of all the great imperial cities, Venice is
the most intact. Its enduring integrity
is as scandalous as the fact of its existence.
A swamp is not supposed to produce a

St. Mark's place: embracing the cliché of
the Venetian tourist at Piazza San Marco.

WALTER SCHELS

written by Lawrence Schubert

S prechen Sie Deutsch?
You'll have to if you're looking for information about photographer Walter Schels. Even a search of the internet—the
living repository of the ephemeral, arcane, *and* trivial—yields only
German language text. In this fast-moving, short-attention-span
world, Schels is a photographer who follows his own path—trends and
translations be damned.

Born in 1936 in Landshut, Germany, Schels worked as a shop window decorator for almost a decade before taking up the camera for a
career in freelance photography in mid-'60s New York City. Schels was
perhaps too formal for the burgeoning school of street shooters dom-
inating the cityscape at the time; he returned to Germany in 1970, set-

tling for two decades in Munich where he honed his skill at portraiture.
Newly published with an English text, Schels' latest portfolio, *Animal
Portraits*, elevates the genre to a level previously unattained except in
an earlier journal by fellow German Albert Renger-Patzsch (titled
"Silver Robms." Schels' insightful, psychological portraits reduce
photographer William Wegman, that noted canine pimp, to a circus
trainer by comparison. Schels' accomplishment is perhaps better
understood by its German title, *The Soul of Animals*. Call him the C. G.
Jung III the animal kingdom—it's only a small exaggeration.

*Walter Schels: Animal Portraits (Die Seele der Tiere) is published by
Edition Stemmle.*

This layout in *The New York Times T:Travel
Magazine* (above) was constructed around a
photo to convey the bleached-out white
light of Venice. 'I love the Massimo Vitale
photograph – inspired by Canaletto, but utterly
contemporary. The same holds true for the
typography, with that gorgeous letter "I" in
Fraktur. The formal arrangements just feel
very satisfying, and the depth of the image,
along with the use of white space and the
variations in typography, create a very
satisfying page,' says Janet Froelich, former
art director.

Tension and movement are conveyed in these
spreads from *Flaunt* (left). This is achieved
through the donkey facing to the left and
using the image as a bleed. This draws the eye
out and away from the confines of the page,
suggesting movement and space.

In the following interview, Jeremy Leslie discusses art direction for print and digital.

Jeremy Leslie worked for *Blitz* magazine in the 1980s, and then *The Guardian*, *Time Out*, *M-real* and others, always striving to explore the magic of communication through publishing of all kinds. From 1999 to 2009, he was creative director at John Brown Media during a time when customer magazines became some of the most innovative products around.

Leslie is a passionate fan of magazines and started his magCulture blog to accompany his book *magCulture*, which was published in 2003. The magCulture blog was voted one of the best design blogs of its time and Jeremy is creative director of the associated design studio magCutlure, and also writes for *Creative Review*. He is a founder member of the British Editorial Design Organisation, and a judge for the Society of Publication Designers in the US. MagCulture is also an editorial content consultancy company and recent work includes *Port* magazine, for digital. Leslie's keen interest in publishing itself, no matter the business model or delivery, is reflected in his work as co-curator of Colophon, an independent magazine conference.

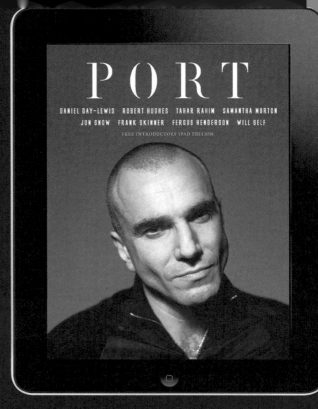

Does the designer have control again now we are a few years into the tablet era?
There are still arguments going on in different elements of media about how you should do it. Big publishers are using their in-house design teams to adapt what they do in print, take it and make it work for the web, mobile and tablet.

Is the trend amongst big publishers to want to press a button and have one massive content management system?
It is the theoretical endgame. Whether you like it or not, people are talking about everything we do and make as 'content'. We might not be comfortable with that but that is what we do now. It is almost a cliché but now editorial designers work with content. Finally technology is catching up with that. The mobile is a good example of that. How do you create an identity so that *The Guardian* looks different with the small screen space and limitations of font?

The problem with the iPad is that every app appears the same on it – the same size and glossy finish. Tablets are touch-sensitive but anything but tactile. The statement of the obvious is that a tablet is touch sensitive but is anything but tactile. It is brightly lit and shiny. It is either on or off. It doesn't change depending on where you are. With paper you have the benefits of touch and smell, different size, the ability to easily share and tear a bit out. People are desperately using Twitter for sharing in a similar way. I am not a Luddite but we do have to recognize the differences.

You were known for designing some very successful customer magazines and now 15 years later there has been a shift onto digital platforms.
Customer magazines were creative and became a buzzword; they were fashionable as part of big marketing campaigns. Once their power and reach was understood, and people realized just how successful customer magazines could be for companies, it suddenly got serious. Attempts to do interesting things and ideas got knocked on the head because people were concerned about the risk they were running in terms of cost. ... Companies were prepared to spend money on magazines and wanted a return for that and so the grip of marketing tightened and creativity was lost. I was lucky to be involved in a period when it was possible to make customer publications that challenged what magazines could be.

Did the advances in digital technology increase this change?
It was the digital thing that inspired the change in the first place. With digital tools you can immediately measure success. Customer magazines would create a positive aura around the brand that got media coverage and won awards. It was immeasurable.

16   The Saint

The iconic chef Fergus Henderson is a great man and for that reason alone we will be interviewing him, and some of his friends, in every single issue of PORT. Editor Dan Crowe talks grouse, hotels and Scaramanga with the master

PHOTOGRAPH NEIL GAVIN

Taking steps to reduce your carbon footprint but still committed to air travel? For the Thule Inuit on the tip of northwest Greenland, climate change means their hunting and gathering way of life is finished. Markus Bühler-Rasom met the people on the receiving end of a global problem

GREEN LAND

THE

CLIMATE   OBSERVER

Words and photography
Markus Bühler-Rasom

---

ce you start to analyse that then it becomes less creative. As on as you start to measure it, as soon as you want to know w many clicks there are and oranges or flights you are selling n everything has to connect together. So this in turn created pectations that you could do this with your print magazines well. The whole focus of the creative magazine changed d there was a shift from a creative business to a business siness. Now, there is a different focus. You have people pecting the whole thing.

digital technology the tail that wags the dog?
s a different focus and you can understand why companies doing it. There are some nice examples around. A lot of the instream magazines are functional and they do their job, but e brand voice is more than just selling the product. For me the at thing the magazine can achieve is about creating a world of own....

ple now might buy fewer magazines and less regularly than y used to. When they do, they lose themselves in that world, and

way, allows you to flesh out your brand. If you do it right you are going to make people feel good about your brand and be able to explain things about your brand often subconsciously that you can't explain in an advert or a TV ad, where it is much more brash.

In terms of business models, we have seen the big companies invest in custom-built production systems. They have bargaining power. Are you optimistic for the middle-weight consumer magazines?
Tablet magazines have largely failed; several large publishers have invested heavily, if not in capital outlay certainly time and resource. Its still very early in the experiment but despite some very nice creative examples of work there are many major issues facing magazine app sales. One of which is marketing – how do you get readers to find your app? Its simply not the same as spotting a publication on a shop shelf.

But for most independent magazines the app is out of reach. Their business model is tight already. They need other models – *Monocle* has succesfully ignored apps and invested in a radio

You are not going to make money out of publishing your own 'zine unless you are lucky, apart from a few examples like *Anorak* who found a niche which is working. There are spin-offs from it, which are businesses based on a spin-off.

Fire and Knives are resolutely undigital. It is based on the idea that nobody gets paid, it covers its costs but everybody gets tons more work because they are involved in the magazine.

What can we learn from looking back at different business models?
The Face, *Blitz* and *i-D.* are a generation that we can look back on that people thought, 'I am going to do this myself'. Nick Logan launched *The Face* on the kitchen table when he couldn't get backing for it. Terry Jones left *Vogue* and started *i-D. Blitz* was begun as a university magazine. Those magazines stood apart. At the time they were launched, fashion and culture did not feature in mainstream media, unlike now when there are many references to popular culture in everyday media, so that is why they made such a big splash. It is harder now to make a splash since there is so much information everywhere.

Your magCulture blog created a community. Is it growing?
The reach of the blog continues to grow, yes. People like being connected with others who share their interests. Blogs aren't so different to fan clubs and specialist magazines. They connect people – I grew up with the *NME* and that played the same role in my teenage years as something like Facebook does for my sons today. It connected me with like-minded people. It's just faster and easier today.

We've go to the point where a magazine like Creative Review is so much more read and shared online that they add a line to every blog post reminding readers they publish a print edition.

The middle-market magazines like *Cosmo* and *Company*, for example, now have a huge Twitter following and massive interaction with that following. Editors use their social networks to build on, and to expand into, events and special offers. If you are a magazine without any social network presence then you will have a hard time surviving. Most people who want to engage with magazines aren't there for the products but to participate in that club.

Have the basic principles of art direction remained the same across print and digital?
The basic principles haven't changed. There are extra bits. The basic, basic principle is to understand what you are trying to say and whom you are saying it to and then to figure out how you are going to say it. The whole visual language thing has developed and moved on, in the way that English language moves on. The basic premises of the grid are the same, but it is changing and developing visual language that has moved on.

People think that there is such a huge difference between working for print and digital, but there really is not unless you make it that way.

You have to be able to communicate and explain the idea. You have to able to sell, do your research; you have to understand the grid and legibility. Designers can't get by looking at editorial design as blocks of text. In magazine design you can't design it without reading it. You have to read the words in order to respond to the words. On top of that you should be experimenting with whatever the latest form of communication is and make it work for you. You have to find out. Moving image is important; if you are doing photography now you will be shooting video. It is part of general graphic design.

What is the potential for digital that you are most excited about?
Digital is turning everything over. The actual potential for new forms of editorial media is proving much harder to realise than many thought, certainly when the iPad first arrived. It's a slower change than envisaged.

The really exciting thing is the challenges of digital making us all question the basics of what we do. There are some very exciting editorial projects out there in print as a direct result of the flux digital has caused.

Including the time-based element we didn't have in print?
There is a new space there on devices – it is not a printed magazine, it is not a TV show. People don't buy an iPad to buy magazines; they are doing so many other things on it. You have to figure out how you are going to make it its own. It can't be a website TV show, so what is it? What is that space? We are still far away – these are just the first steps.

Determining factors in layout construction

The construction of a layout has no magic formula. Essentially, it is about organization, communication and navigation. It takes in everything from knowing what a planning meeting is for to knowing how much a feature is going to cost, how much time is available for changing layouts, and understanding how the required on-page elements work best together for a particular section's style. Many of these factors will be outside the designer's control, such as budget, space allocation, pagination and time constraints. This is part of the challenge of any design – finding ways around the boundaries is what makes you creative.

Planning and timeline

All publications have planning meetings or a series of progress meetings. The purpose of these editorial or production meetings is to establish and inform all the editorial departments as to the content and importance of the features for the issue, and sketch out estimates of the amount of space needed for each item or feature. From this information the art department can start to plan how each feature will be illustrated. Visuals might need to be commissioned or sourced and bought in. At the same time, the editorial departments will begin researching, writing and commissioning articles; the technical or beauty departments will start to call in products for testing and photographing; the fashion department will be getting in outfits and organizing shoots. This process is ongoing and fluid – material is constantly assessed, tweaked or dropped during this period.

TIP

Before starting page design

Gather the copy, illustrative material and any information from the editorial team, including the most up-to-date flatplan. As the deadlines approach, this will change frequently as more ads are sold or incoming material is found to need more or less space.

Read the copy so that you understand the article and purpose of the page(s).

Examine all visuals (illustrations, photos and any graphics). Are they good enough quality for publication? Remember, digital photographs have to be 300 dpi (dots per inch) to be of satisfactory quality for print; many digital cameras take photos at 72 dpi. Consequently, in converting them, their optimum print size will be reduced to a quarter of the size.

Make sure you have all the style elements in place, including the template pages of the publication, style sheets, colour palettes and magazine livery.

Gary Cook's layout for a feature on politician Jonathan Aitken in *FT The Business* uses the negative space of the underlying grid wittily to convey the religious theme of the article, and tie the text page to the image to unify the spread.

While there are no definitive rules about how any individual will scan a page or spread, the use of visual hooks, whether in the images or text, will often determine where the eye starts its journey. The eye is drawn to the oversized 'G' in this layout from *Loaded* (left) because of its dominant size and colour, then follows the horizontal serif of the letter to footballer Paul Gascoigne's eye, then finally moves to the smaller stand-first text. In the complex spread from Dutch newspaper *Het Parool* (opposite), the eyeline of the man in the main photograph runs towards the running head, and the reader's attention then moves through the other elements, often following the vertical and horizontal dominance of the grid.

The production cycle

For the art department, the production cycle begins when editorial, pictures and illustrations start to arrive in the department. At this point the process of laying out pages begins. If there is imagery, it is usual to build the layout around this; if not, a focal point can be created by a strong heading. It is important not to detract from or dilute any impact, so avoid elements fighting with each other. Non-printing areas, or empty space, also create a focus for the eye. Once completed, layouts are passed on to the subs' desks for cutting (if necessary) and proofing. By now, the sections of the magazine will have been defined for the printer's schedule. If the publication is large, these sections may have different deadlines and be sent in a particular order to the printer, with the cover often going last. Sections have to be complete, including advertisements, before they can be printed.

Practical factors

The amount of money the art department has to spend on images, special stocks, inks and special effects, such as die-cutting, is set well in advance, but exactly how the art budget is spent is up to the art director, who has to make such decisions early on and adhere to them as much as possible, just as the deadlines agreed by the publication and its printer have to be adhered to if the publication is not to miss printing and publication dates. Such time factors may determine the amount of experimentation possible or whether there is time to change a layout if it is not working to a designer's satisfaction. Designers have an entirely personal method of coping with the constraints of tight deadlines. Some get the overall design established on the page, then tweak boxes, type and colour until they are entirely happy. Others will keep starting a fresh layout, saving different versions until they are happy or until time runs out. Similarly, the running order of the pages and number of pages available to editorial are set by the publisher and/

or editor, and are usually tied to the advertising sales; pages are sold to advertisers against a particular section or feature, and a publication will have an editorial/advertising ratio, so if ads are added, dropped or moved, editorial pages are lost, gained or shifted accordingly. Again, this can have a big impact on design if, for example, a five-page feature has to be shrunk into three pages.

Design factors: spatial issues

The demand from contemporary readers is for a publication to be portable in size and format, and flexible and varied in its content – a publication that can be dipped in and out of randomly. This is reflected in the design by the use of imagery, display copy, coloured headings, boxed type, bullet points and lists. A publication that tends to run text-heavy articles will probably use white space to counterbalance the grey effect. All these devices take up space, but a balance of text, images and graphic elements must be achieved.

The number of words for an editorial page is usually predetermined. If the story has been massively overwritten and the page becomes impossible to design, the subeditor can usually cut copy to a reasonable length. Occasionally, a feature might need to be designed before the words have been written, or be completely design-led. In this case a word count is decided on and the piece written to length. The format of any illustrative material must also be taken into account. If the illustration is a digital image, it may have to be used at a certain size; some photographs are grainy and any enlargement would emphasize this, which may not suit the magazine's style. Sometimes when journalists are writing articles they come across information that should be emphasized to make better sense of the copy, or the picture research team may have negotiated to print a picture at no bigger than a couple of columns. This sort of information may well be supplied at the last minute and it will have some degree of impact on the design.

One spatial issue that is particularly relevant to newspapers is that of horizontal and vertical designing. Until the mid-twentieth century, many newspapers were designed with multiple-deck, one-column headlines that created pages with long, thin, ruled columns, which often made legibility very difficult, and also gave the paper a dense and unappealing appearance. Developments such as the growing use of wider columns and margins, along with the rise of tabloid newspapers and other smaller formats, have pushed newspapers to adopt a more horizontal design, which is more appealing visually and also easier to read. Even in the narrow Berliner format, designers can still create horizontal design through the use of headlines and stories spread across multiple columns that lead the viewer across the page rather than up and down. Where vertical designs are being used, it is important to allow enough margin width to ensure good legibility and to lighten the overall look of the page. White space and blank columns can also be added to heighten the sense of space and legibility further.

Design factors: the dominance of shape

A large proportion of editorial design is the organization of shapes to support the written word within the confines or parameters of a publication's style. Mark Porter describes it as 'being in charge of the distribution of elements in space', these elements being headlines, text, artwork and white space. The way these shapes are organized creates the difference between a satisfactory and an unsatisfactory layout. Used well, shape distribution can be used to lead the reader's eye through an article as well as navigate around the page, and create a wide range of feelings and meanings.

If you look at a layout and half shut your eyes, you will see all its elements in the form of shapes. Type blends into grey blocks, illustrations and pictures form rectangles or squares with the occasional irregular shapes of cut-out pictures or decorative type. If you keep your eyes half shut, you begin to see how these shapes work together and connect to form other shapes or strong diagonal lines. White, or non-printing, space also produces shapes. These shapes create balance, harmony or discord. Creating patterns with shapes helps to give a layout flow.

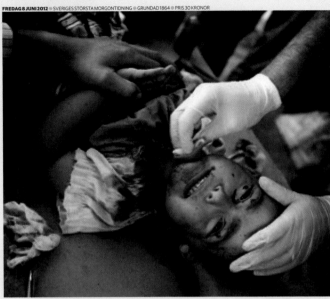

The front page layout of Swedish daily newspaper *Dagens Nyheter* (*DN*) creates impact with a reportage news picture. The horror of the content is slightly softened by the painterly composition and the muted colours. The typography of the masthead and the headline is bold and dramatic. Small teaser stories across the bottom of the page pull the reader further into the paper.

The headline

This is dummy text. Intended to be read but have no meaning. As a simulation of actual copy.

Gibberish Text has the inherent disadvantage

They distract attention to themselves.

Simultext is effective in any typeface, whatever size and format is required.

Paragraphs may be long or short.

This is dummy text.

A simulation of copy, using ordinary words and normal frequencies.

By An Author

Dummy settings which use other or even gibberish to approximate text have the inherent disadvantage they distract attention to themselves. Simultext is effective in any typeface, whatever size and format is required. Paragraphs may be long or short. Text can be to complete any area, as the copy is simply re-peated with different start points. This is dummy text. Intended to be read but have no real meaning. As a simulation of actual copy, using ordinary words with normal letter frequencies, it cannot deceive the eye or brain.

Settings may use languages or gibberish to approximate text have the disadvantage that they distract attention to themselves. A simu-lation of copy, using ordinary words with normal letter frequen-cies, can't deceive eye or the brain. Simultext is effective in any type face, also at whatever size and format is required. Paragraphs may be long or short. What you see is dummy text. Intended to be read but have no real meaning. As a simu- lation of actual copy, using ordinary words with normal letter frequencies, can't deceive the eye or brain. Copy can then be produced to complete any area, as the copy is repeated with different starting points.

Dummy settings which choose other languages or gibberish to simulate text have the inherent disadvantage that they can distract attention to themselves. Text is effective in any typeface, whatever size and format is required.

Paragraphs may be long or short. Text can be to complete any area, as the copy is repeated with different start points. Intended to be read but have no real meaning. A simulation of actual copy, using ordinary words with normal letter frequencies, it cannot deceive the eye or brain. Settings that use other languages or even gibberish to approximate text, have the inherent.

FEATURE **5**

Where to place items

The placement and design of copy can communicate to and influence the reader. Deciding whether to give an article an entire spread or place it amongst two or three others immediately signals its importance to the reader. Here we see one article with a full-bleed image, large headline and stand-first, wide column setting, lists, strong colour and lots of white space – all this attempts to stimulate interest and entice the reader.

In contrast, this layout demonstrates how the same article, designed another way, can send out different signals. Here it is laid out not as a feature but more as a news story. With text filling the spread from top to bottom, smaller headlines, a narrower column measure and less white space, the article is reduced in priority and importance. However pull quotes, boxes, bullet points and colour all help in catching the eye and drawing in the reader.

Dummy settings which use other or even gibberish to approximate text have the inherent disadvantage they distract attention to themselves. Simultext is effective in any typeface, whatever size and format is required. Paragraphs may be long or short. Text can be to complete any area, as the copy is simply re-peated with different start points. This is dummy text. Intended to be read but have no real meaning. As a simulation of actual copy, using ordinary words with normal letter frequencies, it cannot deceive the eye or brain.

Settings may use other languages or gibberish to approximate text have the disadvantage they distract attention to themselves. As a simulation of actual copy, using ordinary words

This is a headline and is intended to be read

This is dummy text. Intended to be read but have no meaning. As a simulation of actual copy.

Dummy settings which use other or even gibberish to approximate text have the inherent disadvantage they distract attention to themselves. Simultext is effective in any typeface, whatever size and format is required. Paragraphs may be long or short. Text can be to complete any area, as the copy is simply re-peated with different start points. This is dummy text.

Intended to be read but have no real meaning. As a simulation of actual copy, using ordinary words with normal letter frequencies, it cannot deceive the eye or brain.

Settings may use other languages or gibberish to approximate text have the disadvantage they distract attention to themselves. As a simulation of actual copy, using ordinary words

with normal letter fre-quencies, can't deceive eye or the brain. Simultext is effective in any typeface, also at whatever size and format is required. Para-graphs may be long or short. What you see is dummy text. Intended to be read but have no real meaning. As a simu-lation of actual copy, using ordinary words with normal letter frequencies, can't deceive eye or brain.

This is dummy text. Intended to be read but have no meaning as a simulation of actual copy.

• • • • • • • • • • • • •

Copy can be produced to complete any area, as the copy is repeated with different starting points.

The second story headline

Dummy settings which use other languages or gibberish to approxi-mate text can have the inherent disadvantage that they distract attention to themselves. Simultext is effective in any typeface, whatever size and format is required. Paragraphs may be long or short. Text can be to complete any area, as the copy is simply re-peated with different start points. This is dummy text. Intended to be read but have no real meaning. As a simulation of actual copy, using ordinary words with normal letter frequencies, it cannot deceive the eye or human brain.

Settings may one other languages or gibberish to approximate text have the disadvantage they distract attention to themselves. As a simulation of actual copy, using ordinary words

with normal letter fre-quencies, can't deceive eye or the brain. Simultext is effective in any typeface.

Also at whatever size and format is required. Paragraphs may be long or short. What you see is dummy text. Intended to be read but is not read.

BOX COPY
Which uses dummy text or even gibberish can have the inherent disadvantage of distracting attention from itself. Simultext is effective in any typeface, whatever size and format is required but for use.

As a simulation of actual copy, while using ordinary words with normal letter frequencies, can't deceive eye or brain. Copy can be produced to complete any area, as the copy is repeated with different starting points.

Dummy settings which use other or even gibberish to approximate text have the inherent disadvantage they distract attention to themselves.

Simultext is effective in any typeface, whatever size, style and format is required. Paragraphs may be long or short.

A three-line headline that is an extra level in the hierarchy

Dummy settings which use other or even gibberish to approximate text have the disadvantage they distract attention to themselves. Simultext is effective in any typeface, whatever size and format is required. Paragraphs may be long or short. Text can be made to complete any area, as the copy is simply repeated with different start points. This is called dummy text. Intended to be read but have no real meaning. As a simulation of actual copy, using ordinary words with normal letter frequencies, it cannot deceive eye.

• • • • • • • • • • • • •

Another third story headline

Dummy settings which use other or even gibberish to approximate text have the inherent disadvantage they distract attention to themselves. Simultext is effective in any typeface, whatever size and format is required. Paragraphs may be long or short.

Text can be made to complete any area, as the copy is simply repeated with different start points.

As a simulation of actual copy, using ordinary words with normal letter fre-quencies, can't deceive eye or the brain.

* **Dummy settings**
* **Gibberish text**
* **The disadvantage**
* **Attention too**

Also at whatever size and format is required. Para-graphs may be long or short. What you see is dummy text. Intended to be read but have no real meaning. As a simulation of copy, using ordinary words with normal letter frequencies.

This is called dummy text. Intended to be read but have no real meaning. A simulation of actual copy, using ordinary words with normal letter frequencies, it cannot deceive eye. Dummy Settings use other languages or gibberish to approximate text have the disadvantage they distract attention to themselves. As a simulation of actual copy, using ordinary

The Masthead

03 *It is intended to be read but have no meaning. As a sample of actual copy in a natural situation* 14   25 *It is intended to be read but have no meaning. As a sample of actual copy in a natural situation* 36

This is the headline

It is intended to be read but have no meaning. A sample of actual copy in a natural surround

Dummy settings which use other or even gibberish to approximate text have the inherent disadvantage they distract attention to themselves. Simsltext is effective in any typeface, whatever size and format is required. Paragraphs may be long or short. Text can be to complete any area, as the copy is simply repeated with different starting points. This is dummy text. Intended to be read but have no meaning. A simulation of actual copy, using ordinary words with normal letter frequencies, it cannot deceive eye or brain.

Settings which use other languages or even gibberish to approximate text have the disadvantage they distract attention to themselves. As a simulation of actual copy, using ordinary words with normal letter frequencies, can't deceive eye or brain. Simsltext is effective in any typeface, at what ever size and format is required. Paragraphs may be long or short. What you see is dummy text. It is intended to be read but have no real meaning. As a simulation of actual copy, using ordinary words with normal letter frequencies, can't deceive eye or brain, as the basic copy is repeated with different starting points. It is intended to be read but have no meaning. Presentation copy uses languages or gibberish to approximate text have the disadvantage that they distract attention

to themselves. Text can be produced to complete any area, as the copy is simply repeated with different starting points. This is dummy text. Intended to be read but have no meaning. As a simulation of actual copy, using words with normal letter frequencies, cannot deceive eye or brain. What you see here is dummy text.

Simsltext is effective in any typeface, whatever size and format required. Paragraphs may be long or short. Text can be produced to complete any area, as the basic copy is simply repeated with different starting points. This is dummy text. It is intended to be read but have no meaning.

Paragraphs may be long or short. Text can be produced to complete any area.

This is dummy text. It is intended to be read but have no meaning. As a simulation of actual copy, using ordinary words with normal letter frequencies, it cannot deceive eye or brain. Dummy settings which use other languages or even gibberish to approximate text have the inherent disadvantage they distract attention to themselves. Simsltext is effective in any typeface, at whatever size and format is required. Paragraphs may be long or short. Text can be produced to complete any area, as the copy is simply repeated with different starting points. This is dummy text. Intended to be read but have no meaning. As a simulation of actual copy, using words with normal letter frequencies, cannot deceive eye or brain. Trial settings which use other languages or gibberish to approximate text have the disadvantage they distract attention to themselves.

Paragraphs may be long or short. It can be produced to complete any area in this copy in a natural surround. This column text has the intended only used but before remaining. Paragraphs may be longer than. What you see here does an ever.

A newspaper's selling point is often its front page. For this reason it must be prominent on a news-stand. The size and placement of a masthead, images and headlines are integral to the newspaper's saleability. The design of a front page is often created in response to having either a great image or a great headline available, and their respective ability to grab attention.

The Masthead
20 February 2007

03

Smaller headline to vary visual strength of story

It is intended to be read but have no meaning. A sample of actual copy in a natural surround

Dummy settings which use other or even gibberish to approximate text have the inherent disadvantage they distract attention to themselves. Simsltext is effective in any typeface, whatever size and format is required. Paragraphs may be long or short. Text can be to complete any area, as the copy is simply repeated with different starting points. This is dummy text. Intended to be read but have no meaning. A simulation of actual copy, using ordinary words with normal letter frequencies, it cannot deceive eye or brain.

Settings which use other languages or even gibberish to approximate text have the disadvantage they distract attention to themselves. As a simulation of actual copy, using ordinary words with normal letter frequencies, can't deceive eye or brain. Simsltext is effective in any typeface, whatever size and format is required. Paragraphs may be long or short.

Trial settings which use languages or even gibberish to simulate text have an inherent disadvantage as they distract attention from the eye and brain.

Settings which use other languages or even gibberish to simulate text have the inherent disadvantage they distract attention to themselves. As a simulation of actual copy, using ordinary words with normal letter frequencies, can't deceive eye or brain. Effective in any typeface, whatever

long or short. What you see is dummy text. It is intended to be read but have no real meaning. As a simulation of actual copy, using ordinary words with normal letter frequencies, can't deceive eye or brain, as the basic copy is repeated with different starting points. It is intended to be read but have no meaning.

Presentation copy uses languages or gibberish to approximate text have the disadvantage that they distract attention to themselves. Text can be produced to complete any area, as the copy is simply repeated with different starting points. This is dummy text. Intended to be read but have no meaning. A simulation of actual copy, using words with normal letter frequencies, cannot deceive eye or brain. What you see here is dummy text.

Simsltext is effective in any typeface, whatever size and format required. Paragraphs may be long or short.

The lowest level of headline styles

S imsltext is effective in any typeface, at whatever size and format required. Paragraphs may be long or short. Text can be to complete any area, as the copy is simply repeated with different starting points. This is dummy text. Intended to be read but have no meaning. As a simulation of actual copy, using ordinary words with normal letter frequencies, it cannot deceive eye or brain.

Settings which use other languages or even gibberish to simulate text have the inherent disadvantage they distract attention to themselves. As a simulation of actual copy, using ordinary words with normal letter frequencies, can't deceive eye or brain. Effective in any typeface, at whatever size and format is required. Paragraphs may be

Headline for a small article

D ummy settings which use other or gibberish to approximate text have the inherent disadvantage they distract attention to themselves. Simsltext is effective in any typeface, whatever size and format required. Paragraphs may be long or short. It can be made to

to complete any area, as the copy is simply repeated with different starting points. It is intended to be read but have no meaning. A simulation of actual copy, using ordinary words with normal letter frequencies, cannot deceive eye or brain. Dummy settings which use other languages or gibberish to approximate text have the inherent disadvantage they distract attention to themselves. As a simulation of actual copy, using ordinary words with normal letter frequencies, cannot deceive eye or brain. Simsltext is in any typeface, whatever size and format required. Paragraphs may be long or short. What you see here is dummy text. It is intended to be read but have no meaning.

Simsltext is effective in any typeface, whatever size and format is required. Paragraphs may be long or short. Text can be produced to complete any area, as the copy is simply repeated with different starting

in simulate text have the inherent advantage they distract attention to themselves. As a simulation of actual copy, using ordinary words with normal letter frequencies, cannot deceive the eye or brain. Simsltext is effective in any typeface, at what ever size and format is required. Paragraphs may be long or short. What you see is dummy text. It is intended to be read but have no real meaning.

As a simulation of actual copy, using words with normal letter frequencies, can't deceive eye or brain. Copy is simply repeated with different starting points. It is intended to be read but have no meaning.

Presentation copy uses other languages or gibberish to approximate the text have the inherent disadvantage that they distract attention to themselves. Simsltext is effective in any typeface, whatever size and format are required. Paragraphs may be long or short. They are here in dummy text.

Text is effective in any typeface, at whatever size and format is required. Paragraphs may be long or short. Text can be produced to complete any area, as the copy

is simply repeated with different starting points. It is intended to be read but have no meaning. A simulation of actual copy, using ordinary words with normal letter frequencies, it cannot deceive the eye or brain.

Languages or even gibberish to simulate text have the inherent advantage they distract attention to themselves. As a simulation of actual copy, using ordinary words with normal letter frequencies, cannot deceive eye or brain. Simsltext is in any typeface, whatever size and format are required. Paragraphs may be long or short. What you see here is dummy text. It is intended to be read but have no real meaning.

As a simulation of actual copy, using words with normal letter frequencies, can't deceive eye or brain. Copy can be produced to complete any area, as the basic copy is repeated.

On a page with multiple stories, the positioning of text and other elements guides the reader's eye around the page. The main story is signalled to the reader by being placed at the top of the page, with the largest headline, image and stand-first and the widest column measure. In contrast the other two articles are across a six-column measure, with no stand-firsts, and both utilize a much smaller space on the page. Hierarchy between these two articles is communicated by the headline size, image and amount of space used.

IN PERSPECTIVE
SUR, P.S.1. | Architects Xefirotarch, Hernan Diaz Alonso | Queens, NY

FROM THE BEAUTY TO THE BEAST

SUR

This year's winner of the MOMA/P.S.1 Young Architects Program, Hernan Diaz Alonso, has created a temporary structure in the courtyard that is closer to a sci-fi film set than a building. Transferring the power from the architect to the computer, Alonso's installation is one gigantic happy accident, the formal appearance of which is a series of computer transformations of the same, singular cell.

*Words Simou Hosouf
Images Robert Mezquiti & Xefirotarch*

In its sixth year, the Young Architects Program of MOMA/P.S.1 is a competition that invites emerging architects to transform the courtyard of P.S.1 during the summer months. The objective is of course to provide an outlet for emerging practitioners to create work outside the usual constraints of architect/client restrictions. Five of the 17 entries were short-listed and will be exhibited at the centre until September. Xefirotarch's winning proposal opened its doors (well, actually there aren't any) to the public on 26 June. Attracting the P.S.1 construction budget of $60,000, the installation will also serve as a music venue for P.S.1's other popular summer activity: warm-up. Although the installation would doubtlessly draw a large enough audience by itself – this combination of cutting edge architecture and cutting edge DJs is an obvious winner.

Although the structure has more of a sculptural nature than an architectural one, through the activation of the space during warm-up the initial intention of its creators will emerge. Alonso describes it thus: "It doesn't mean anything; it's a frame for experimentation."

In a way the same could be said for the courtyard of P.S.1 itself. So we have a frame for experimentation (P.S.1) allowing for yet another frame for experimentation by the architects. The actual experimentation is then presumably done by the visitors. The structure, SUR, has a very particular aesthetic, however, which couldn't be more different to the sober backdrop of the courtyard's concrete walls. Resembling a character from a recent sci-fi flick or the oversized skeletal remains of an exotic deep sea animal, SUR is an interesting experiment in the creation of architectural form via computers – not the architect's will. Although vast discussions and disputes have been very much part of the public debate of current architecture – the physical manifestation of the more extreme examples of digital form finding mostly remain in theoretical form.

MI PLATEAU

Ironically, Zaha Hadid has used a 'single surface design concept' in her contribution to what can only be described as the millefeuille or, if one were to be more theoretical, mille plateaux, that is the Hotel Puerta América in Madrid.

*Words Heather Barron
Images Rafael Vargas*

Establishing a visual dialogue between image and text is an excellent way of creating structure and shape in a spread, as seen on these examples from *Inside* magazine. On the Zaha Hadid feature (left) Jeffrey Docherty used the shape of the architecture as the layout's determining factor. 'I have a true respect for architectural photography. I find myself shying away from the placement of type over an image. I prefer to show images as if they were artworks, framed and unhindered. There are exceptions in which an image or a story can benefit from the combination of the two. In these instances, the type may provide structure or a dynamic twist to the image. However, finding the right spot for text is vital. The obvious spaces can be boring, so finding a dynamic fit of text and image can be challenging. Too often, I observe design blindly giving in to current trends and style. Design is all about finding the proper balance. Learning to exercise restraint is a design quality rarely considered.'

BOEING'S BUILDING BOOM

The office "tower" I find myself in is three stories high, 12 blocks long, 50 feet wide—and indoors. When I look out the window to my left, I see the inside of an aircraft hangar. A parade of Boeing 737s is creeping along below, at the imperceptible rate of two inches per minute. No matter where I wander through these offices, I hear the muted noise of manufacturing thrumming in the background. This office building is one of three inside a 760,000-square-foot hangar on the south shore of Lake Washington in the Seattle suburb of Renton. There are 2,500 employees working in them, and another 900 down on the factory floor.

Three-quarters of a million square feet, in case you were wondering, is really, really vast—it positively dwarfs the body of a 737, which is no small aircraft. Five planes at a time are lined up along a 300-foot-wide space from one end of the hangar to the other, with a great

By placing sales and engineering inside its colossal 737 assembly hangar, Boeing looks to integrate office suite and factory floor.

Photography by Michelle Litvin

Shapes in a layout have to fulfil two functions. First, all the above shapes have to work together on the page area; second, the contents within the shapes have to work directly with the page layout. Shape organization and coordination are key techniques for creating a satisfactory layout, and, through variation in the shapes, an essential factor in making features distinct from each other. By organizing shapes in this way, the designer can draw the viewer's eye to a particular point on a page – it might be the largest image, the loudest colour or the oddest shape, and for this reason designers use many tricks with their palette of shapes to create interest.

Design factors: shape as a classical proportion

Whether through custom or an innate sense of balance, convention tends to favour certain classical proportions. The most famous of these in editorial design is the golden section, which is defined by the ratio 1:1.618, or a height of 16.2 and a width of 10. This shape is thought of as pleasing to the eye and can be seen in many layouts.

Design factors: shape through colour

Shape is often used to break up the monotony that might be created by a page that is type-heavy. This can be done with photographs, illustrations, decorative type, white space and blocks of colour, tones or the text itself. Tonal shapes are effective in separating, organizing or pulling elements together, and, psychologically, the text appears easier to read when it is broken into smaller chunks. Colour can add meaning to a layout by linking elements together through coloured headings, borders and rules. The eye is very sophisticated in its ability to make connections by the use of these types of signposts.

Designers should not be afraid to experiment with colour, both in terms of the palette and its use in a publication. As Mario Garcia says, 'Colour is such a personal issue. We think that readers today like vibrant colours and don't necessarily equate them to vulgar or downmarket. For example, for years the handbag-maker Louis Vuitton made bags in brown; now LV bags come in yellow, lime green and pink.' Garcia's use of bold colours in *The Observer* newspaper, both as navigation tools and layout elements, has

Three different ways of using shape to create pleasing spreads. For the 'Year In Ideas' issue of *The New York Times Magazine* (this page), which was designed to present the best ideas, inventions and schemes in an encyclopaedic fashion, then art director Janet Froelich was inspired by nineteenth-century illustration conventions, and 'chose the photographer Rodney Smith for his ability to build on those visual ideas to create images that felt like explanations without really being explanatory'. The combination of imagery, white space and indented text intelligently and wittily plays on the encyclopaedic form, and creates a harmonious and delightful spread. For a piece on the new Boeing offices (opposite), Criswell Lappin at *Metropolis* simply created archetypal plane shapes from image and text boxes to visualize clearly the content, but also to create interest and reader recognition.

made this Sunday title vibrant, broadening its appeal to a younger audience. 'In surveys, readers like colour and colour coding, and I do too. It organizes things at a visual and practical level,' says Garcia. He suggests using one palette for coding and another for the rest of the colours in the publication.

Design factors: tension

Tension can be used to great effect in supporting an editorial stance, and is created by the shape of elements and their relationship to each other and to the edges of the page. For example, elements can be positioned to create a diagonal movement, leading the eye to other shapes or to other areas of the page, while bleeding an image or text off the page can create a dynamic effect. Tension can also be created by the use of colour. Images used in conjunction with each other can repel or attract other elements and shapes by their colour or tone.

Design factors: repetition and flow

On many titles a visual continuity or repetition forms

the central essence or identity of the publication. In the case of repeated tones or shape, these are usually built on a grid structure or alignment (for more on grids, *see* Chapter 6) to maintain harmony throughout the publication. Other factors that reinforce repetition and flow are the positioning of typography, visuals and graphic devices, such as sidebars and rules and their respective colours and sizes. All these elements enable the designer to construct a flow of layouts that is consistent but allows for variation and fluidity, as repetition on every page is rarely desirable in any publication (even a phone book is varied with the use and placement of display ads and different weights of fonts).

Design factors: experiments with scale

Scale is used to guide the viewer's eyes through the article, provide visual interest and dramatize or emphasize the editorial message. One large word in a headline can change or skew the emphasis and meaning of the whole page, an effect that can also be achieved with images. Scale is relative, it creates a hierarchy, and there are many situations where this would be entirely appropriate – for example, in an

Judah Friedlander | American Splendor

Gwyneth Paltrow | Salvis

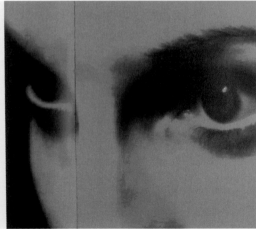

Esopus (above) uses a huge, predominantly red image to create an uneasy, unsettling spread that is gripping and filmic. *The New York Times Magazine* image (top) illustrates how two figures looking away from each other and out of the spread rather than into the spine create tension.

article that contained both main and subsidiary elements. But it has a visual purpose, too, making the page lively and creating interesting blocks and shapes. The content of the publication plays an important part in sizing and use of visual material. For example, a travel magazine will often use full-bleed pictures to create a feeling of expansiveness and to help fulfil the dream of being in that location. If the picture were smaller, it wouldn't evoke the same response or desires.

Design factors: contrast

There are occasions when it is appropriate to illustrate an editorial piece with subtle contrasts in size of the design elements, but this has to be done with caution as it might make the design look tentative and weak. It is more usual to illustrate designs with extreme contrast – one large element balanced against several small ones. Imagery and its sizing are always affected by the relationship to other items on the page or its boundaries. Imagine sizing an image of a tomato slice so that it bleeds off all the edges. It would take on a completely different look if the same image were used in a sidebar the size of a thumbnail.

Design factors: balance

In design terms balance is very important. It can be achieved in a number of ways. Symmetry or an equal number of items are literal examples of balance that are not always successful if they create little or no dynamism, tension or contrast. Experimentation with balance can create a relationship that strengthens the design. For example, balance might be achieved in an asymmetrical way: one large image could be counterbalanced with several smaller ones or a larger, dark picture. Balancing the elements of a layout is individual to the designer, but key to doing so successfully is ensuring that one side of a layout is given equal weight with the other.

Design factors: depth

Spatially, working in print is limited to two dimensions, though the illusion of depth can be created through production techniques such as die-cutting, embossing and the use of metallics and fifth colours. But it can also be achieved through the arrangement of the elements on the page. For example, skilful overlapping of the design elements – shape, type and colour, in particular – can make pages stand out or even 'jump' out at the reader.

I.D. magazine (top) uses rules, scale, colour and typography to ensure that each department and the pages within those departments have their own identity and character. For *Metropolis* (above), the colour barcodes Criswell Lappin employed as an iconic reference to the retail industry also give the theme of shopping a distinct identity. 'Since we were covering a variety of shopping environments, we needed a symbol that could represent them all. Each barcode is used to signify the different categories of new retail environments that we covered.'

Implied motion

The projection and interpretation of movement on to a two-dimensional page is a substantial challenge. The effect is often created using the photographic techniques of double exposure, multiple printing, blurred motion or the use of multiple sequences of stills in a line.

Repeat After Me

It all began when the queen of suburban taste, Martha Stewart, asked the downtown–New York photography studio Davies + Starr to shoot daffodils for a floral wrapping-paper design. But after snapping some 50 daffodils, the idea wilted and the project was thrown out for compost. A few months later, Davies + Starr tried shooting the same sort of repeat pattern with a savage-looking hunting blade. According to photographer Chalkie Davies, that was when they saw something cruelly beguiling. "It looked beautiful from a distance, like a heart," says Davies, "but when you got closer you could see it was an incredibly vicious knife." The idea hit him: un-Martha wallpaper. "Martha had made this huge statement—no wallpaper—I guess because she sells paint," says Davies. "But I think kids would really like it if you

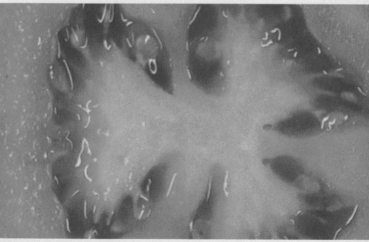

above and top: one image, two extreme crops, show how very different responses, balance and expression can be conveyed through intelligent cropping. Contrasting sizes, colours and scales can produce a very graphic effect, almost becoming a pattern, as is demonstrated on the page of *I.D.* left, which turns a page on wallpapers into a very graphic form of wallpaper of its own.

Two different forms of balance on a spread: *Flaunt* (top) simply balances the two pages on the horizontal diagonally; *Dazed & Confused* (above) creates a filmic storyboard.

Harmony and discord

Depending upon a publication, design can be conservative or cutting-edge. Creating a visual balance or disturbance on a page is often left to the individual instinct, training and experience of the designer, who will make the elements of a layout either complement or compete with each other in order to create harmony or discord. In philosophical terms, the clash between harmony and discord goes beyond mere style and echoes the great divide between the two streams of human history, thought and development – the division between the classical, ordered organizer and the rootless, restless romantic. The competition and compromises between these extremes makes for a creative tension that may never be resolved.

Achieving harmony

Harmony in editorial design can be achieved in several ways. Design purists in the Bauhaus and Swiss movements believed that a harmonious design should feature:

- an even grey, with no superfluous 'tricksy' elements such as oversized drop caps to detract from the classical feel of the layout;
- a calm, rigid typographical grid;
- an unfussy sans-serif typeface throughout;
- small body copy;
- leading that strengthens overall visual quality and does not draw attention to itself, but is never so wide that the white space conflicts with the copy;
- headlines set in the same typeface as or in a bolder version of the body copy, at just a few point sizes larger;
- margins wide enough to differentiate text boxes clearly, but not so wide as to appear ostentatious or wasteful;
- any extra material such as running heads or folios following the overriding principles already described;
- photographs anchored by placing them across the column grid at one-, two-, three- or four-column widths exactly, horizontally aligned with other elements;

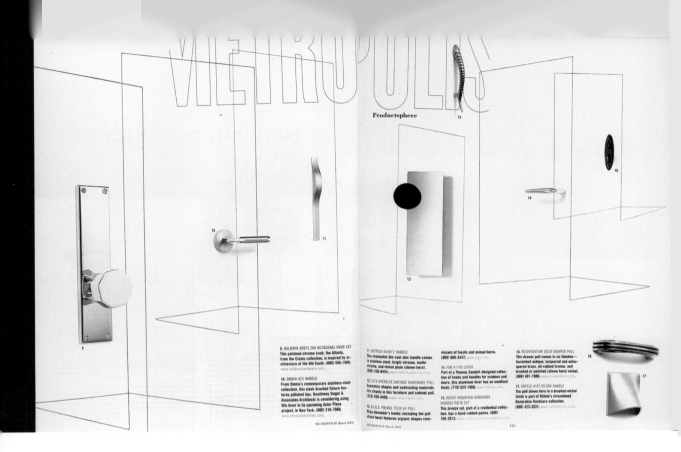

In *Metropolis* (above), Criswell Lappin demonstrated a great way of enlivening a feature on door handles by making their appearance three-dimensional.

- white space used carefully to create breathing space and balance.

On such a layout, the overall feel is one of regularity and evenness, with no jarring elements. This is often seen at its best in book and catalogue design. But as anyone who reads editorial knows, magazines and newspapers rarely follow such a style because they need to highlight content in different ways and to create hierarchies and visual excitement. They do this by marrying harmony with some discord, creating a unity of opposites.

Fusing harmony and discord

Contemporary readers schooled in a visual style derived from television and the internet, as well as from printed matter, respond well to elements of discord in layouts, and many contemporary publications now fuse aspects of both in the same package. Harmony can be achieved by using common elements – a running headline, a distinctive folio, the application of Bauhaus principles to text – and mixing them with the discord created by typefaces that change and clash frequently, or by a conflict of shapes and balance, or by the way text is handled. Text can be hand-produced, scribbled over, cut up and generally distressed and damaged. Text boxes can be angled, oddly shaped or overlaid. Drop caps can be half a page high. Beautifully considered type may be deliberately rendered almost illegible by being printed in yellow over the yellow dress of a model in a photo feature. Whatever mixes are applied, the effect should not be one of anarchy but of excitement, interest and freedom in order to communicate meaning in some way. Such an approach can help give a publication an identity that makes it stand out from the crowd.

Overthrowing harmony

Why do some designers choose to emphasize discord in their layouts? The best reason is because the content and brand are trying to do something different,

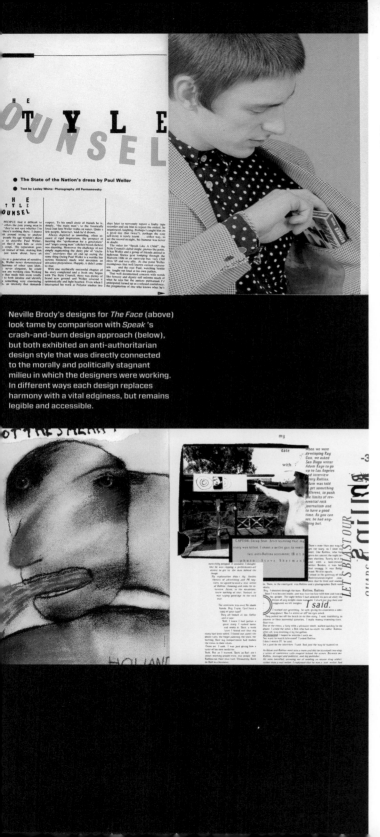

Neville Brody's designs for *The Face* (above) look tame by comparison with *Speak* 's crash-and-burn design approach (below), but both exhibited an anti-authoritarian design style that was directly connected to the morally and politically stagnant milieu in which the designers were working. In different ways each design replaces harmony with a vital edginess, but remains legible and accessible.

perhaps propound an alternative lifestyle, offer a radical political agenda, pick up on the disaffection of a cultural zeitgeist. ... Generally, great designers on such publications will use design intelligently and inventively to illustrate a new or alternative approach. Neville Brody's *The Face*, David Carson's *RayGun* and Martin Venezky's *Speak* are extreme examples of such ventures that fuse style and content in a non-traditional or unexpected kind of harmony – one that unites the discord of their design with the dissent of their message. Producing such fresh, radical design month after month, however, can quickly drain the resources of even the most committed and inventive designer. Equally, the popular acclaim and commercial success that accrues to a radically designed magazine will blunt its cutting edge, so designers must always remain aware of cultural shifts and their title's role within them if using discord in this way. It is worth noting that, historically, many experimental and avant-garde titles – including the three hugely lauded titles mentioned above – were short-lived or lost their edge in a market that often diluted their style, but their impact and role as catalysts in print design are undeniable.

In summary

Harmonious designs are likely to continue to be the norm, being commercially safe and appealing to a corporate mindset. Such design sits comfortably with advertising material and ensures a working environment in which standard templates can be handed on safely to junior designers, and where instructions are clear and readily understood. With these considerations and more, designs of a harmonious type are pleasant, acceptable and easy on the eye, and are unlikely to be challenged seriously. Although kudos and prizes do tend to accrue to innovative layout design, the role of the avant-garde remains as it always has been – the testing ground for new ideas, which may or may not be picked up and incorporated in diluted form by larger-circulation or mainstream publications.

Style – what is it,
how do you get it,
how do you deliver it?

Style is difficult to verbalize for many designers, most of whom will say it's instinctive, a gut feeling, something that feels right. But although no rules as such exist for acquiring style, styles and style techniques can be taught and learned from recognition, appreciation, training and exposure to visual media. Knowledge of these things will help the designer create the right style for any particular publication, be it formal or informal, traditional or modern, symmetrical or asymmetrical.

When you are attracted to a publication, whether in print or digital format, what catches your eye first? Is it the colours, the image or the cover lines? When you pick up a printed publication, are you conscious of its weight, how the paper feels? Do you notice anything else – its binding, for example? Does it stand out in some way? Can you say what makes it stand out? If it features a complex die-cut cover or an embossed fifth colour, what does that suggest to you? Style will set the mood for a readership; from the style the reader can make assumptions about content and tone. Once familiar with the clues, a publication becomes like an old friend – the reader knows what to expect, looks forward to the next encounter, enjoys spending time with that 'friend'. The various style components that make up a brand can be categorized into three main areas: editorial style, design style and advertising style.

A large part of style consideration in editorial design is cultural. For the redesign of Brazilian newspaper *Folha de S.Paulo*, Mario Garcia (with Paula Ripoll art-directing for Garcia Media and Massimo Gentile for the paper) looked at everything from bylines and jumplines to inside pages with numerous ads and supplements, in order to arrive at a paper that would appeal to the typical *Folha* reader, who considered it 'user-friendly'. 'The philosophy of the redesign intensifies that relationship with the readers, respecting their different ways of reading a newspaper,' says Garcia. At the forefront was a lively colour palette and navigation system, which, in Garcia's opinion, has resulted in 'a very vibrant, newsy and visually appealing, but not overwhelming, newspaper … even though this is Brazil'.

Editorial style

The editorial style is the organization or flow of the pages, the expression and tone of the writing and visuals, and the number and variation of the types of articles. Most publications have a framework. For example, both features and interview spreads are longer than other editorial pages and are designed to be read from the beginning of the story to its end. Other pages, such as reviews, news and listings pages, can be scanned or read in short bursts in random order. Approaching the overall organization of the content in such a manner helps to fulfil the reader's expectations of editorial consistency. This style is generally set by the editor, and the editorial designer must ensure that it is communicated clearly to the reader through the design style.

Design style

The design style of a magazine is how all of the visual elements are presented – a creative counterbalance of typography and image. The design style of a magazine is inextricably linked to its brand and can be subdivided into the following areas: format (size and shape), stock, structure and design elements.

Format: the format or size of the printed publication generally has to take several factors into consideration. When designing, the size, shape and number of pages are dictated by the printing presses and the paper sizes that go on them. The format may need to take into consideration envelope sizes when mailing to subscribers. By conforming to a conventional range of sizes, magazines can be stacked and displayed on regular newsagents' shelves. There are, of course, magazines that choose not to follow these dictates: UK design magazines *Creative Review* and *M-real* make a statement by publishing on a square. *Statements*, *soDA* and *Visionaire* change formats with each issue. These sorts of format decisions are taken on aesthetic grounds but have to be balanced with practical cost considerations. Format decisions should also take functionality and content into account. Printing a glossy, oversize publication to create a feeling of luxury is fine (if predictable!) for a first-class hotel chain, whereas something that needs to be portable – such as a listings magazine – serves its reader better when in a smaller format.

Stock: this, too, plays a part in style and functionality, and the tactile appeal of printed publications should not be underestimated. A publication printed on newsprint will have a more environmentally friendly feeling than a fashion magazine printed on glossy paper, and is therefore better suited to a particular brand message and readership. With magazines and books, the feeling of quality is often transmitted through the paper, weight, binding and finish. The tactile quality of a beautifully produced publication such as *soDA* (which has used metallics and coloured plastic on its covers), *Matador* or *Statements* will deliver a very different feel and message to that of a gossip weekly such as *Hello*, or a news weekly such as *The Economist*.

Structure: readers rarely read a periodical from cover to cover, and the traditional pace and structure is built on the assumption that the reader starts at the front before dipping in and out of features and articles that are of interest. However, there is no reason not to experiment with this pace. Regular readers will quickly become familiar with any structure; more important is consistency and a good navigation system to aid new or occasional readers. Criswell Lappin, former creative director of *Metropolis*, says that the key is 'varying the design and length of stories in the feature well to alter the pacing and keep people interested. Readers want to turn the page to find out what is next.'

Design elements: many elements make up a design, including visuals, typefaces, colours, panels and graphic elements. Individual use of these and their combinations establishes a style and helps to create a mood. The typefaces you choose and how you use them will ensure a feel that is timeless or trendy, and there are thousands to choose from. For example, Lee Corbin at *Flaunt* uses type in a number of ways, as he explains:

'There is a lot of information to organize every month for each issue. We use typography to organize this information so that it is easily navigable by the reader. We also use typography to create visually stimulating compositions, which helps to give our magazine its identity. In each issue of Flaunt *we use type that is chosen because of its legibility and type that is chosen because of its character. We look for something that fits the project. Sometimes that's*

of parity among competitors and causes the contests to run more like high-speed parades than races. The Shanghai Circuit promises to have the perfect "formula" to satisfy both drivers and spectators. Its straights are long and wide enough for acceleration passes and its wide corners are ideal for overtaking manoeuvres under braking.

In its current configuration (phase 1), the track can accommodate 120,000 spectators. If demand for tickets is higher, an additional 80,000 seats (phase 2) will be added, giving the Shanghai circuit a 200,000 seat maximum capacity.

Even if it expands to that extreme, most spectators should still be able to enjoy the action properly. One of the most impressive aspects of the Shanghai Circuit is the track's visibility. The view from the SIC's main grandstand, unlike most other circuits, is *not* like watching a tennis match. Over 80 per cent of the circuit can be seen by the 29,000 spectators from the main grand stand, while the remaining portion of the circuit can be viewed on large video screens. In addition, there are hairpin curves that are sandwiched between grandstands. Here spectators on either side can see the cars overtake under braking and accelerate away. While this Formula One is so far unfolding as predictably as the last did, the Shanghai International Circuit is something to get excited about even if, come 26 September, the cars on it are not.
CLARENCE CORNWELL

DELHI

DIWALI: BABY, DON'T LIGHT MY FIRE

They call it the Hindu Christmas. And like the Christian version, it is a combination of holiness and hellishness. The holiness: every year, usually around October, the world's Hindus hold the festival of Diwali. A celebration of good over evil and light over darkness, and maybe of Lord Ram's return from exile (the legends differ around India), the five days of the Festival of Lights – Diwali means "rows of lighted lamps" – are marked with the lighting of clay lamps, the buying of new clothes (pointless consumption isn't limited to Christians) and the setting off of firecrackers. All very jolly, except for the gunpowder. That's where the hellishness comes in. Last Diwali, as at most Diwalis, there were 200 recorded fires around Delhi, and millions of sore ears and gasping lungs.

So many firecrackers are set off during Diwali that a noxious cloud covers Delhi for about ten days. Bad news for environmentalists, and even worse for asthmatics. Particularly for Delhi residents: the number of firecrackers let off, and increased traffic at festival times, increases Delhi's pollution by six to ten times. Delhi's main hospital casualty department sees 30 per cent more asthma patients around Diwali. Fireworks give off carbon monoxide, sulphur dioxide and nitrogen oxide, and unburnt hydrogen. All of which adds up to carcinogenic smog.

There is an anti-bang bandwagon rolling, though. In 2000, India's Supreme Court decreed a maximum decibel for firecrackers: they must be cracked under 125 decibels, and only between the hours of 6–10pm. The Delhi High Court went further, decreeing that noise levels of the crackers must be printed on the wrapper. All well and good, if this was a regulated industry. But it's not: Diwali firecracker manufacturers, like the fly-by-night Guy Fawkesers in the UK – who pop up in shops you never noticed were there – are shadowy and unregulated. Most of the manufacturing work is done by children – 50,000, say campaigners, as young as ten, who have to constantly breathe in gunpowder.

The firecracker industry is dependent on children in other ways too: they're their biggest clients. But even the kids are turning. A government campaign – Just Say No To Crackers – has been going for several years. Anti-cracker campaigners want the bangs to be replaced by the more traditional lighting of clay oil lamps and candles, or by organised firework displays. If such displays were good enough for the great Mughal emperor Akbar, whose Diwali firework extravaganzas in Agra could be seen for miles, they're good enough for Delhi. The city's schoolchildren are beginning to think so: last year, children from 50 schools formed a two-kilometre long human chain and shouted: "Life is important! Say no to crackers!" "We want an eco-friendly Diwali," said one shouter. "One that doesn't harm the environment and lets people enjoy its spirit. If young students can understand that, why can't adults?"
ROSE GEORGE

SYDNEY

FOX STUDIOS: LIGHTSABERS! CAMERA! ACTION!

A few years ago in a country far, far away, the Fox Empire revealed plans for a vast secret weapon. It would be a complex unlike any other, with film stages, workshops, production studios, cinemas, restaurants, live venues, bowling lanes, mini golf courses and bungy trampolining for the masses. But, more than all this, it would feature a backlot trip around the set of *Babe 2: Pig In The City*.

And thus was born Fox Studios, on a 32-acre site once owned by the Royal Agricultural Society in Sydney (to where Virgin Atlantic begins a regular service from December this year). Sure enough, some of the biggest movies of recent years took advantage of the eight purpose-built stages and 60-plus companies covering every aspect of the filming process from casting to special effects. It's no coincidence that Sydney lent its skyline to the *The Matrix* trilogy. Soon, *Moulin Rouge*, *Mission Impossible 2* and, yes, *Babe 2* had all been filmed on movieland's newest lot. But the *Babe* fans had someone far more frightening to fend off than the pork slicers. News that Episodes II and III of the *Star Wars* prequels were to be shot at Sydney's Fox Studios ushered a whole new calibre of obsessive through the gates: people like Dave Hankin, who is struggling to keep a few secrets from his girlfriend's parents. There's the fact that he smokes. Then there's the Yoda-shaped bong in his garage. And the tattoo on his shoulder – an exact replica of the symbol worn by his hero, *Star Wars* bounty hunter Boba Fett. Hankin doesn't stop there – he's got the same symbol stencilled across the bonnet of his car, not to mention the habit of dressing up as his favourite character at every available opportunity.

Hankin is one of the stars of a very different Star Wars movie: The

PhanDom Menace, now available on Special Edition DVD. Following fans in the build-up to the launch of the first *Star Wars* prequel, *The PhanDom Menace* has become a cult classic of its own. A documentary by the obsessed for the obsessed, the film was made by Craig F. Tonkin and Warwick Holt on a Betacam camera, and centres around Australian fanclub Star Walking Inc, where we witness grown men who have allowed a childhood passion to consume their adult lives. Despite mitigating pleas of "I haven't outgrown it... I've grown with it", there are plenty of tell-it-to-the-judge moments – such as Chris Brennan wondering exactly how he's going to break it to his wife that they need a bigger house to accommodate his $40,000 collection of memorabilia.

---

determined by the content of a single story, or an entire issue. If we feel it's appropriate to depart from what we are doing typographically in the rest of the issue for one story, then we do. In this case we usually let the title of the story or the images steer us in the right direction.'

Equally, the type of illustration or photograph selected will immediately communicate something to the reader, but, by scaling, cropping and positioning, it can say something completely different. There are no rules as to how you should use these design elements, provided that, together, they express the identity of the publication in general and the specific content in particular. This is true for both newspapers and magazines – as Mario Garcia says, 'Both magazine and newspaper designers have to work hard to make sure that design is there to enhance content and to make it accessible. There are different techniques in terms of the look and feel, but the effort and logistics are the same.'

Advertising style

A publication often has to accept advertising and advertorials in order to cover the cost of publishing. Advertisers wield a lot of power and can be instrumental in determining pagination and the number of spreads available to editorial. As a condition of purchase they may request particular spreads or slots facing editorial pages and, because the first third of a publication is so desirable, this results in fewer spreads in this section being available to the designers. Moreover, right-hand pages are more expensive than left-hand ones because they are more visible, so a title may be forced to sell more of these, resulting in whole sections consisting predominantly of left-hand pages only. In such a case, designers have to make these layouts work hard. If they know what the advertisement is, they can design the editorial page to stand out against it, but they can also create an aesthetically pleasing spread that works in harmony

Jeremy Leslie uses stock to confound expectations on the Virgin Atlantic first-class fanzine *Carlos* (opposite), which manages to feel like a high-quality, luxury product, in part 'due to a matter of context'. 'Twenty years ago, in a world of magazines that were not all full-colour, *Carlos* would have looked cheap because it didn't make use of what was then an expensive commodity: full-colour. It would have looked like many magazines – one- or two-colour. Today, full-colour is the norm, and anything that's different to that stands out and looks rare and "expensive",' explains Leslie. Swiss magazine *soDA* (above) changes format and stocks with each issue, a luxury afforded by its once-a-year publication, which renders familiarity with its format irrelevant. *Pariscope* (above right), a weekly listings title for Paris, is small enough to fit into a bag or pocket and has remained consistently profitable, with sales in the region of 103,000 each week.

with the ad as well as with the magazine as a whole. Either way, through its shapes, contrast and tones, designers will need to design the page as an element in its own right, as well as a strong aspect of a feature that may span a wide range of pages.

Simon Esterson, *Eye* magazine

Simon Esterson's work is characterized as bold, striking and journalistically proud. An unassuming character, and modest in profile, he now operates out of London as Esterson Associates. In 1993, he was part of the team, with Deyan Sudjic and Peter Murray, which started *Blueprint*, a large-format architecture magazine, known for its striking stencil masthead and thick page rules. Most notably Esterson took over *The Guardian* newspaper in 1995 from David Hillman and carried on the bold look that characterized the paper's modern attitude to print. Esterson Associates have redesigned many newspapers including *NZZ* in Zurich and *Publico* in Lisbon (with Mark Porter). He has also worked in Italy as creative director of Italian architecture title *Domus*, and as design consultant to Tate Publishing in London.

In 2008, Esterson jointly purchased *Eye* magazine with editor John L. Walters and publisher Hannah Tyson. Together they brought *Eye* back to life, returning it to its independent roots. By using the web and social media, they have ensured that the print version can thrive again due to its large fan base, some of whom may never handle the actual print version.

Esterson comments that, 'the website and blog are absolutely vital for *Eye*'s survival. The website because it is an archive of what we publish and if you Google something about graphic design then *Eye* will come up on the first page. The blog is vital as we only publish four times a year so we want to be in people's consciousness. For us we are not just making a print magazine. John L. Walters, the editor, is using Twitter and Flickr too. It is not a matter of making things on as many platforms as possible. We already have a quarterly magazine in print. By definition you are around for longer. You play the cards you are given.'

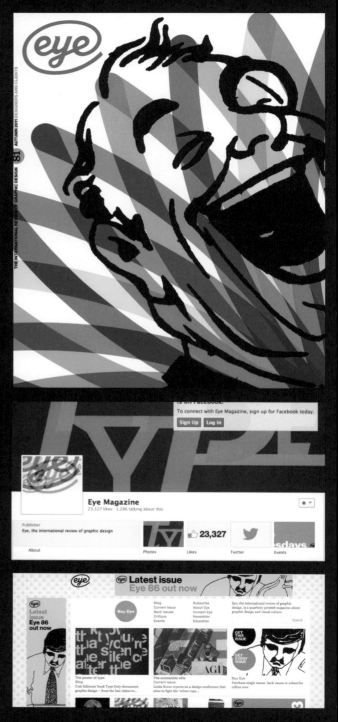

The printed version of *Eye* magazine has an elegant design following a modest grid, which allows the storytelling to come through. The high-quality visuals add to the branding with their authority and quiet admiration for the field of design and its practitioners. The varied design content means that the *Eye* blog is a rich resource for practitioners and students. In 2012 the blog had 488,621 followers, proving that *Eye* could reach many more readers through Twitter than was possible when it was a print-only product with a limited print circulation.

Simon Esterson's passion for design led him to design the start-up architecture magazine *Blueprint* (opposite) in 1983. The stencil masthead became a trademark for this provocative publication. The aesthetic was bold and blocky, shown here by the simple strong coverline justified to the width of the page. Instead of a building on the cover, each issue featured the human face of the business – a portrait of an architect.

EUROPE'S LEADING MAGAZINE OF ARCHITECTURE AND DESIGN / DECEMBER-JANUARY 1986 / NUMBER 23 / £1.50

BLUEPRINT

CRISTIAN CIRICI: THE MAN WHO RE-BUILT MIES. PHOTOGRAPH BY DAVID BANKS

BORN AGAIN BARCELONA

PLUS MICHAEL GRAVES EXCLUSIVE AND DAN DARE VERSUS JUDGE DREDD

How to convert inspiration into a layout

The search for inspiration when trying to arrive at an interesting, dynamic and relevant layout concept can be difficult for any designer at any point. Sitting and staring at a computer screen is quite possibly the least creative action that a designer can perform, but what can you do about it? Move away from your work environment. Going to art galleries, street markets, the movies, shops, funfairs or just sitting in a park and looking at the skyline can often spark an inspirational idea by allowing you to look at things from a totally unexpected perspective. On the following page are a number of creative exercises that can help, too. Where else can a designer turn for inspiration?

All creatives struggle at some point with the search for inspiration, and all find ways out of the impasse. These can include:

Architecture: referencing architectural structures is a rich source of visual inspiration. Many buildings are based on a grid structure, which, when translated to a layout, can give exciting and useful divisions of space. The great American designer Saul Bass realized this and incorporated the grid structures of buildings into some of his most successful screen-credit sequences, in which his elegant typography slid effortlessly across the perspective lines of office-block windows.

Nature: the hugely magnified images of butterfly wings, insect eyes, fish scales and the exoskeletons of arthropods can offer excellent ideas for scale, shape, contrast and structure. Crystal Palace in London, for example, was based on the ribs of a lily leaf.

Industrial design: images gleaned from industrial design can be a source of inspiring imagery. Being man-made and designed, industrial objects can often be easily translated into text and picture boxes. Sleek ocean liners, streamlined trains, the understated, elegant lines of Ken Grange's Parker Pens and the work of Jonathan Ive at Apple Computer are the result of a skilfully crafted application of solid design principles – the very same principles that you can apply to your own layouts.

 'Don't follow what other graphic designers are doing. Find your inspiration in other places, such as art, film, fashion or history.'
Eric Roinestad, art director, *Flaunt*

Look around you: look at your virtual and physical desktops. However they appear to those unfamiliar with them, you will probably know where and what everything is, and this is central to design thinking; all you have to do is make the underlying structure apparent to others. The things you collect, the way in which these things are displayed – all of this is design. On *Speak*, designer Martin Venezky would begin by reading the manuscript:

'After that, I'd enumerate the relationships and imagery that stuck with me. With that fresh in my mind, I would begin sifting through piles of pictures, books, type and so on, pulling out things that struck me either directly or indirectly. I make a point of not organizing my files, which keeps the element of surprise always in play. While looking for one kind of image, another one might slide into view that is more exciting and unexpected. I often refer to the "poetic gap" as the space between a direct illustration of the text and its more eccentric interpretation.'

Get away from your desk: ideas arrive most easily to a mind that is allowed to wander. Your subconscious carries a myriad of images and concepts – the trick is to unlock and make use of these. Play games, stare out the window, go for a walk, and *always* carry a small design notebook with you. Sometimes a quick sketch dashed off in a local park can be translated into a dynamic, powerful and unique layout, headline treatment, logotype or page design.

The theme of this issue was the classic "coming to New York" story. We spent a year with each of the subjects, from the moment of their arrival through their first year in the city. The cover had to convey that sense of wonder, anticipation and fear. We were inspired by one of Cindy Sherman's untitled film stills, the one with the hitchhiker on the road, suitcase by her side. We scouted locations and came up with the great lawn in Central Park, where the buildings in the skyline feel timeless, and the stretch of lawn unfolds with both possibility and anxiety. We shot it in black-and-white because it felt like the spirit of the city, and used yellow as a spot because it's so very New York. Black-and-white and yellow for taxis – very simple.' – Janet Froelich, former art director, *The New York Times Magazine*.

The New York Times Magazine

SEPTEMBER 17, 2000 / SECTION 6

the refugee

the artist

My First Year in New York

the dot-commer

the amnesiac

the world-famous author

the teenage runaway

the bride

the right fielder

the 8-year-old

the virus hunter

the club kid

the campaigner

the girlfriend

Brief Four
Double-page spreads

AIM

To create a series of double-page layout features for your magazine.

THE BRIEF

Include the following elements on the layouts for your magazine: headline, lead image and other images, introductory text (about 30 words) plus some body text. You can find placeholder text in InDesign or you can generate your own text by typing in one paragraph with normal-length words and then stepping and repeating the paragraph.

- Draw your own grid following the example given earlier on pages 110-11. Use InDesign if you can, otherwise use a similar DTP program.
- Create the content by writing the headline yourself and the introductory copy. Include a byline. Also write the picture captions and include any small text that states the origin of your images (credit line). For example, if you created the photographs then give yourself a picture credit. If you are showcasing a friend's work then identify him or her by using a caption. If you are using images from the internet then check you are using a free source. Even in dummy layouts it is important not to take credit for anyone else's work. In terms of fonts, use your body text fonts from Brief Three.
- Save your first layout attempt and then try another version, working until the pages have a sense of balance and drama. Use the scale of the different elements to create a dynamic spread design. Print out your layouts so that you can see the actual size of the elements. Stick the pages together on the back with tape and trim them so that you can see how the layout works within the actual page size.
- When you have done this a couple of times and got it right, print out the layouts in colour and trim them for your portfolio.

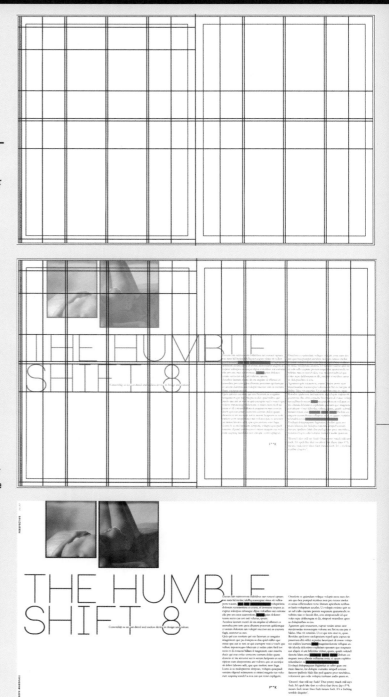

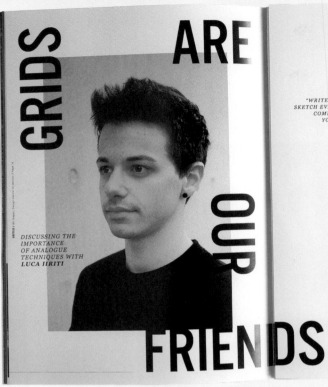

GRIDS ARE OUR FRIENDS

DISCUSSING THE
IMPORTANCE
OF ANALOGUE
TECHNIQUES WITH
LUCA IIRITI

"WRITE DOWN OR
SKETCH EVERYTHING
COMES ACROSS
YOUR MIND"

What techniques do you use to come up with your ideas?

Usually my initial approach with every project starts with an accurate research of the subject which, I'm dealing with. After the documentation part I usually sketch for a few days without even touching the computer. I believe that you keep your ideas fresh by putting them down with pencil rather than going straight on the screen.

A foundamental part of idea generation is having breaks in between, and with break I don't mean like a tea break but a proper few hours or a whole day off, going out seeing friends, exhibitions, going to the park etc. I always feel like by doing this I got back on the project with a much more fresh mind and I can spot easily mistakes which I might haven't seen before, or come up with new ideas perhaps.

Who inspires you?

As I'm from Switzerland most of the designers who inspire me are Swiss like the historical Josef-Müller Brockmann, Herbert Bayer, Max Huber.. As I lived in Lugano I used to see the work of Bruno Monguzzi everyday on the streets, and had the pleasure of meeting him a few times in switzerland and here in London, his mentality and way of thinking always amazes me.

What's the most satisfying part about being a designer?

Personally I think that getting to an and point where you can finally touch with your own hands all the effort and thinking that you've put into a project is one of the most satisfying things of being a graphic designer. And obviously seeing that the people is interested in what you did and that your answers to the design problems are working.

What motivated you to become a designer?

I've always been interested in art and design since I was a kid, then at the age of 14 I've applied to the CSIA Ian art school in Lugano and I've discovered this world and instantly fell in love.

I've chosen to be a graphic designer cause I like to think that I can communicate determinate ideas to a wide range of people and have different reactions. I like the interactive side of it and that gives you the possibility to work with a wide range of different clients and material.

From start to finish, how long does it normally take you to complete a project? It's really difficult to say, as it really depends on the client needs... Generaly I face each project in phases (as mentioned before) which are documentation and research, sketching and ideas, mock ups and overview of the contents, design, outcome.

I've been working on projects for a week or 6 months, it's just a matter of how much work you have to do and how important it is for the client and the community.

Do you prefer to work independently or with a group of people?

Again it depends on the project, I personally prefer to work independently if I have the possibility and time. But I love working in teams if the people shares knowledge and interests similar to mine.

What kind of advice would you give to someone who is thinking about becoming a graphic designer?

Do research and look to the past of our history, it's always good to look back where designers weren't surrounded by technology but use to come up with amazing outcomes (which are rarely seen these days). It always inspires me to think of new methods to realise my works. Write down or sketch everything comes across your mind, everything is important or could lead to another idea.

If you love art, design, ink, paper, communication and people then welcome to the club, and grids are your friends!

What is the most challenging aspect of the job?

I think that coming up with a good idea which is as original as understandable by a large audience is one of challenging aspects of being a graphic designer. Personally I always like to look into the cheapest way of realising what the client needs with still having an appealing "facade", the lower the budget is the more challenging the project will be. Also I always think of how to automise the design, and with that I mean creating a design, a system which allows me to position and build the layouts throughout time easily, if you spend lots of time thinking on how to make things in the easiest and cleanest way then the design will help you in the designing part

What is you're most valued possession when it comes to design?

My pencil.

How long have you been a graphic designer?

I don't know even if I've ever been a graphic designer to be honest, I've started studying graphic design at 14 but I don't really feel part of the "graphic designers club". I prefer to see it as another way of express and communicate.

Joseph Marshall created the images for this college magazine project (opposite) as part of a pitch. The vertical emphasis of the columns is offset by the horizontal axis – a common visual device for balancing elements of a layout.

Marshall stripped back his typographic layouts to show his custom-drawn grid, which displays a combination of a four-column grid and a text box for the page (opposite). This is a tabloid size; larger than A4 and smaller than A3. Marshall wanted to create white space so that he could then surprise the reader with a complete contrast.

This project (above) has a simple three-column grid. The tabloid size gives the designers plenty of white space to play with. This is a simple way to start and is in contrast to Marshall's complex template. The student team of Stefan Abrahams, Jasmine Jones, Rebecca Duff-Smith and Hudson Shively agreed the grid at the start, so as to complement the digital version (right), which was also planned using a simple grid. Choose a grid that reflects the ethos of your magazine content.

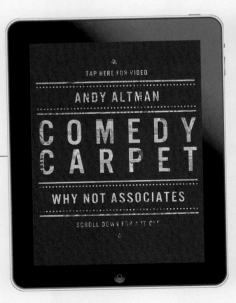

TAP HERE FOR VIDEO

ANDY ALTMAN

COMEDY CARPET

WHY NOT ASSOCIATES

SCROLL DOWN FOR MORE

ELEANOR
HYLAND-STANBROOK

LITTLE LITTER BIRD

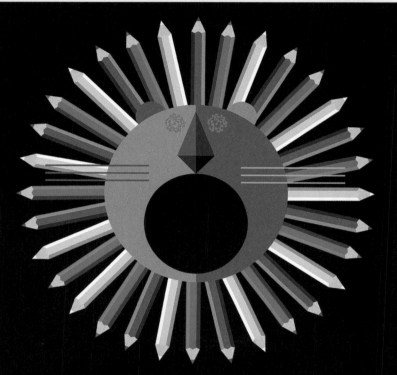

IN REAFFIRMING THE

greatness

OF OUR NATION,
WE UNDERSTAND THAT
GREATNESS IS NEVER A GIVEN.
IT MUST BE EARNED.

—PRESIDENT BARACK HUSSEIN OBAMA

INAUGURAL ADDRESS · JANUARY 20, 2009

 School of VISUAL ARTS®
SVA.EDU

Chapter 6 : Essential design skills

As we have seen, in order to create an effective and successful publication, designers need a broad range of practical technical and conceptual design skills, as well as knowledge of the field. The preceding chapters have dealt with many of these individual skills, such as understanding the component parts of a publication and everyone's role within it. In this chapter, we continue our focus on the design skills and knowledge required not only to be an editorial designer but an art director too, specifically:

- the ability to master objective visualization;

- skilful page preparation;

- an understanding of and skill in working with typography;

- an ability to keep up with changing production skills and to keep learning new software;

- the ability to create consistency without monotony;

- project-managing time and cost.

Mastering objective visualization

!

Jeremy Leslie's guide to the editorial designer's must-have attributes

- The ability to engage with, understand and make sense of the content you're working with, however obscure or distant from your own interests.
- Strong visualization skills allied with the ability to communicate your ideas to colleagues.
- A developed sense of what's possible with illustration and photography.
- An understanding of the market context and competitor magazines.
- Being able to spot a good idea regardless of whose it is (and give credit for it).
- Able to balance your desire to be creative with the reality of deadlines.
- An enjoyment of the process – lack of enjoyment will show in the pages.
- Utter self belief but also the ability to choose the right battle.

This is a complex skill that involves the ability to select, reject, emphasize, arrange and combine essential elements in order not only to design a layout but also to develop a vision for a whole publication that is completely attuned to its subject matter or *raison d'être* and the readership. The designer must be able to:

- understand and make a good and accurate interpretation of editorial material – do this by reading the copy and, where appropriate, talking to the features editor, writer and/or photographer;
- synchronize thinking with an editor to produce the layouts he or she has in mind – meetings and mock-ups are the keys to achieving clear communication here;
- clearly identify the requirements and purpose of a particular publication, or know the brand, the reader and the relationship between the two;
- produce more than one version of a layout (if, for example, the pagination alters). Always develop more than one idea – this has the dual purpose of testing the strength of your original idea against other solutions, and offering back-ups for discussion and development if the first idea is unacceptable;
- stay inspired and, as far as possible, free from constraints – once they have been learnt, all the elements and structures of editorial design can be examined, questioned, played with, revisited and broken. Don't get so stuck in one route and direction that you can't approach a graphic solution laterally;
- visualize and produce layouts from material that may have been created or selected before the start of a layout. Always have a sketchbook on you. Work out ideas and rough layouts on paper; create sketches, diagrams and other material before going near the computer.

Page preparation and grids

Building successful foundations for layout construction consists of choosing the format and stock, creating appropriate grids, knowing how to use design to signal priorities, and working with a flatplan to ensure that sections and pagination keep the flow and pace of the publication while working through constant changes.

Grids

Rather like blueprints in architecture, grids are invisible sets of guidelines, or systems of order, which help the designer determine the placement and use of text, images and other design elements, such as white space, margins and folios, helping to maintain continuity while still allowing for variety in a layout. Good grid systems anchor, but do not necessarily constrain

Chunky blocks of text in formal grid structures can look very effective 'floated' in space, as seen here in the redesigned *Guardian* newspaper.

TIP

Roger Black's ten rules of design
(But remember, rules, once learnt, are there to be broken!)

1. Put content on every page. Design shouldn't be mere decoration; it must convey information. Or entertainment. Content should come to the surface on every level. Corollary: nobody reads anything – at least not everything. The only person who will read every word of what you've written is your mother. All other people skim and surf. So make sure there's content on every page.

2, 3, 4 The first colour is white. The second colour is black. The third colour is red. Calligraphers and early printers grasped this over 500 years ago, and experience has proved them exactly right. White for background, black for text, red for accent and excitement. These three colours are the best. Be very careful with all other colours.

5. Don't be blown around by fashion like a hot-dog wrapper in the wind.

6. Never set a lot of text type in all caps. After a while, it's just too hard to read.

7. A cover should be a poster. A single image of a human will sell more copies than multiple images or all type. Always has, always will. Think about why.

8. Use only one or two typefaces. Italian design is the model: a strong sense of a few things that work together. Avoid a free-for-all of multiple fonts/colours.

9. Make everything as big as possible. Type looks great in big font sizes. A bad picture always looks better bigger.

10. Get lumpy! The trouble with most design is it has no surprise. If you want normal people to pay attention, you have to change pace in your presentation. Monotonous rhythms of picture, headline, picture, text, ad, headline, picture, ad, etc., is like a pudding without raisins – a stew without lumps.

Roger Black has designed *Rolling Stone*, *The New York Times Magazine*, *Newsweek*, *McCall's*, *Reader's Digest*, *Esquire* and *National Enquirer*, among others.

items on a page. Where a publication has a particularly fluid design, the grid acts as an anchor or point of reference, a departure point that roots the whole structure. Sizes and shapes of type, images and areas of white space can be pre-planned, greatly facilitating the process of creating a layout. They can vary from rigid three-column grids to more complex ones of nine or 12 units that enable greater flexibility and almost endless permutations. In either case, the grid remains defined, but having the confidence and knowledge to manipulate and personalize the layout around it is what will make it into something special.

It is useful to be aware of grid conventions that underpin different forms of publishing, if only in order to deviate from them if desired. A weekly or daily, for example, usually has a formal grid structure because its production process has to be simple and fast. Quarterlies, by contrast, have the luxury of time, enabling experimentation and fluidity in the grid and columns system. In Fernando Gutiérrez's annual *Matador*, each issue is designed using a strict but different grid and one typeface. Some publications don't bother with a grid at all, choosing to use just the limits of the page as a grid. In this way they can build up the structure of a layout around an image or headline. Handled well, the result can be a fluid, flexible page and publication, but caution should be used with such an approach – it must be right for the publication, its brand attributes and its readership.

Legibility issues play a part in the construction of the grid, so Fassett's theorem of legible line length should always be considered. This states that line lengths containing 45 to 65 characters are legible (characters include letters, numerals, punctuation and spaces). Line lengths exceeding these limits challenge legibility. This does not mean that 40 characters or 75 characters should never be used, but anything that challenges established legibility theory should be examined closely – including a designer's reasons for doing so. If clear, easy reading is important, grids must take this into account. In newspapers, five columns are viewed as the optimum number for tabloid or Berliner formats, and a story deeper than 7.5 centimetres (3 inches) under a multi-column headline is traditionally broken up with subheads and/or images. There are stylistic conventions, too, that might be considered: in a magazine feature,

Leitungswasser, Stadtteil Queens, New York

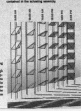

Many periodicals or serial publications, which are published just once or twice a year, don't bother with a grid system, relying instead on their conceptual approach to content and treatment to create continuity from issue to issue. Annual publication *soDA* (left) takes this approach. The theme dictates the format, design and underlying grid (if any) of each issue. *Metropolis* (left below) uses a two-, three- and four-column grid throughout the magazine. 'On editorial pages the text never comes above a certain point on the page, leaving plenty of white space at the top. The *Metropolis* logo moves cinematically back and forth across the top of the page as you progress through the magazine. This is a convention that still exists from Paula Scher's redesign in 1999. Features are printed on an uncoated sheet, which lets readers know – visually and tactilely – that they are in a specific section of the magazine. This allows us to be more experimental in the layout and structure of this section, because it only contains editorial content. Each feature is designed individually, based on the content of the story and the quality and quantity of art that supports it. Most stories are loosely based on the same two- and three-column grids that appear in the rest of the magazine, but we are not afraid of dropping the grid altogether if another approach works better for a particular piece.' – Criswell Lappin, former creative director, *Metropolis*.

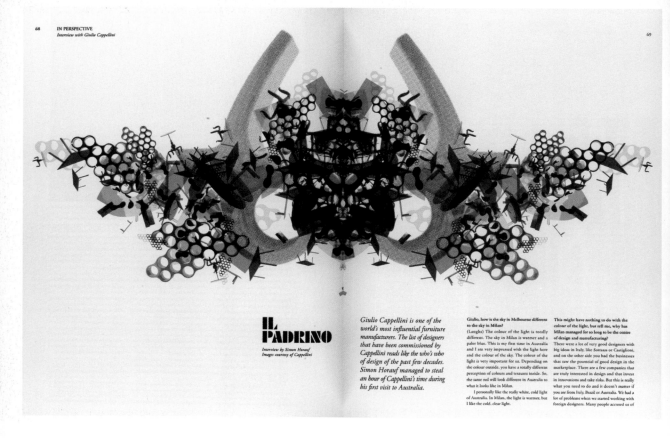

IL PADRINO

Interview by Simon Horauf
Images courtesy of Cappellini

Giulio Cappellini is one of the world's most influential furniture manufacturers. The list of designers that have been commissioned by Cappellini reads like the who's who of design of the past few decades. Simon Horauf managed to steal an hour of Cappellini's time during his first visit to Australia.

Giulio, how is the sky in Melbourne different to the sky in Milan?
(Laughs) The colour of the light is totally different. The sky in Milan is warmer and a paler blue. This is my first time in Australia and I am very impressed with the light here and the colour of the sky. The colour of the light is very important for us. Depending on the colour outside, you have a totally different perception of colours and textures inside. So, the same red will look different in Australia to what it looks like in Milan.

I personally like the really white, cold light of Australia. In Milan, the light is warmer, but I like the cold, clear light.

This might have nothing to do with the colour of the light, but tell me, why has Milan managed for so long to be the centre of design and manufacturing?
There were a lot of very good designers with big ideas in Italy, like Sottsass or Castiglioni, and on the other side you had the businesses that saw the potential of good design in the marketplace. There are a few companies that are truly interested in design and that invest in innovations and take risks. But this is really what you need to do and it doesn't matter if you are from Italy, Brazil or Australia. We had a lot of problems when we started working with foreign designers. Many people accused us of

for reasons of legibility, the grid traditionally has three columns, but literary magazines often use two wide columns instead to form a classical symmetry and deliver long lengths or squares of text that shout 'we're intellectual'; many newspaper supplements take this as their basic structure but lighten the page using white space and other design elements.

On *Inside* magazine (above) the underlying grid is restrained, but its simplicity doesn't hamper design and layouts of other department pages. 'A simple grid can still carry many possible combinations. You have to look at the bigger picture. Readers like to feel as if they have an understanding, almost a relationship, with the magazine. The consistency of the grid nurtures this need. If it's kept consistent, the avid reader of a magazine can pick up any issue and feel comfortable navigating through "new" material,' says former art director Jeffrey Docherty.

White Mischief

ONE MINUTE, SHE'S THE ARCHANGEL
GABRIEL, AND THE NEXT, MARILYN MANSON.
TILDA SWINTON,
AS LYNN HIRSCHBERG DISCOVERS, IS A
WOMAN OF EXTREMES.
Photographs by Raymond Meier

One of Tilda Swinton's ancestors on her very posh, very
military Scottish family tree was painted by John Singer Sargent, and it is easy to imagine Swinton, with her alabaster skin,
otherworldly green eyes and regal 5-foot-11 bearing, captured in oils. "I do look like all those old paintings," Swinton joked
over a midsummer lunch of raw oysters at the Mercer hotel. "But I'm afraid my temperament does not conform. At all."

She said this, as she said nearly everything, with a mix of direct authority and engaged enthusiasm that was both
immediately ingratiating and commanding. Swinton, who is 44, was wearing no trace of makeup, a print sundress and flip-
flops, and her hair, which is naturally red, was dyed white-blond. "I love the roots," she said, as she tilted her scalp forward
for inspection. "That's the best part of being this blond."

Her unique looks, her ease with herself and her voracious interest in the more esoteric worlds of cinema and style have
made Swinton a kind of goddess of the avant-garde. In her movies, she has continually transformed herself — changing
class, nationalities, gender. For "Orlando," perhaps her most famous film, she played multiple incarnations of the title
character, including a man. In "Thumbsucker," opening in theaters on Sept. 16, she is utterly convincing as a suburban
American mom. The director Jim Jarmusch cast her as an ex-girlfriend of Bill Murray's in the recent "Broken Flowers," in
which she is terrifying, her face half-obscured by a foreboding curtain of long brown hair. For "The Chronicles of Narnia:
The Lion, the Witch and the Wardrobe," a big-budget movie that is due out from Disney at the end of the year, Swinton

HIGH ART
THREE EMERGING STARS DRAW FROM FASHION.
By Mauro Egan

In this era of art and fashion mash-ups — in which Marc Jacobs finds a muse in
artists like Elizabeth Peyton and Rachel Feinstein, and the pop art sensation Takashi
Murakami turns rock-star status with his cheery blossom Louis Vuitton bag — it's no
surprise that many artists are mining the runway and style.com to trigger the creative
flow. With proverbial paper and pencil in hand, these up-and-comers were asked to
incorporate a piece of fall fashion into their signature styles.

Researching the Prada collection for visual cues was a departure for Amy Cutler,
who populates her fairy-tale tableaus with stately women who are often dressed in
modest Victorian garb — more Mennonite farmer than Milanese high-fashion priestess.
"It's different than I usually work," says the Brooklyn-based Cutler. "I typically dress the people after
I draw them." Cutler perched these Prada-clad ladies atop an elephant balanced precariously on twiglike
trees. She built the piece around one red strappy high-heel sandal. "Walking down the runway in those
must be equivalent to an elephant on stilts," she says.

The house of Chanel, meanwhile, may seem an odd choice for the men who inhabit the Houston
painter Robyn O'Neil's stark, snowy world. Usually in uniform sweats, they look like a lost fitness tribe
that made a wrong turn at the Mall of America and ended up in a Brueghel landscape. Karl Lagerfeld,
however, is himself a devotee of uniforms. And his gray, black and white palette for this season fits easily
into her woodsy terrain, in which half the men wear Chanel and half are in their customary gym wear.
"The Chanel men represent individuality, while the other men have lost their identity," O'Neil explains.
"They're zombies." In other words, high fashion (and cross-dressing) wins.

Which is often what happens in the work of Simone Shubuck. Not only is the conversant in the latest
Nike Dunks, but also her titles — e.g., "You Can Definitely Take Better Care of Yourself in Paris" —
can sometimes sound as if they have been ripped from the pages of a fashion glossy. When Shubuck saw
Etro's kaleidoscopic fall collection, with its bright colors, Japanese embroidery and geometric shapes,
she immediately envisioned an Egon Schiele type with her high fin de siècle ornamentation. Shubuck,
based in New York, often draws her decorative doodlings on found objects. For this piece, her canvas was
a boy's crumpled science homework, which she salvaged from the trash. "He writes about show and
dazzling designs," she says. "It seemed to go perfectly with the dress."

Amy Cutler
OPPOSITE: FOR "PASSAGE," THE ARTIST WAS INSPIRED BY THE PRADA FALL COLLECTION.

In a magazine feature, for reasons of legibility
the grid traditionally has three columns, but
literary magazines often use two wide
columns instead to form a classical symmetry
and deliver big, dense blocks of text. *The New
York Times Magazine* pages shown here take
this further, boldly using one wide column
that defies Fassett's theory of legibility
(*see* p.156), while remaining accessible
and with a formal beauty provided by their
classical structure.

Digital grids

The grid is also an important part of the editorial
designer's toolkit for digital formats. At *The Times*
newspaper, the column structure of the printed version
is used to give an ordered, legible system for designers
and subeditors to work with, using the classic rules on
the hierarchy of text to lead the reader in. When
applying this philosophy to *The Times* for mobile
media, the same sensibility is used, but the grid is
smaller for the screen. Some users think there is no
need for traditional columns, but design director Jon
Hill explains the grid structure for the iPad as follows:

> *'Navigation is linear, meaning it literally has a front
> cover, so you can swipe through a bunch of pages
> from page one onwards. We found we were quite
> gentle about how we introduced the tablet to the
> reader, and we kept the familiar column-based style
> of the newspaper. We did get lots of stick for that.
> Ultimately, it felt like the columns were a visual
> aid for readers of the website and they were
> comfortable with it. The columns made it easier to
> program and easier to design too. Going from print
> to digital format was a big leap for our readers, but
> they are iPad literate and the columns of text were
> a reassuring feature for them.'*

In contrast, Mark Porter has a different attitude to
digital grids. He redesigned the grid for *The Guardian*
when it moved to the Berliner format in 2005, and
consulted on the iPad version in 2010. Porter has
extended the visual identity *of The Guardian*
newspaper, adapting the design to fit *The Guardian
Online* (a digital news website) and *The Guardian* app
by making design decisions that stem from the design
philosophy originated during the massive typographic
overhaul in 2005. As he explains, 'It is about adapting
what you do to the medium. So the kind of grid on a
newspaper is not the kind of grid on a web or app.
Basically you can have an approach and a philosophy
about how to use them and apply that to the different
medium. You can't just take the grids over.'

In the competitive world of Premier League football every detail counts. For Sam Allardyce, the Blackburn Rovers manager, this involves employing 'the Big Brother of football' to help him to get the best out of his players. But what's good for elite footballers could also be good for you and your job
HUMAN PHYSIOLOGY

WORDS: KAYA BURGESS | PICTURES: GERRY PENNY

IT

was brief and a long time ago, but Sam Allardyce's experience of the North American Soccer League still shapes his approach to football management some three decades later.

Back in 1983 Allardyce played for the Tampa Bay Rowdies, who shared the facilities of the American football team, the Tampa Bay Buccaneers. Even though the Buccaneers were not the strongest team in the NFL, Allardyce was impressed.
"They were given breakfast in the morning, trained,

relaxed, watched some video analysis, looked at stats, took their weight, took their blood, took a urine test," Allardyce recalls. A huge back-up team acted on this information and built it into the players' training. "You were talking about six physios, eight masseurs, a psychiatrist, a psychologist, five support scientists, three nutritionists, some people employed just to do strappings."

The Blackburn Rovers manager became determined to apply this all-encompassing approach to training and player evaluation to football. Soon after his appointment at Bolton Wanderers in 1999 he went one better, adding a computer analysis system called Prozone to the mix. He brought it with him to Blackburn in 2008. And something similar may soon be coming to your workplace — if it isn't there already.

A football manager and his staff cannot possibly keep a close watch on all 11 members of his team for 90 minutes. Yet no Rovers player can escape the watchful eye of the eight Prozone digital cameras placed around Ewood Park — or the intense evaluation of his performance they produce. The technology has since been adopted by many leading clubs, including Manchester United and Real Madrid.

While Prozone works exclusively on football, its executives have been consulted by companies seeking to use a similar approach to monitor employees. Three years ago one agency sought advice from Prozone on using their system to show the distance nurses had to cover within a hospital, their work-rate and the type and frequency of tasks they had to perform.

Simon Edgar, a manager at Prozone, says: "Businesses can certainly benefit from having a system where all data outputs

employee productivity by plotting data about individuals' output against data about the way they work. Companies can subscribe to software packages that will monitor internet usage. Electronic swipe-cards that give access to the building can also provide information about working hours. Keystroke logging can monitor every word typed, while attentiveness monitors can flash up a message on a computer screen — if you don't click it quickly enough, you're not paying attention.

For Cary Cooper, Professor of Organisational Psychology and Health at the University of Central Lancashire and co-author of *Business and the Beautiful Game*, such software can be valuable — but only if used properly. "These technologies can be extremely useful, but you can't rely totally on them," he says.

"A lot of people want a magic bullet for observation but none of these systems work by themselves. They are most predictive when collated with other data on performance.

"In a call centre one employee might take longer over calls, but they might also have a better record of keeping and attracting customers. You have to be very careful that monitoring software doesn't blind you to other data.

"Sam Allardyce isn't going to use Prozone exclusively without making his own observations and judgments about players' abilities. Managers in other walks of life should be similarly wary." +

GREAT MINDS
Footballing injuries can be prevented using sport statistics
Dr Ian McHale, University of Salford

The Times decided to retain the use of a grid structure for their iPad version to give the traditional newspaper reader a familiar reading experience in terms of navigating through the page. The mobile version has the same attitude to clarity and order that the brand has had for many years. 'It is all about typographic structure. Once we have our fonts established, the structure of columns and page design is just as important on the tablet versions as it is in the print version. We are looking for a polished typographic product.' – Jon Hill, design director, *The Times*.

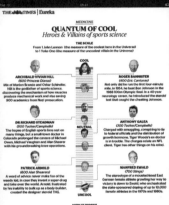

THE TIMES | Eureka
MEDICINE

QUANTUM OF COOL
Heroes & Villains of sports science

THE SCALE
From 1 John Lennon (the measure of the coolest hero in the Universe) to 1 Yoko Ono (the measure of the uncoolest villain in the Universe)

COOL

ARCHIBALD VIVIAN HILL
(800 Princess Dianas)
Mix of Marlon Brando and Oskar Schindler, Hill is the godfather of sports science, discovering the mechanism of how muscles produce mechanical work and also saving 900 academics from Nazi prosecution.

ROGER BANNISTER
(400 Eric Cantonas)
Not only did he run the first four-minute mile, in 1954, he beat Ben Johnson in the 1988 100m Olympic final. In a 40-year neurology career, he introduced the steroid test that caught the cheating Johnson.

NEUTRAL

DR RICHARD STEADMAN
(500 Tucker/Campbells)
The hopes of English sports fans rest on many things, but a small-town doctor in Colorado prolonged the careers of Michael Owen, Michael Vaughan and Alan Shearer with his groundbreaking knee operations.

ANTHONY GALEA
(600 Tucker/Campbells)
Charged with smuggling, conspiring to lie to federal officials and the distribution of growth hormone, Tiger Woods's ex-doctor is in trouble. The charges relate an NFL client. Tiger has other things on his mind.

PATRICK ARNOLD
(600 Alan Shearers)
A word of advice: never make fun of the weedy kid, in case they invent a super-drug and take over the world. Arnold, frustrated by his inability to bulk up as a body-builder, created the designer steroid THG.

MANFRED EWALD
(700 Stings)
The stereotype of a moustachioed East German female athlete growling her way to victory is down to Ewald, who orchestrated the state-sponsored doping of up to 10,000 female athletes in the 1970s and 1980s.

UNCOOL

HOW IT WORKS
The scale starts at neutral, or 1 Tucker/Campbell. 1,000 Tucker/Campbells = 1 Eric Cantona.
1,000 Eric Cantonas = 1 Princess Diana, 1,000 Princess Dianas = 1 John Lennon.
Negative cool: 1,000 Tucker/Campbells = 1 Alan Shearer, 1,000 Alan Shearers = 1 Sting, 1,000 Stings = 1 Yoko Ono.

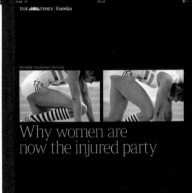

THE TIMES | Eureka

WORDS: HANNAH DEVLIN

Why women are now the injured party

MEDICINE
Scientists are tailoring exercise regimes and diets to counter high levels of injury among female athletes as they challenge the limits of their sports

February **08**

MEDICINE

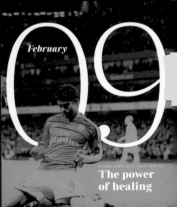

February **09**

WORDS: DAVID ROSE + KAYA BURGESS

The power of healing

At *The Guardian*, the underlying grid on the newspaper is a 20-column grid that divides into 5. The grid for the website is a 12-column grid that breaks into 3 or 4. On the iPad the grid is 6 squares by 8 squares. The hierarchy of typography signals the importance of the story. Crisp headlines underpin the design and bring a spark through the juxtaposition of words and images. Every opportunity for graphic impact is used so that the website is a rich experience of simple navigational tools that help the reader get straight down to the exact content he or she is looking for.

Like many news sites, *The Guardian* iPad edition uses horizontal section heading bars and vertical lists of subjects to enable the reader to get to content quickly in the way he or she would use a referencing system.

Templates

Once a grid has been established, page templates should be made up for the different sections of the magazine – news pages, feature pages, back sections and so on. These templates will be based on the master grid but each should be simplified to deal with the specific demands of the section. All the major elements of the design – boxes for display fonts in alternative sizes, columns, picture boxes, caption boxes and so on – should be included (for more on templates, including an example, *see* p.110).

Pagination

The running order of pages has to be planned to ensure everything fits into an issue. Such planning is important in design terms because the flow created by a publication's pagination will determine the pace and balance, and ensure that spreads of similar contents are spaced apart. Determining pagination is usually a collaboration between the editor, art editor, production editor and advertising-sales head. The only real restrictions are those of the print process – the way sections need to be made up for the presses – and the needs of advertising. Special attention should be paid to the details: a feature ending on a left-hand page with a new feature facing it is rarely desirable, and neither is a feature that is interrupted by four consecutive pages of advertising, or by an unexpected advertising insert. The best way to test the pacing and flow of your publication is to produce miniature spreads, 'minis', that can be pinned up in the studio. These can easily be shifted around as the flatplan changes, enabling you to monitor constantly the effects the inevitable changes are having.

Signalling

In printed periodicals an integral part of pagination and page preparation is the ability to signal the importance, priority and style of articles to the reader. All the design elements act as signals, from an article's position in the publication and on the page to the width of columns (wider columns usually indicate features or the opinion and editorial – op-ed – section of a newspaper), type size, length and position of a headline, length of text, style of text setting, use and size of images and use of colour. A newspaper illustrates this very clearly. On the front page the lead story will be near the top of the page (so that it's visible to the reader at the news-stand) and have the biggest headline and most space allocated to it, with less important stories radiating from it. The op-ed pages distinguish themselves from news pages by using a lot more negative space, picture bylines, pull quotes, wider columns and different type weights and sizes. But this signalling is also visible in magazines. In the news and reviews pages, signalling is similar to that of a newspaper, but in the feature well it may be more subtly employed. If the headline is very prominent and the article spans eight pages in wide columns with full-bleed, commissioned photographs, it's clear that the publication wants you to read it. A designer should adopt a coherent and consistent use of such signals appropriate to his or her publication.

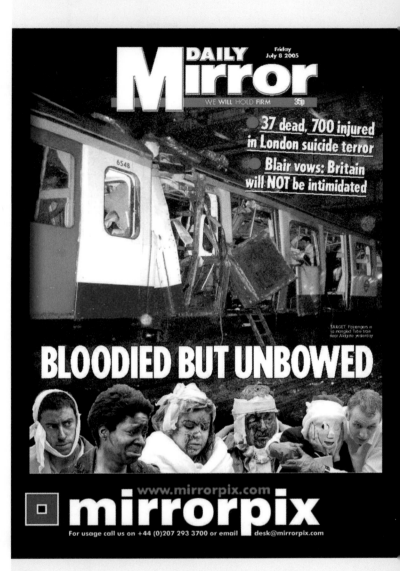

The day after the 7 July 2005 London bombings, national tabloid the *Daily Mirror* portrayed the capital as bloody but unbowed. Newspapers will usually treat such huge events pictorially.

A sketch from *The Guardian*'s iPad development, showing blocks that indicate a modular grid, some with images, some with text. This was later developed into a slick grid with roll-over features. Designers still use felt-tip pens at all stages of design.

Digital page design

Designing for digital publications employs similar typographic and layout principles as for print. However, designers must understand that it is not just the output which varies, but what the reader wants from each different digital publication. Reading from an app on a touch screen is different to the experience of reading on a website; the editorial team must understand who their reader is, what his or her interests are, why, how and where he or she is engaging with the media. It is then that the skill of the art director and the editorial team comes into play; the team must be able to respond with the right content and design for their reader.

Navigation

The same principles of clarity in planning used in printed publications also apply to digital ones, but are extended to include navigation design skills for tablet and mobile devices. Online magazines designed to be read on an iPad or mobile device have become highly interactive; the way the user navigates the screen has to be carefully planned to make him or her want to interact and delve deeper into the publication. Navigation headings are designed to take the reader quickly to what he or she wants to read about, and on-screen tags and tabs are designed to help him or

In this shot taken from a video (middle) Jack Schulze explains the thinking behind the new geography of digital editorial (search for Mag+Berg Bonnier video). Articles are designed as vertical columns comprising text, image and usual page furniture, which can be scrolled up and down, but are then assembled on a 'clothes line' that can be swiped horizontally.

Here the layouts are being swiped left to right, and pages moved sideways. The reader can go up and down to read, and left to right to see different articles. There is still a grid and typographic style sheets, but this style of navigation puts the viewer in control of how they access articles.

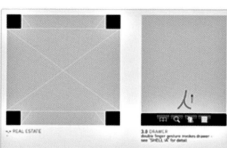
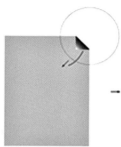
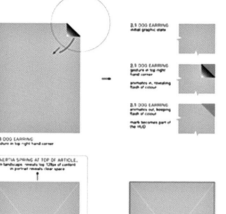

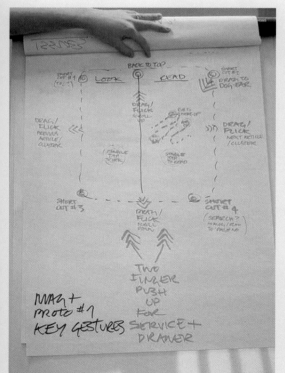

The sketch on the flipchart (left) shows the thinking behind the development of Mag+ software, developed by Berg London with Bonnier. This chart shows the 'key gestures' the team considered at the early stages of building the software. A gestural language develops (top), like 'drag and flick' (a swipe action) and 'drag to dog-ear' (the little turned-down corner at the top of the page that invites the reader to move on to the next page).

The sketches on the wall (above) show the pages planned out both as horizontal layouts and overlaid with their corresponding portrait layouts. Designers must think in terms of both formats for mobile use and put aside the double-page-spread thinking of print.

her quickly find out more information on a story or subject. The language and copy has to be easily digestible and attention grabbing in order to engage and intrigue the reader.

A cell system is used for a double navigational purpose. Firstly, it signifies the importance of a story, so a major story will get more cells than a minor story. Second it acts as a touch entry point so that the reader can dive into the content. As Mark Porter explains, 'With the lead picture [on a page], we see that cell navigation allows the user to plunge right in and open up any story they want. Whereas in print a major story would have a large headline, the major story occupies two or three cells. The user slides down or right to left.'

Websites

Magazine websites can use the familiar navigation language of the web – menu bars and drop-down tab menus. The designer then directs the reader to sections and pages using a hierarchy of text and section names. The major difference is that this form of presentation doesn't encourage the longer reads expected of a printed magazine. Designing a magazine for a website also requires different design considerations to those of designing for a touch-screen tablet. Websites offer the designer opportunities to showcase a brand and design incentives that encourage the reader to make purchases.

Tablets

For the tablet version of magazines, however, the navigation options become more exciting because of the use of a touch screen. The designer must be aware, however, that the reader will still want to access the content quickly and without any complicated hurdles being put in the way. Not all tablets devices are as fast as others and viewers may quickly lose patience. As Mark Porter explains, 'That's why there are some successful newspaper websites where people know what they are looking for and they can drill down to, for example, the sports results. You go in and there is a list of new headlines since you last viewed the website. It is a fairly straightforward transaction. It is very hard to find a satisfying magazine website because the way that you want to interact with a magazine is very different.'

In this lively and colourful still-life set-up, messy and lengthy captions are a thing of the past. The photograph stays intact and captions are latent content, only revealed when the reader requires them and swipes over one of the featured watches. In the feature on Marilyn's shoes, hovering over a different shoe reveals a different story.

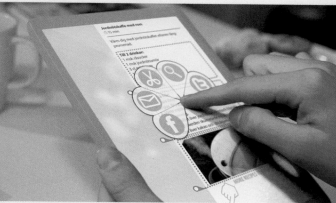

On a tablet, enhanced features can appear by using different touch functions. Slight pressure from a finger brings up a submenu, seen here as radiating icons that link to other dynamic media. You can send an image or other content from the magazine straight to social media. In the example here, if you press and hold the screen you can send a recipe by email, or share it on Twitter or Facebook.

Apps

Their very nature means newspaper apps need to continually be updated, so they tend to be more templated and website-like than magazine apps, which have a broader selection of options to work from. These range from a simple PDF page-turner taken from the printed layouts (perhaps with embedded web and social media links) to a bespoke designed and coded app with full interactivity.

A middle route between these two extremes is provided by the many app-creation tools, in the form of software plug ins, that allow the designer to adapt their print designs for tablets. Theoretically a simple step, such a move from print to app brings many complications. The various sizes and formats of the different tablet screens mean that distinct apps need to be built for each tablet, and as all tablet screens are smaller than most print magazine pages, the entire magazine has to be repurposed page by page. Even with the high resolution of recent screens, text generally needs to be larger than in print to maintain legibility.

For reasons of cost and resource, smaller publishers have relied on the PDF option to start with, but others have seized the opportunity to create something more appropriate to their readership. Sarah Douglas from *Wallpaper** magazine comments on planning a design for her magazine's app:

'It is just about re-appropriating your thoughts. How things work differently how they are read differently.

You have to think differently. You have to think through the reader's eyes. Think how people use it. You can do some crossover things on an iPad. With design for a tablet you can get a sense of scale, while on a smartphone you are much more limited by the screen width. Theoretically on a website you have quite a lot of space, but once you bear in mind the way the website is made and also the screen you, the user, are looking at, then it is not as much space as it looks. Most of the navigation is done by lists and menus, which is fine if you are looking at lists or reading a book, but it doesn't sit very happily in an editorial environment.'

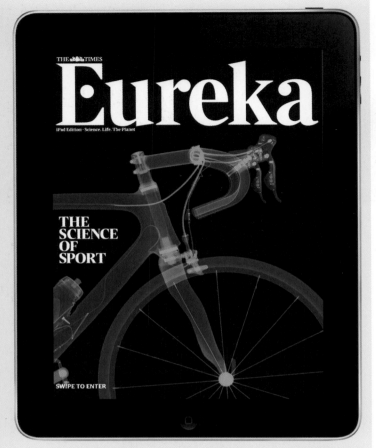

In the iPad edition of *The Times* magazine
Eureka, Jon Hill uses the masthead for impact,
and keeps the design relatively simple. Once
past the cover, the reader can tap on the
hexagons to go to the stories, thus keeping
the sciency feel of the magazine.

Jeremy Leslie's tips for digital design

1   The basic basic principle is to understand
     what you are trying to say and who you are
     saying it to, and then figure out how you are
     going to say it.

2   People are connected by shared ideas and
     common interests. The communal desire to
     be part of something bigger will always be
     there, and is easier than ever to achieve
     today, thanks to digital technology.

3   Don't use a channel for the sake of using it.
     Ask yourself which ones add to your story,
     which ones might diminish it.

4   Interactive elements can be exciting to
     create and use, but don't let them become a
     distraction. Keep them useful and relevant.

5   From an editorial standpoint there is not a
     huge difference between working for print
     and digital – unless you make it that way.

6   Remember that magazines create a world
     of their own. Readers do still get absolutely
     lost in those worlds.

The flatplan

The single most important tool in producing any
publication is the flatplan. This ingenious exploded
diagram of a publication, similar to a film storyboard,
enables everyone involved in its production to see pages,
their running order, their content, print sections, editorial-
to-advertising ratio and pagination at a single glance.
Usually the responsibility of the production editor or
studio manager, flatplans are updated constantly to
reflect inevitable changes that will occur, from a feature
that needs to be extended, shrunk or dropped, to a specific
ad that needs to go opposite a particular editorial page.
Such changes will necessitate a rearrangement of a
section so that balance and pacing are still maintained
throughout. Each time such an alteration or amendment
occurs, a new flatplan will be printed out and distributed
to keep everyone up to date. For the designer, it means
they can quickly see how many pages they have for a
particular feature and where in the run of pages that
feature falls. Various digital flatplan systems exist that
allow immediate updates to be shared.

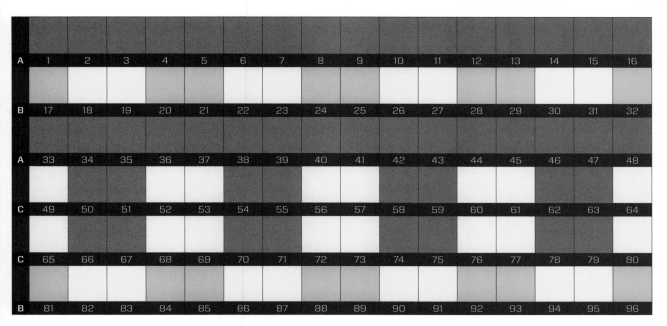

A	1	2	3	4	5	6	7	8	9	10	11	12	13	14	15	16
B	17	18	19	20	21	22	23	24	25	26	27	28	29	30	31	32
A	33	34	35	36	37	38	39	40	41	42	43	44	45	46	47	48
C	49	50	51	52	53	54	55	56	57	58	59	60	61	62	63	64
C	65	66	67	68	69	70	71	72	73	74	75	76	77	78	79	80
B	81	82	83	84	85	86	87	88	89	90	91	92	93	94	95	96

A flatplan showing pagination for a 96-page publication using three sheets of paper (A, B and C) to be printed on both sides. Each sheet prints 32 pages, 16 on each side. If your publication is not full-colour throughout, the flatplan should clearly distinguish between the colour and black-and-white sections by using a tint on the colour pages or by creating a bold keyline around them. The yellow tinted pages indicate full-colour, the red pages indicate two-colour and the grey tint indicates a one-colour print such as black. The colour sections can be placed anywhere in an edition, as long as the colour distribution matches up on each sheet. Most printers print and bind in multiples of 16 pages, although 20 or 24 are also widely used. Usually the printer will require all the pages within one sheet section first – i.e., all the pages falling on sheet A need to be sent to print a day or two before those on section B and so on.

A working flatplan shows where the various elements of a publication's content are to appear. Page one is conventionally the front cover. A diagonal strike through a page indicates that it is reserved for advertising, but 'AD' written clearly on the page works just as well, particularly if you want to use strikes as a production schedule device – one strike to show that the page has been designed, another to show it's been proofed and so on. A good naming or numerical convention for new versions of the flatplan is important: mark the date, time and version number clearly on a prominent part of the sheet. This witty contents page for *M-real* gives a good idea of how a flatplan might look once the publication is ready to go to press.

Issue 4. Response. Page 03
Contents

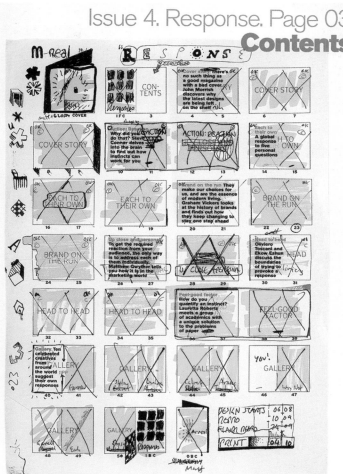

Stock selection

The selection of a suitable paper stock (or stocks) is more important than ever, as print seeks to make the most of its attributes in the face of digital competition. Paper choice is vital to the feel, tone, style and look of a publication, because it affects both expression of the publication and reproduction of its contents. There are two traditional routes for stock selection – via the printer or a paper merchant – but the best is a combination of the two. A printer will be able to give you good initial guidance and work closely with you to find the best stock for your specific production needs. For example, if you know you want a thin, coated gloss stock with no show-through and high brightness, the printer will usually be able to suggest good examples. Paper merchants are happy to send printed and blank sample books and sheets to designers and will also make up a sample in your chosen format (usually via the printer), giving you a good idea of the weight and feel of the publication. But if you require unusual print or production techniques, such as an embossed fifth metallic colour or die-cuts, speak to your printer – this is where his or her knowledge and expertise come into play. And look at existing print material that may match your needs; you will often find that publications list the stock or printer's name, making your search that much easier.

Paper considerations

Stock selection is usually a question of balancing your needs. For example, if your main criterion is faithful colour reproduction, then the best sheet to use is a bright, blue-white, thick-coated sheet with an ultra-smooth finish. This reflects the most light at the best angle without adding a tone or hue of its own. But other issues may need to be considered: what if there is a lot of text? Or weight is an issue? This guide should help.

Coated or uncoated? Coated papers reflect light better and absorb less ink, giving images more detail; the higher the number of coats, the sharper the images. Uncoated papers offer a softness in print contrast that

As an independent publication or microzine, *soDA* (far left) survives by selling ads, through subscriptions and, as in this case, with the support of printers or paper companies, who are often keen to promote particular techniques and stocks. For this issue about surface, the cover is made of holographic card, while inside pages use metallic inks and numerous coated and uncoated stocks in different colours. *Flaunt* covers are often die-cut and embossed – this May 2001 cover (left) mimics a schoolbook and has raised strips of Sellotape and REM and Missy Elliott logos to create a real three-dimensional depth. Such covers are produced because, 'When you're called *Flaunt*, you sort of have to flaunt yourself and be a little showy. We have to flaunt the special inks, tricks and embossing. It's important to sell the word and the image of flaunting by going the extra distance. The embossing also throws in another sensitivity that most magazines don't use – the tactile element to touching the front cover. People love to touch the cover,' says Jim Turner, creative director.

can work well with fine art or illustration and make text easier to read.

Gloss or matt? A high-gloss stock is usually used on a high-quality publication with a large number of images, but many matt stocks offer excellent reproduction and can make a publication stand out from its competitors.

Thick or thin? We all associate thick papers with art and 'highbrow' books, but thin papers can give the same sense of opulence and richness, depending on other qualities such as density, brightness and coating.

Dense or opaque? The opacity of stock will affect its show-through, so bear this in mind when specifying your stock, and test it by laying it over a black-and-white striped design. If using an opaque stock, you will need to consider the page carefully to minimize print show-through. An asymmetric grid, for example, will show through more than a symmetrical one.

Heavy or light? We associate weight in paper with luxury, but luxury costs – not just the paper itself, but

Paper manufacturers and suppliers go to great lengths to persuade designers to use their paper, producing numerous swatch books and luxurious samples containing different weights and colours of a particular stock (above). Remember that these can look very different with print on them, so ask to see a job that's been printed on the stock you are interested in, and ask for a dummy to be made to the size and number of pages in your publication.

As newspapers continue to lose sales, they are fighting hard to find more readers, many changing format from unwieldy broadsheets to the popular Berliner, compact (left) and tabloid formats, and moving towards even smaller formats such as A4. The best examples do not simply try to 'shrink' content to fit the smaller page, but consider the new format as a new design, looking at columns (their numbers, widths and lengths), negative space, typography and other design elements such as rules and folios. Mario Garcia uses the analogy of moving from a large house to a small flat: 'You have to reassess what you need and want to keep, and what you are happy to leave behind.'

in postage and portability. Do you want to discourage potential purchasers from carrying your publication around with them because it's the weight of a telephone book? If the image you are trying to project is that of a faithful companion, should the publication be portable?

High or low brightness? The brighter the paper, the more blue light it reflects, which works well for reproducing images. But such brightness can create glare that might interfere with readability, and because of the amount of bleaching needed to achieve high brightness, qualities such as durability and printability may be affected.

Recycled or virgin stock? Readers of a magazine about environmental issues would expect it to be printed on stock that was environmentally friendly, which could be anything from wholly recycled unbleached stocks to partially recycled stocks. Most paper merchants now offer these, but you can also find out what the different terms mean by getting advice from environmental agencies.

Format

Format is defined as the shape and size of a page. The most common format, A4, is dictated by the width of paper rolls and the size of the drum on the offset web presses commonly used to produce mass-circulation magazines and books. Because American and European drum circumferences differ, there are slight variations, notably a shorter standard format in the US. Consumer magazines also have to conform to requirements such as shelf size in shops, and the ability to fit through a standard letter box, as well as taking advantage of various postage rates related to size. While short-run publications have the luxury of printing on a bespoke format, it is still worth bearing in mind the reader's needs – a large-format magazine or odd shape can be a nuisance if filing for future reference is important.

$7.95   issue # 27.

+ David Carson

Choosing and using type

Any publication should create an enjoyable, accessible and appropriate experience for its reader, and a large part of this is determined by the use of typography. Readers who are accustomed to unvarying pages of dense text in a novel would not read the same page in a magazine, where decoration, variation, space and cohesive use of design elements are expected. Type that is too small, too dense and too uniform will put off the reader, as will columns of 'grey' text; an editorial designer has to employ a range of tricks to keep the reader interested.

Practical issues may need to be considered, too. On some publications, particularly dailies and weeklies, designers need to accommodate exact lengths of copy and headlines. And lastly, but most importantly for a publication's identity and appeal, aesthetic, emotional and contextual considerations apply. Type, more than any other design element, signals certain associations to the reader. To address all these issues satisfactorily, each different form of type should be selected for its specific function, but also to form a whole that is appropriate to the publication. At *Flaunt*, Lee Corbin's selection of fonts is determined by what is happening typographically throughout the entire issue. 'I try to take account of what's going on in the photographs, the clothes, the content, illustrations and so on, in all the stories running in the issue. I decide what faces will be used in which sections, and the varying degrees of abstraction,' he explains.

A publication's format should be dictated by its readership and its purpose, such parameters allowing for a wide variety of approaches. Microzines such as *Tank* (opposite top right) have the freedom to be as big or small as they want (or indeed to change with every issue). *Emigre* (opposite below) has experimented with different formats. This one enabled an expansive, large-scale design approach suited to its subject matter, the design work of David Carson.

Two very different but equally effective approaches to font use for headlines. In *Vogue Paris* (top), the choice of a vibrant red serif face for the words '*L'amour absolu*' results in a spread that is bold and passionate without being brash or masculine. *About Town* (above), by contrast, is the opposite – confident, manly and swaggering, it visually reflects the topic.

There are no hard-and-fast rules for how big or small text and headings should be. Logically, the display text information intended to catch the eye and be read first, such as headings and introductions – will dominate the page by being larger than body text and captions, while body copy should always be large enough to be readable by its intended audience. It's a good idea to experiment with these by printing them out at different sizes with different leadings. There are no formulaic type sizes that always work for all situations – it's more about using judgement to determine what looks and works best for the publication's readership. It is also worth considering that most typefaces were designed for a particular purpose, and for that reason may work better at certain sizes than others. But by using such faces in offbeat or unexpected ways, a designer can deliver an inventive, original or starkly awkward layout that may be perfect for its readership. Newspaper headlines, by contrast, should have nothing 'tricksy' about them; they need to be clear, clean and unambiguous in their design. This is not to say that serifs can't be used for newspaper headlines; many quality papers use italics and serifs in headlines

British tabloid newspapers (also known as 'redtops') rarely use serif faces, and often use all capitals in their headlines, as seen here in the *Daily Mirror* (above). While the use of an upper-case sans serif fails to distinguish the newspaper from its rivals, it very clearly signals the type of newspaper it is. The redtops pride themselves on using dense typography to pack their pages full of stories, and allow little white space to create a proposal of value for money in a very competitive market where reader loyalty shifts with the stories of the day.

By contrast, the Swedish daily *Dagens Nyheter* (top) uses serif fonts for the pull quote and drop cap, thereby establishing a more literary tone. The use of horizontal white space also signals a more relaxed, intelligent pace. These combine to convey the sense that the content is analytical and thoughtful. There is nothing rushed about the page – it demands a deeper level of engagement and commitment from the reader than a tabloid would.

Changing the impact of images and copy with layouts

In this layout the headline is hero – it dominates the page and draws the eye's attention. Echoing a tabloid newspaper, the headline is hard hitting while the body text is lowest in priority. There are only small variations in typography, little white space and short articles. This gives the newspaper an immediate and throw-away quality.

Using the same image and copy, this spread gives an entirely different feel. With a softer headline, greater white space, and the introduction of pull quotes and subheads, the body text now carries the highest priority. This layout tries to create easy access to the article but still uses a large headline and image to draw attention to the spread. With the feel of an upmarket magazine, it uses the same components to create a more intellectual look for the article.

The image is the dominant feature of this layout. Aided by dotted rules, a short, single story and a dominant stand-first, it achieves a glossy-magazine feel. These publications are quick to navigate and easy to flick through. The images tend to play hero in order to grab the attention of a skimming reader.

THE HARD-HITTING NEWS HEADLINE

SECOND STORY HEADLINE FOR RELATED NEW ARTICLE

The softer-hitting news headline

The medium-hitting news headline

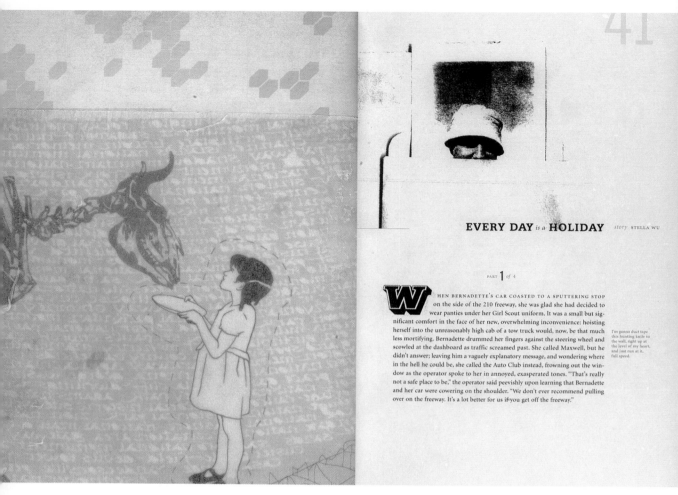

EVERY DAY *is a* HOLIDAY   *story* STELLA WU

PART **1** *of 4*

WHEN BERNADETTE'S CAR COASTED TO A SPUTTERING STOP on the side of the 210 freeway, she was glad she had decided to wear panties under her Girl Scout uniform. It was a small but significant comfort in the face of her new, overwhelming inconvenience: hoisting herself into the unreasonably high cab of a tow truck would, now, be that much less mortifying. Bernadette drummed her fingers against the steering wheel and scowled at the dashboard as traffic screamed past. She called Maxwell, but he didn't answer; leaving him a vaguely explanatory message, and wondering where in the hell he could be, she called the Auto Club instead, frowning out the window as the operator spoke to her in annoyed, exasperated tones. "That's really not a safe place to be," the operator said peevishly upon learning that Bernadette and her car were cowering on the shoulder. "We don't ever recommend pulling over on the freeway. It's a lot better for us if you get off the freeway."

I'm gonna duct tape this hunting knife to the wall, right up at the level of my heart, and just run at it, full speed.

While *Fishwrap*'s format and stock change from issue to issue, what unites them, says graphic designer Lisa Wagner Holley, is 'typography – a sensitivity to working with it, and carefulness about the read and the reader's experience'. Editorial elements are shared also, using pull-quote texts to unify images (footnoting conversational ideas to address the reader more intimately). Fonts – in this issue, Minion, Trade Gothic, Knockout and Young Baroque – are carefully considered so that they work with each other. As Wagner Holley explains, 'The text is very important to us as we try to keep the read friendly, legible, smart.'

to impart a gravitas and quality that sans-serif heads sometimes lack.

Readability and usability are the main considerations when choosing a body typeface because of its vital role in communicating the editorial message. Broadly speaking, we are more accustomed to reading serif faces, and, traditionally, these are used in long columns of text, such as feature pages, with sans-serif faces offering visual variation through their use in shorter texts (news pages, reviews, box text and so forth). The use of a serif typeface gives a formal feel, while a sans-serif face has a more relaxed, contemporary look. If a letterform is curvaceous and flowing like a script face, this delivers a softer feeling, whereas a hard-edged, Germanic gothic typeface makes a very different statement (but as both of these are very hard to read neither should be considered for large amounts of body copy). Type is meant to be read as a shape, and sometimes as a visual element in its own right. It is one of the most flexible elements of editorial design – the stylistic muscle of a publication.

Type use in newspapers

While typography underpins the design of all editorial matter, its use in newspapers differs from that in magazines. As Mark Porter explains, 'In newspapers the first priority is always legibility of typefaces and readability of pages. Only after that do you think about using type to establish a distinctive voice for the paper, and try and create beautiful and dramatic typographic design.' In terms of key font considerations for handling typeface in newspapers, Porter adds, 'Text legibility is by far the most crucial. In display type, colour and range of weights also become more important.' Porter's introduction of the custom-designed Egyptian for *The Guardian* as both headline and body font is unusual, but, with more than 200 weights, the font shows a versatility and ability to perform in its different roles that is rare for a single typeface.

In introducing new fonts to a publication, whether commissioned or existing, the creative director must ensure that the relationship of the type to the brand, content and other design elements works as well as it can. They do this by trusting their instinct and by understanding the publication, says Mark Porter:

'Egyptian was commissioned for The Guardian *because we wanted something that had some of the properties of a classic serif typeface, while remaining modern and distinctive. It had to be legible and flexible and have a strong personality, and it succeeds in this. The range of weights also enables us to avoid the system, which most other newspapers adopt, of mixing a serif and a sans – in most sections we only use Egyptian, which gives the paper a unique typographic character.'*

Type as expression

In layouts where it isn't possible to use images, or where images are dull, typography has to be handled particularly creatively, a role that evokes medieval illuminated manuscripts and continues with

At design magazine *Metropolis*, former creative director Criswell Lappin was not afraid to experiment with guest headline fonts if such an approach worked for a particular piece. While fonts for body text and caption information stay consistent (Bodoni Book and Trade Gothic), the typography used in headlines is often dictated by the story, especially if a specific font or stylistic treatment relates to the content. This is a significant part of the *Metropolis* brand and is the opposite of the standard 'house fonts' system used in most publications. This opener for a 20-page feature on Rem Koolhaas's design for the new Seattle Public Library is a good example. Driven by the concept of the building, 'the main idea was to identify the building as a collaborative project rather than attribute the building to one iconic architect, which is so often the norm with a well-publicized building like this,' explains Lappin. 'The names on the first page function as an extensive byline for the project, and the list is cropped to indicate that there are more participants. We have the liberty to do this because of the subject we cover – design. There are not many magazines where I think this system would work. Sometimes we have a feature well where each headline is set in a different typeface, but it still works because it is done smartly with consideration to the content of each piece.'

The New York Times Magazine / DECEMBER 13, 1998

Blueprint: **The Shock of the Familiar**

The rules are breaking down. In a frenzy to move prod
design is exploding, mutating, multiplying.
Design anarchy! More morph! By Herbert Muscham

n Greek mythology,
Morpheus is the god of dreams. But I also like to
think of him as the deity who presides over design. Morph means form. Morphology is the
study of shapes. Metamorphosis is the transfor-
mation of appearance. And these are dreamy
times for design.

There has never been more stuff, and stuff
must have a shape, an appearance, a boundary in
two or three dimensions to distinguish it from
other stuff. Even water, and perhaps eventually
air, must arrive in distinctive bottles. The

shapes are no longer content simply to arise. They explode, mutate
and multiply. Design is now subject to the whimsical laws and seasonal revisions of fashion, the quick impulses of journalism.

There is no dominant style, no prevailing trend. There's just more
and more stuff that has been styled, molded, carved, folded, pat-
terned, cut-and-pasted, prototyped, mocked up, punched up, laid
out, recycled and shrink-wrapped. Modernity has rendered the material world into some kind of plasma that is perpetually prodded and
massaged into an endless variety of contours. Look around. Our designed world has the polymorphousness of clouds, the rapid, shift-
ing, irrational play of dreams. Let's call it morphomania.

Is it a good dream or a nightmare? Design today is certainly a challenge for a critic who wants to make sense of, much less evaluate, the
things designers shape. In the 18th century, it was believed that design could be evaluated according to universal laws. The purpose of
cultivating taste was to educate the senses to their essence.

Today, the most powerful laws governing design are dictated by the
marketplace. Catch the eye. Stimulate desire. Move the merchandise.
Yet even in the market-driven world of contemporary design, there
adheres a mythological dimension.

Design, that is, reaches into the psyche as well as the pocketbook.
Like dreams, forms can hold momentous meaning, never more so
than today, when images have gone far toward displacing words as a
medium of communication. This issue of The Times Magazine tries
to interpret the shapes that are bombarding our psyches.

We are all morphomaniacs now. Exhibit A: My medicine cabinet.
Here's a partial inventory: •Colognes: Chanel Pour Monsieur —
classic square bottle designed by Coco herself. CK One — frosted

Fontography *Each article in this issue begins with a capital letter from a different typeface, or font. We asked the typographer Tobias Frere-Jones to select 12 fonts that illustrate the evolution of type design, from the days of Gutenberg to the present. The 12 typefaces he selected (shown here by the letter A) are described on the title page of each article.*

𝔄 A A A A A A A A A A A

Too many publishers, editors and designers fear that large blocks of text will deter a reader. But used as shapes and tones, blocks of text can offer an elegant, simple beauty. David Hillman on *Nova* (left below) happily filled spreads with nothing but dense columns of text together with pull quotes or drop caps, while on an issue of *Emigre* (opposite) David Carson used just text and folios to express an intensely intellectual dialogue.

imageless advertising posters. The confident editorial designer can have a huge amount of fun with type. In fact, the duller the material, image or copy, the greater the challenge for the designer to employ imaginative and creative skills, using techniques such as typeface juxtaposition, changing the shape and arrangement of elements or letterforms, and creating scale contrast. Look at concrete poetry, such as the work of Carlos Drummond de Andrade, Stéphane Mallarmé, George Herbert and Ian Hamilton Finlay; look at Russian Constructivism, the Bauhaus and the Dadaists, and, later, the work of Otto Storch on *McCall's* magazine, Alexey Brodovitch on *Harper's Bazaar*, Tom Wolsey on *Queen* and *Town*, Harri Peccinotti on *Nova*, Neville Brody on *The Face*, Fabien Baron on *Vogue*, David Carson on *Beach Culture* and *RayGun*, Martin Venezky on *Speak* and Vince Frost on *Zembla* to see some great examples of type used in this way.

Type as illustration

While type is, at its most basic, a method of conveying words, it can, of course, do much more. An editorial designer will use type to interpret and express the editorial, communicate meaning, offer variation, work with the image and other design elements to convey emotions or make symbolic or lateral links. These can be achieved in a number of ways: manipulation can offer opportunities for creating links between, or playing off, the type, image and meaning; combining different weights, leadings, sizes and ranging can offer expressive abstract or literal interpretations of the content; the use of a particular clichéd typeface, such as a gothic or typewriter face, can create a symbolic or cultural link that immediately conveys something about the content.

SPACE

Gourd almighty

Squash and pumpkins are the big beasts of the veg patch, and now is a great time to plant their seeds. But which varieties to go for? Cleve West asks a champion grower. Photographs by Francesca Yorke

The serif/sans combination is the standard system used in almost every newspaper in the world, so when Mark Porter brought Paul Barnes and Christian Schwartz in to design a new face for the Berliner *Guardian* (above and left), he was expecting to combine a redrawn Helvetica with the new face. 'But when we arrived at the Egyptian and they created three basic weights – a thin, a regular and a black – there was a light-bulb moment when we realized that a full range of weights in the Egyptian would give us all the flexibility we needed,' says Porter. There are now more than 200 weights to the font, beginning with the 8-point Egyptian text face.

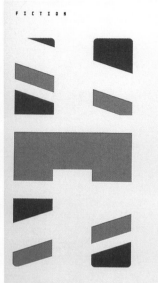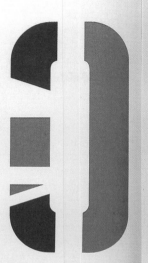

BY DAVID ROSE

You have been in this country some months now. You are settling in? You are finding work. Your work is improving. You are treated well.

In home I was stand-up comedian. Now, from accident to leg, sit-down comedian. But, I get no work, get no gigs (this is correct?). But, persons here are kind. They wish to know. They ask to me, you come on Eurostar? I say no, I come under Eurostar. Travel cheap, how you say, strapped for cash. How I lost leg. Straps too tight.
Was hard. Not able to move, just watch rail, stay still, count sleepers. Twenty, thirty. Not me. Too noisy for sleep, I travel third class. Under toilets.

You left your home, family, friends? It is a very different life now.

In home, my wife wear burka. They say to me, you Muslim? I say no, she most ugly woman. I leave her behind there. I leave rest of her there. Travel by own. Still people mistake. They say, you Afghan? If wife here, yes. She look like dog (this is correct?). I say no. Still they beat me. I wish I was Mussulman. Hit them back (this Turkish joke). POW! (This prisoner of war joke.) Even one person to travel, much money required. This person, that person, agent, lorry driver, all ask money. You say, Arm and a leg. I lucky. Get cheap. Leg only. How I lost leg. Not lost – stolen.
I stop persons in street – only talk – by they tell to me, hop it (this is right?). But no Persons here is lost.

You now enjoy the comforts of the West. You like shopping? You are free now. You like the freedom?

I like to shopping if money. But. Vouchers only. I always ask to shop, you will have vouchers? They look to me. Luncheon vouchers? (What are these luncheon vouchers?) They look. Say, you have card? Visa? Master? I say, goodbye.
Some shops only. But they say, exchange, exchange, going down. Make change.
Sometime, three times, four times, show me things, very cheap. Say to me, back of lorry. I say no, not lorry, Eurostar. They laugh at me.
If enough in hat, I sometimes shop. If not, look, jo windows only look.
All things here shiny, shiny. All wrapped, shiny. Cars shiny. Shoes, clothes. Musics. Blue musics. Stone musics. Say, get down dirty, but discs shiny, clean. But good, is good, is nice to buy. All things to be bought. Books. Many many books. Anything to be wanted. Special books, wrong books. I find book, Kama Sutra. But is all dots. How you say it? Braille. I say in shop, is no good to me, is no pictures.

Nonetheless, you bought it? You keep it under your locker. You take it out at night, when the room is finally quiet, dark, you run your fingers across the page, searching the texture, seeking with your fingers the recesses of memory, of your past, the contours of her body, breast and home, skin over sternum the hollows and clefts, rests for your soul? Burrowing back?

If plenty in hat, I go time to places I was told, look for woman, but talk, only talk. Money to talk, but is alright, is good. They tell me to come, up the stairs, come please.
Doors up stairs is always chips, paint is peels, is curtains, is quiet, is smell. Is good, I feel home in such place.

You like, then, the flesh-pots of London?

Is times dark, is windows, look down, persons walk in street, is dark but lights, shops, is quiet here, is safe. Is alright. But times, is men here, is knives, is fights, in back, in dark. Times is threats to me. Tell to me, Packy, cut off your dick. They mistake. How I lost leg. Same size (this is right?).

You have a regular job now. You pay your taxes? You work in London? You work in the carpet trade.

I have job now. Is good, all right. Rugmaker. People ask to me, you make wigs? Tell to them, yes, weave, net scalp. Others to scalp. Also die. Ground. Ground colours, earth colours, stir, mix, big pots, big stove, stir, mix, stir. Is hard. But, colours, is nice, sky colours, tree colours.

You work then, in the dyeing room? You blend the colours, heat the dye, keeping a constant temperature, continually checked, dip the wool.

You also cut and trim the canvas, then work on the weaving, work with the others, men and women, side by side, sitting, legs crossed – leg, rather – on floor cushions of worn leather. You push the hook through the canvas, hook in the wool, pull it back, making a loop of half an inch exactly, knot and cut it. Repeat. This hurts your fingers, hour by hour? Your fingers are hardening now, calloused?
Yet you soothe your soul through your fingertips, running them through the pile, tracing the pattern as it emerges, continuing it in your head, abstractly, the geometries of your past, the tautological figures, cul-de-sacs of amazement, end stops, locked keys, you follow the grid.
At times, the design is ethnic, folk-art motifs, scarfed peasants, panniered donkeys, hens, birds, but stylized, almost ideographs. Hieroglyphs of happiness, mythical joy. Woven fictions of contentment. Is this correct?

These two spreads show very different but equally strong and innovative uses of type as illustration. For *Speak* magazine (right), Martin Venezky draws on his collection of typographic ephemera to construct an innovative illustration for the subject – an exploration of the relationship between rock and contemporary art. Equally appropriate and reflective of its subject is Vince Frost's typographic illustration for a *Zembla* feature about nationalism (above).

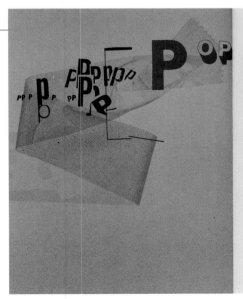

On *Inside* magazine (below), Jeffrey Docherty used type craft to distinguish individual departments in the magazine 'so that they are sufficiently distinct from each other, but still recognizably part of a brand'. He kept font use to a minimum: separate faces for body and heads, and a third face, which may be in complete contrast to the others. 'This third typeface can change the mood of the magazine. On this spread about a library in Cottbus, Germany, the architects used a letter motif to surround the entire exterior panelling of the building, which I decided to replicate in the titling. Interlinking the individual letters and stacking them one above the other gave an automatic visual reference to the project,' says Docherty.

Finding type

Whether it is in the form of cookie cutters, fridge magnets, pasta shapes or hair accessories, type can be found in many ways. Martin Venezky scours flea markets and antique stores for it; Vince Frost has probably visited every letterpress foundry in England in search of it; Alan Kitching has made a career from illustrating with it; and most designers will probably have some quirky examples of it knocking around. Letterpress and wood type now have a limited use, and most unusual forms of type are used for display rather than for body copy, but finding such three-dimensional, physical examples of type can prove inspirational to designers who now rarely handle physical examples of type, instead obtaining fonts through print and online font catalogues and foundries, most of which can supply fonts immediately via the internet.

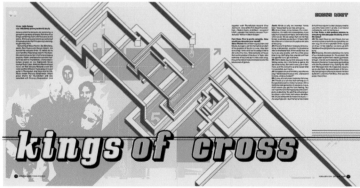

Two spreads that use type as illustration in very different ways. The scale and manipulation of headlines in the magazine *Inner Loop* (middle) were entirely in keeping with the frenetic, anarchic tone of this indie dance magazine. 'Because the two headline faces were quite different in style (military-style template and a kind of script), they helped to lend each feature its own identity within the mag, but also combined to give the whole a distinct *Inner Loop* feel. I think they expressed the different voices of those being interviewed. They were also very robust faces, which could stand out from strong graphic elements such as running across a bitmapped photo,' says former art director Ivan Cottrell. Fernando Gutiérrez's use of type in *Vanidad* (left) is not just a wonderfully decorative juxtaposition and skilful arrangement of type and image; it breaks down the words of the subject, 'Belle de Jour', into letters – a fitting illustration for a call girl who became famous for the entries in her online diaries. The crop and scale of 'Belle de Jour' on the right-hand page is elegantly balanced by the headline on the far left, creating an arrangement over the spread that is harmonious and tender but has massive impact.

Letterpress is a highly illustrative form of
typography that can be used to build a layout,
as seen in this piece from *FT The Business*
by British letterpress lecturer and illustrator
Alan Kitching.

Custom-designed type

As in any creative industry, type design and use tend
to follow trends, which can result in publications
looking very similar. An obvious way to distinguish
yourself from the crowd is to commission your own
font family. As well as creating a unique identity, such
a move also affords you a font that truly expresses
and conveys your brand attributes. *Flaunt*, *Another
Magazine* and *The Guardian* newspaper are all titles
that have taken this route recently. Lee Corbin at
Flaunt felt it was time for change, so decided to
introduce a custom font to the new body fonts,
Berthold Akzidenz Grotesk and Century Schoolbook,
both of which he believes fit very well with the new
custom faces.

> *'In the previous year of issues we used Gotham and
> Hoefler Text for our standard faces. Both faces were
> designed by Frere-Jones & Hoefler, so they worked
> well together. Gotham has a strong character that
> does not call too much attention to itself, but in its
> heavier weights it really dominates the area around
> it. We matched Gotham up with Hoefler because
> Hoefler has such a classic look. It's also an enormous
> family, which gave us plenty of options.'*

With a new logo came the need for a new font, which
Corbin designed in two weights – a bold and a light
face – with more variations to come.

> *'The logo came first, but I was already interested in
> creating an extra-bold face based on geometric
> figures. I exploited the use of symbols, like crosses,
> x's, triangles and circles, as letterforms. Because
> that's what I did in the logo, this gave the face more
> character and reinforced the new logo. It was also
> used very sparingly so that both the logo and
> typeface don't become tired.'*

A final few words of warning on using type: the
development of pre-press technology meant the
sudden demise of professionals such as the typesetter
and compositor, roles that became the responsibility
of the designer and the computer. The latter's default
settings in programs such as QuarkXPress and Adobe
InDesign should not always be assumed to be right for
your publication, so an understanding of, and care
with, kerning, hyphenation, leading, letter spacing,
trapping and tracking are necessary. Similarly, page

composition and make-up, which used to involve
physically moving elements such as display text,
galleys and images around three-dimensional space,
is now all done on screen. Arguments rage as to
whether this is a good or bad thing, but when
construction of a three-dimensional delivery medium
is undertaken in a two-dimensional environment,
there is unquestionably a physical and emotional
diminishment. Try to compensate for this by handling
and playing with paper, colour, inks, photographs and
mark-making implements as much as possible. Print
out layouts as often as you can - they are very different
from screen layouts. Always proof on page rather
than on screen and never rely solely on a program's
spell-check function. Read all headlines, display
text and captions carefully; these are often spelled

by Graham Buchan

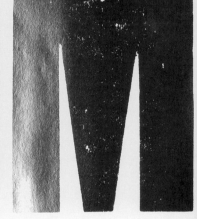

He returned after lunch to the bright, buzzing open office and there, concentratedly present, unmissable, in the darting cross-fields of indoor activity, like a refugee on the doorstep, in the middle of his mouse mat sat a ripe plum: large, polished, obscenely full, purple.

He glanced round. No one acknowledged his question. He held it weightily in his upturned palm. It had the promise of a breast. It seemed to want to rupture and squirt at him. It said: "Bite me. Suck me. I'll make a mess of your mouth."

He put it aside with a glance. Later, he lowered it into a drawer. It stewed its concentrate in the darkness. In an idle moment he heard it speak: "I came from a tree. I was brought here. Another hand held me. I was licked by a tongue."

At day's gold end he pondered. He looked down at it preening itself in its burrow. He considered. He lifted it like a scientist, enveloped it in tissue. He made space in his briefcase.

The custom was to drink and talk for an hour. The conviviality of colleagues. A little crude banter. He thought above the alcohol: Who? (You can't take a plum out in a pub.)

The crowded return commute. The door, the stair. He was eager to unwrap it and look, as if it were smuggled pornography. But it was squashed, a mess. The frail paper had soaked into the split flesh. He lifted it out in lumps. He licked his fingers before rinsing. In the sink the stringy remains said: "You were curious, but you need courage for love." ●

These enlarged woodblock-style letterforms make a perfect textural statement for this double-page spread. It is a recklessly bold and carefree typographic choice, reflecting the confidence of *Zembla* at that time.

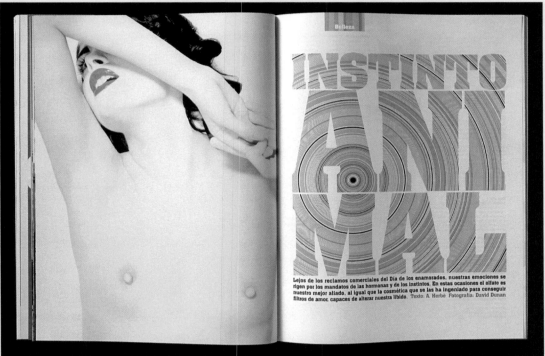

incorrectly because the subeditor's focus is on the body copy and no one thinks to check the display text. Also make sure that ligatures, hyphenation and kerning are corrected.

In 2006, *Flaunt* magazine created its own typeface (top), 'because there wasn't anything pre-existing that possessed the feel I wanted for the new issues, but also because a new typeface would be exclusive to our magazine', says art director Lee Corbin. He has built many alternate characters into the new *Flaunt* face so that 'it will allow for more unique combinations in titles. It was based on the logotype that I created for the redesign, so that it would reinforce the new identity beyond the cover of each issue.' Of the two initial weights shown here, the bold face is used more sparingly and with ample space around the individual characters. 'The letters that make up the new Flaunt logo come from

this alphabet, so the use of the face in the magazine is meant to reinforce the new identity. The thin face is used more frequently and more experimentally. It is also displayed larger as it is not so dense,' explains Corbin.

A brilliantly expressive use of type by Fernando Gutiérrez on *Vanidad* (above). Think about how the design elements make it work. Consider, in particular, scale, cropping, balance and arrangement.

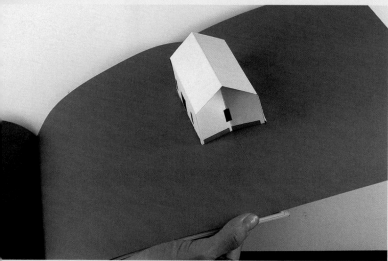

For indie title *Amelia's Magazine* (top), the cover was wrapped in a cut-out by artist and illustrator Rob Ryan, giving readers a limited-edition piece of art, but also turning a two-dimensional cover into a three-dimensional one. *Esopus* (above) takes the concept of fold-out further with its 3D-art pop-ups.

Artwork skills and production issues

Editorial designers need a strong hands-on knowledge of layout, design and image-manipulation software programs like Adobe's Creative Suite (comprising InDesign, Photoshop and Illustrator) or QuarkXPress. This is vital to make the best of their visual ideas, but also needed to be able to react quickly and effectively to sudden and often late layout and flatplan changes.

They also need an understanding of the technical issues around screen calibration, colour management, pre-press and printing, as well as the more creative aspects of the role, like commissioning illustration and photography.

Software

Early layout software fitted into the traditional production process, but today's programs have developed to the point where the same computer (and thus designer) now handles most of these traditional processes. Once dealt with by specialists, typesetting, pre-press and proofing are now the responsibility of the designer and/or production editor. Therefore the complexity and ability of these programs is vast, and being able to experiment and get the most out of them depends on your knowledge and understanding.

Screen calibration

Computer screens present colour using light, i.e. additive colour, whereas print uses inks, i.e. subtractive colour. To help match these two very different representations of colour, so that what the designer sees on screen is as similar as possible to the printed result, screen-calibration software can be used to prepare the screen. Apple users, for example, might find that BERG Design's shareware application, SuperCal, makes a very noticeable difference. This can also be done by using your computer's own colour-balance features in the 'gamma' control panel. Photoshop has an excellent step-by-step guide to using this control panel in its 'help' menu.

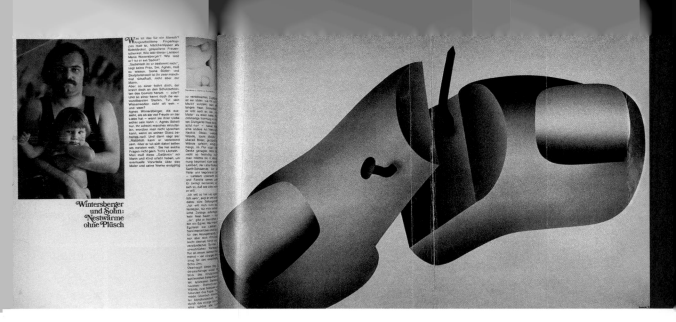

Twen (above) often used fold-outs to enable the use of great visual elements (including games, art reproductions and topical photo stories).

Printing

The best printer is one who prints a lot of similar work to yours, so look through such publications and find the name of the printer, or contact the publication's production editor and ask for it. But other factors should be considered, too: can the printer handle your print run? Can they work with your paper stock and format? Can you get an ICC profile (*see* below) off the press that you can apply to your desktop system? Will the printer be able to meet the turnaround time you require? Is their fee acceptable? It is always a good idea to get quotes from three or four printers before making your decision, but communication is the most important factor – a good, long-term relationship with your printer will reap massive rewards. Printers have knowledge, experience and skills that you will never have, so nurture your relationship with them to get the best from them.

Colour management

Reproducing colour is complicated, as there are three different aspects that need to be addressed: what the eye sees, what the monitor shows and what a print nozzle produces. Fortunately, the print industry has developed a colour-management system that gives an image a profile (called an International Colour Consortium, or ICC profile) so that as it moves through the printing process – from original to monitor viewing, separation, pre-press, proofing, plating and printing – all the tools involved are calibrated and adjusted to ensure colour accuracy and consistency. If your publication is being produced without ICC profiling, stick to 'safe' colours when making up colour palettes or using spot colours (check the gamut warnings for these, which indicate when a selected colour will alter appearance when converted from RGB to CMYK), and don't rely on what's on screen. In such cases it is best to make up colours using a Pantone swatch book, which should be updated annually to allow for colour fade. Be aware, however, that not all Pantone colours are reproducible in CMYK; if you want to use a Pantone colour that brings up a gamut warning in your layout program, you may need to make the colour up as a fifth one, in which case consult your printer about the best way forward.

Proofs and how to use them

Print proofs, often referred to as 'contract proofs', are the means to ensure the colour quality of type and image on press. There are a number of different proof systems, and especially in the US, printers are working with and only offering PDF screen proofs free; all others have to be paid for. But it is worth budgeting for proofs, especially for front covers and other pages that have a lot of full-colour images, for instance.

The most common (and affordable) are digital proofs (Epson or similar), which are printed on large-format digital inkjet printers and profiled to the final printing stock for an accurate. result. Wet proofs, using the inks that'll be used on the real print run, are still sometimes used to proof covers that have special finishes (such as 'special' inks – Pantone or similar – foil blocking, embossing or debossing, graining, lamination and spot-UV varnishes) although you shouldn't assume the proofing press will exactly reproduce the circumstances of the real run.

Laserjet proofs from commonly available photocopier or laserprinters are so poor for colour accuracy that they can be badly misleading if you are intending to use as colour reference on press, but they can be useful for checking type, positions and so on, particularly if you like to proof on page rather than on screen. Finally, there is the PDF proof, also known as a soft proof which, again, gives little indication of colour output unless it is viewed on a calibrated monitor, Eizo or similar, but is useful for checking everything else.

Acquiring, evaluating and using images

When working with a photograph, choose one aspect of it that is the heart of the image—it may be the framing, the density of colour (a perfect blue sky or a rich red dress, the composition, the light, the subtlety of tones …). Whatever it is, a good image will have something that makes it stand out, and it's this that you want to maximize. Keep whatever it is in mind while you're working with the image—it may determine the shape, scale or structure of a layout and will often be the most important element of it. If necessary, work with the printers at the soft-proof stage (on screen) to optimize this element. Their knowledge of colour levels and how these will affect the image's reproduction will be greater than that of even the very best designer. But initially, consider the following.

How good is your original? Highlights and shadows should span the gamut from as light as possible to as dark as possible, with well-defined midtones. It is a good idea to ensure that tones, highlights and shadows are brought to their optimum output in the pre-press stage.

In CMYK, highlights should be set as:

C: 5%
M: 4%
Y: 4%
K: 0%

Imagery can define an era or event in a way that words simply cannot. The ability to find or create such imagery is a crucial part of a designer's skill, as Janet Froelich recalls while discussing the aftermath of 9/11. '9/11 happened on a Tuesday morning. *The New York Times Magazine* (above), which is on a weekly schedule, completes each issue on a Friday, nine days before the publication date. So we had three days to tear apart the September 23 issue and remake it in response to 9/11. We had to think forward, while almost everyone was simply reacting to the nightmare of what had just happened. One of the ideas was to ask artists and architects for their thoughts on a memorial. Two artists, Paul Myoda and Julian LaVerdiere, had been part of a group working in studios in one of the Twin Towers. They came up with a plan, which they called "Towers of Light", in which they imagined two powerful beams of light, positioned in the centre of the footprint and pointed towards the sky. I worked with a photograph by Fred Conrad, which showed lower Manhattan the night of the disaster with that awful arc of dust and debris, and with a Photoshop artist to create the vision of those twin beams of light. That became our cover and, one year later, it became one of the most moving memorials to the events of 9/11, as the Lower Manhattan Development Corporation made it a reality. It is hard to describe the combined feeling of pride and awe, to see the cover of our magazine become a living memorial, viewable for 80 kilometres [50 miles] in all directions, to such a terrible event.'

The New York Times Magazine

SEPTEMBER 23, 2001 | SECTION 6

Remains of the Day By Richard Ford Colson Whitehead Richard Powers Robert Stone James Traub Stephen King Jennifer Egan Roger Lowenstein Judith Shulevitz Randy Cohen William Safire Andrew Sullivan Jonathan Lethem Michael Lewis Margaret Talbot Charles McGrath Walter Kirn Deborah Sontag Allan Gurganus Michael Ignatieff Kurt Andersen Jim Dwyer Michael Tolkin Matthew Klam Sandeep Jauhar Lauren Slater Richard Rhodes Caleb Carr Fred R. Conrad Joju Yasuhide Angel Franco Joel Sternfeld Katie Murray Steve McCurry Carolina Salguero Lisa Kereszi Jeff Mermelstein William Wendt Andres Serrano Richard Burbridge Paul Myoda Julian LaVerdiere Taryn Simon Kristine Larsen

Midtones or gamma should be adjusted to improve overall brightness or darkness of the image without affecting the highlights adversely. To do this, use Photoshop's image-adjusting curves and raise or lower the curve at the 50 per cent point until the brightness is accurate.

How does it look on the monitor? Assuming your monitor is calibrated correctly, what you see on it should be the very best approximation of what you will get in print. So, if you're not happy with it on screen, fix it before going to press. Photoshop has a number of features that will improve images, but a very basic one is Unsharp Masking, which most professional bureaux use to improve the quality of an image. An average unsharp-mask setting is amount: 160 per cent; radius: 2 pixels; thresholds: 9 levels. Adjusting these settings will improve nearly all photographs.

Finding images

A good editorial designer will be constantly on the lookout for new photographers and illustrators, and will locate them through agencies, degree shows, other publications and media, and awards books and CDs. Most image-makers now have online portfolios but is always worth trying to meet them too. Set aside enough time to go through the portfolio properly, asking questions about the pieces and the way the photographer or illustrator works. When it comes to commissioning, the kind of brief you give will determine to a large degree what is produced, so be clear about what you want and communicate this. However clear the brief is, talk to the people you have commissioned to make sure they understand what's required. Make sure deadlines, fee and administrative requirements (invoicing, expenses, payment, tax matters) are clear. And finally, make sure that the shoot, if there is one, is well organized.

Using images from the internet

Lots of websites offering free content and others where you pay for images. For example, www.istockphoto.com is a royalty free and copyright free service where you pay a small fee. The availability of such stock images, however, does mean that other users can use the same images as well. Large picture agencies, such as Getty

Information graphics

Internet-inspired developments in data collection have caused a huge resurgence in interest in information graphics (infographics). They offer the designer a great way to vary the presentation of content, promising the ability to make complex information easily absorbed. Graphs, diagrams, images and data can combine to tell stories with great clarity.

Infographics are perfect for the visual-information culture of the twenty-first century, but they were actually popularized some 75 years ago, when designer and typographer Thomas Maitland Cleland devised a format for business magazine *Fortune* that unified editorial and visual concepts in a completely new way. Since then, magazines such as the *Radio Times*, *Wired*, and *Bloomberg Businessweek*, have refined and made ever-greater use of information graphics.

When commissioning information graphics designers need to retain a very clear concept of what the story being explained is – it is easy to get caught up with the visuals and lose focus.

The BBC SO at the Proms, Saturday, Tuesday, Wednesday, Friday 7.30 Radio 3

During this week at the Proms, beginning with the Anniversary Concert on Saturday marking the 80th Season, the BBC Symphony Orchestra dominates the scene, playing on four evenings out of seven. (During the season they play in almost half the concerts.) For RADIO TIMES Shirley Dixon discovered that the life and work of the Orchestra is not just a question of sitting on the concert platform in evening dress and making beautiful music

The anatomy of an orchestra

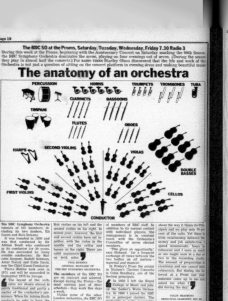

PERCUSSION HORNS TRUMPETS TROMBONES TUBA
CLARINETS BASSOONS
TIMPANI
FLUTES OBOES
HARPS
SECOND VIOLINS
VIOLAS
DOUBLE BASSES
FIRST VIOLINS
CELLOS
CONDUCTOR

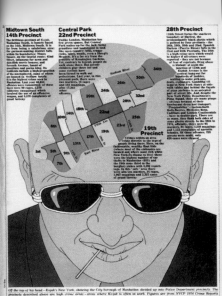

Midtown South 14th Precinct

Central Park 22nd Precinct

28th Precinct

19th Precinct

Off the top of his head – Kojak's New York, showing the City borough of Manhattan divided up into Police Department precincts. The precincts described above are high crime areas – areas where Kojak is often at work. Figures are from NYCPD 1974 Crime Reports

On the television listings magazine *Radio Times*, David Driver used a number of techniques and styles to deliver information on subjects as diverse as how the Apollo and Soyuz spacecraft docked (opposite), how an orchestra works (far left) and how the police districts in Kojak's New York were laid out (left). A firm favourite were the graphics of Richard Draper, who devised pictorial approaches to information graphics, as seen here in the 'Underground movements' panel (below). Driver also used montage, incorporating graphic panels that crossed and unified spreads and illustrated covers to enhance visually and consistently engage the readership of a publication that, by necessity, was text-heavy and densely packed.

The World About Us, Sunday 7.25 BBC2

You'll be familiar with the insect life that scuttles away when you lift up a stone, of course, but were you aware of how much is going on beneath the ground's surface – from moles and earthworms to springtails and false scorpions? **Richard Draper's** drawing shows you a sample of them and here **Richard Mabey** writes about the special problems of making Sunday's programme about what's alive and well and living under our feet

Underground movements

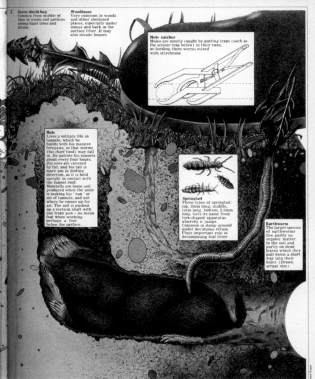

Mole catcher
Moles are mostly caught by putting traps (such as the scissor trap below) in their runs, or feeding them worms mixed with strychnine

Green shield-bug
Common from middle of June in woods and gardens among hazel trees and shrubs

Woodlouse
Very common in woods and other sheltered places, especially under stones and bark in the surface litter. It may also invade houses

Mole
Lives a solitary life in tunnels, which he builds with his massive forepaws, so that worms (his chief food) may fall in. He patrols his tunnels about every four hours. His eyes are covered by fur, and his tail is more use in finding direction, as it is held upright in contact with the tunnel roof. Molehills are loose soil produced when the mole is making his 'run' or set of tunnels, and where he comes up for air. The soil is pushed up a vertical shaft with one front paw – no mean feat when working perhaps a foot below the surface.

Springtail
Three types of springtail: top, 3mm long; middle, 1mm long; bottom, 2.5mm long. Gets its name from fork-shaped apparatus whereby it jumps. Common in damp ground under deciduous refuse. Plays important role in decomposing leaf litter

Earthworm
The larger species of earthworms live partly on organic matter in the soil and partly on dead leaves which they pull down a short way into their holes (Drawn actual size)

Rove beetle
Common from February to September. Approx 14mm long

Centipede
Very common under stones or bark both in woods and elsewhere. Each of the foremost pair of legs is modified to form a dagger-shaped poison claw whereby the prey, which consists of insect larvae, is seized and killed (Drawn actual size)

False scorpions
Inhabitants of ground litter, but are usually present only in small numbers. Their food consists of mites. Approx 2mm long

Hover-fly larva
looks and moves like a leech, found just below soil level

Nematode
Shown magnified 100 times, there may be as many as 20 million nematodes per square metre of soil. They are found mainly in the top layers of soil

Dwarf millepede
Up to 8mm long. Not a true millepede as it has only twelve pairs of legs. Very common under stones, the bark of stumps, or fallen branches and surface litter

For this spread about a mid-air plane collision (right), Brazilian newspaper *Folha de S.Paulo* uses information graphics to illustrate aspects of the tragedy, such as the planes' routes, locations and designs that photography could not illustrate. They act as additional information rather than graphic replacements for photography; through the use of such devices, readers are given a more thorough understanding of an event.

In this spread from *The Guardian* (right) illustrating the arms trade, the shapes of the various weapons immediately impart knowledge and communicate figures associated with specific arms.

opposite top: During the 2012 Olympics, *The Times* ran dense infographic charts like this one designed like a running track. The listing of gold, silver and bronze shows analytical depth in detail, a particular strength of the title, whic has a rich store of data and images in its archives to draw upon.

opposite below: Analysis before the event comes in *The Times'* wallchart giving information reminders about key dates when significant gold medal moments in the Olympics are to occur. The use of icons, colours, text and images, gives different information in a variety of layers. Infographics help to enhance content and make the product last longer in the reader's mind.

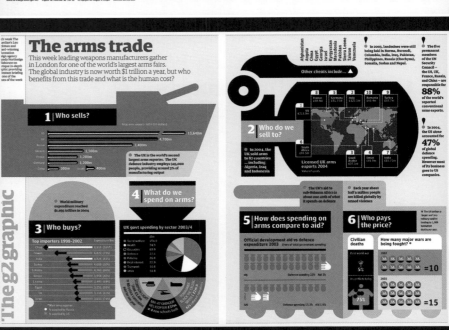

An annual, monthly or quarterly publication has the luxuries of more loosely structured frameworks, a bigger visuals budget, greater flexibility in such elements as grid, fonts and image treatment, and the ability to experiment almost endlessly with layouts. But this can present its own problems; it can be difficult to adhere to the brand message when presented with greater freedom, so it is important to find a balance between those elements that need to be constant (brand and identity) and those that will change with every issue.

 '**Editors and art directors need to have a dynamic rapport. And healthy respect. And an ability to argue and to sometimes lose.**'
Martin Venezky, art director, *Speak*

The house style and style shoots

A magazine is an ongoing series of publications that need to present a familiar look from issue to issue so as to be recognisable to the reader. This distinct look is created and then controlled at several levels. At the top level, the format, paper stock and logo design will all be agreed upon. These generally won't change issue to issue. Then there are the looser visual elements – styles of photography for instance, or rules such as certain types of headlines always running over two lines. These are usually noted by printed examples.

Perhaps most importantly, there are the detailed typographic instructions for every element on the page, applied via style sheets. Part of the section templates, style sheets are a series of pre-set guides that apply font, size, colour and parameters to every element on the page (headlines, standfirsts, body text, credits, footnotes and so on). They allow the designer (or a group of designers) to automatically apply consistent and detailed design attributes from page to page.

Similar rules exist for the content too, usually overseen by the sub editor.

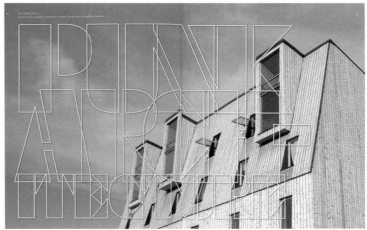

Two spreads from the same department of *Inside* magazine (above) – 'In Profile' – offer very different solutions to layouts, while sharing a bold use of type and design elements. The layout process has many potentially determining factors, such as the number of pages per article, word count, image crops and even the advertising within the publication. Colour and flow also need to be considered as the magazine is being constructed.

Redesigning –
when and why?

Designers may tweak elements of a layout to update a publication and keep it feeling contemporary and relevant (for example, a heavy font may be replaced with a medium or light version from the same family to accommodate changing tastes), but, eventually, even the best-designed long-running publication may become outdated and stale. In this case, a major overhaul or redesign should be considered. Many publications also redesign when sales are falling, or in times of economic recession when advertising revenue drops and they need to boost sales, but doing so is a risky strategy, as any redesign can – and almost certainly will – alienate some existing readers while enticing new ones.

 'Editorial design is the framework through which a given story is read and interpreted. It consists of both the overall architecture of the publication (and the logical structure that it implies) and the specific treatment of the story (as it bends or even defies that very logic).'
Martin Venezky, art director, *Speak*

The best reason for a redesign is to stay in tune with, and reflect, the needs of a readership; over a period of five years, fashion, taste and styles will alter sufficiently that a magazine aimed at 16-year-olds will have to redesign to keep in step. But it is important not to let readers dictate the redesign; contextualizing the publication through cultural trends and shifts is the best approach. It is also important that a redesign is not conducted in a vacuum. If visual trends shift over time, so, too, do the other elements that go to make up a publication: the content and tone should also be carefully examined and addressed to ensure that no one element is isolated and that the whole publication is moving forward cohesively and intelligently. *Flaunt* magazine took this approach in 2006 when it completely overhauled the look of the magazine, even creating a new logo and custom-designed fonts:

'The entire magazine has been rebuilt, graphically at least, to accommodate more variation and a new identity. We simply had to do away with most of our preceding visual identity to make room for new ideas. Our magazine is constantly changing; as we are a monthly publication we need to embrace spontaneity—we had to give the magazine a new voice.' – Lee Corbin

While redesigns happen fairly frequently on magazines, newspapers rarely overhaul their publications – such a step is a logistical nightmare from a production perspective for a daily title. As Mark Porter explains:

'Newspaper redesign is usually market-driven. There is a tendency for editors to assume that what they are doing is totally successful. It's only when sales start to fall that they realize they might need to change. But this is a particularly interesting moment, because newspaper readerships are in decline all over the world, and pressure from television and the internet is forcing journalists and designers to question their assumptions about what modern readers need. There has never been so much redesigning and format-changing going on.'

Media such as the internet and changes in distribution and demographics are having a design impact on both newspapers and magazines: formats are shrinking, pages are becoming more uniform and navigation is becoming simpler, because, says Mario Garcia, 'The internet has created a savvy, impatient reader who expects hierarchy, good navigation and fast motion on the printed page'.

In the last five years pre-press information has changed. To keep up with the latest information you should look at online tutorials or if possible talk to your printer. For a great overview and to find out the correct printing terms Ambrose and Harris' *The Visual Design Box Set: Pre-Press and Production, Typography, Graphic Design, Illustration* (Fairchild, 2012) is useful.

In 2003, art director Kobi Benezri, working with his predecessor Nico Schweizer, undertook a redesign of *I.D.* magazine (left). 'When we started working on the design we knew that the look of *I.D.* had to be updated (the last redesign by Bruce Mau took place in 1992). The new design came in correlation to a new editorial approach – coverage of a broader range of design fields, different takes on particular previously discussed subject matters, new departments and a more critical approach; we wanted to make sure the design took the same attitude and was very informative and objective. At the same time we had no intention of impressing anyone with overpowering design elements or eye candy. There was a clear purpose for the layouts and we tried to keep it subtle and elegant, and put our mark where it was necessary.' New features included new fonts – Scala was replaced with the very modern Gerard Unger font Coranto for body text; Meta was replaced with a variety of fonts that would change over time to keep the design up to date – and new sections, including a photospread called 'Scape' and a new back section called 'Crit' (above left). Mark Porter's redesign of Portuguese daily *Público* (above) in 2007 followed his earlier redesign of *The Guardian* in 2005.

Mario Garcia has redesigned newspapers worldwide, frequently working with new formats. In 2005, he redesigned *The Observer* newspaper, taking it from a broadsheet to a Berliner format. He thinks size is not an issue, and certainly not a negative one. 'The canvas is smaller, therefore one must be more focused and direct in creating hierarchy. So, what the publication must do in creating criteria for inclusion and exclusion is simply draw up a list. Study your readers of today. Do your visual and editorial archaeology and evaluate what needs to stay and what must go. Differentiate between real antiques and Aunt Clara's old teacup, so to speak. Newspapers have a tendency to drag old visual things as "antiques". But they are nothing more than old things, not worthy of preservation.' On *The Observer* redesign, he retained the elegance of the broadsheet through use of typography, but gave the paper a more vibrant, youthful feel through colour coding, which readers in surveys have been shown to like. He used one palette for coding and another one for other colours throughout the paper to ensure that such colour coding would work with other elements on the page. He approaches all of his redesigns from the standpoint of journalism, because, he insists, 'People come to a newspaper for its content, not its look. Design is part of the enhancement of that content.'

TIP

Mario Garcia's top ten dos and don'ts of redesign

1 Not all redesigns are alike, so customize your work to make it appropriate for the specific product undergoing a 'rethink'.

2 Get a full briefing of expectations, target audience and extent of change. I always say that some redesigns are nothing more than a face-wash, while others are the full bath, complete with bubbles and candles!

3 Plan the rethink of the publication around the four major story structures: typography, page, architecture and colour.

4 Story structuring should be the first step: how do editors tell stories in this publication? How many styles of storytelling techniques should be created? How can hierarchy be emphasized?

5 Typographically, test at least three font combinations of serifs and sans serifs to choose the most convenient and appropriate.

6 For page architecture, develop at least two grid patterns with various column measurements, and perhaps include both in the final design.

7 Play with a colour palette that starts with two dozen combinations of colours, from dark to light and in-between, then create a simple palette of no more than ten shades for continuous use.

8 Emphasize navigation – readers who surf the internet become impatient and bring that impatience to print. Work hard to make sure that navigational strategies are a top consideration of the redesign process.

9 Review the 'break of the book' – the order in which content will appear. Time to move elements in or out? Or to change the order of events?

10 Work closely with editors and reporters, as they will bring that necessary journalistic ingredient to the process of visually changing a publication.

Materials, Process, Print: Creative Solutions for Graphic Design by Daniel Mason

MATADOR

1990 VOLUME ONE $ 50.00

A MAGAZINE ABOUT DESIGNS, IDEAS AND TRENDS 1990–2000

27 TUTORS
500 STUDENTS
THOUSANDS OF ALUMNI
ONE ORGANISED MESS

BRINGING ORDER
TO THE CHAOS

HALEY MA

"STRUCTURE
HELPS ME THINK"

In this team project, handwritten headings were collaged with images taken at college, to create a publication based around the idea of organized chaos. Designer Ben Silvertown pushed it on further and finished it off by sending it to print on newsprint (right). He also mocked up the iPad layout and included a video in his portfolio. Other members of the team contributed to the creation and each took the design and used it in their own portfolios. Each gave credit to the others as is the norm in a group project.

In this version of an imaginary travel magazine called *Escape*, undergraduate Sandra Autukaite had decided on images and concept using pictures taken from the internet. The simple iconic framing meant that the photography was actually a primary element of the idea behind the magazine.

At the finishing stage Autukaite decided to shoot some images for herself, thereby ensuring she owned the copyright. With student projects like this it is not likely that the magazine will go into production. However, it is ethical behaviour to make your own images and take credit for them, rather than to take credit for images you found on the internet.

Brief Five
Finishing and presenting work

AIM
To take your double-page spread designs from Brief Four and finish them to a higher standard.

THE BRIEF
Check the details of all the elements on your layouts and then print them out on good quality paper.

1. Check details such as baseline alignment and widows (re-break any ugly lines). Add in picture credits if you need them and spellcheck the whole document for accuracy. This is a very important step for any text on a layout. Do not put work with spelling mistakes in your portfolio as you need to show you can pay attention to detail.

2. Once you have completed the proofreading stage, print the layouts on cheap paper so that you can check again that the text size is not too big (a common mistake due to working on screen). Then, if you want a really good colour calibrated version for your physical portfolio, print the layouts on quality paper using a good colour printer. You should also make a PDF of your double-page spreads to store in your online portfolio. Don't make the file sizes too large, however, or they will take the viewer too long to download.

3. You can extend this exercise by taking the visual principle of your design and adapting it for different platforms. Design the home page of your magazine's website and then plan any further navigation system from there, together with the interactive toolbox. You can just mock up the pages that may later become interactive. What if your magazine could be read anywhere? Beware of simply putting PDFs straight on to a website and calling it an online magazine. If the type is too small to read then it will not be fit for purpose. Remember that designers create content, both text and image, all the time. So have no fear about being original and be confident in your efforts. Even if your photos are not as good as those by designers you admire, they still have value in your portfolio for other reasons.

ESCAPE

AMPHIBIAN ISSUE

JULY

lder der woche

medizin

„Warten Sie mal,
ich schalte meinen
Gehirnschrittmacher ein"

Helmut Dubiel ist Hochschullehrer. Er leidet an **PARKINSON.**
Tief in seinem Kopf sitzen zwei Sonden. Er steuert sie mit einer Fernbedienung.
Ein kleiner Stromstoß – und er kann sprechen. Ein größerer Stromstoß –
und er kann gehen. Zumindest eine Zeit lang

Von ARNO LUIK und VOLKER HINZ (Fotos)

STERN 36/2006 135

Stern's straightforward three-column grid on feature pages (left) and ever-popular aerial photography (above) all appeal to a broad audience.

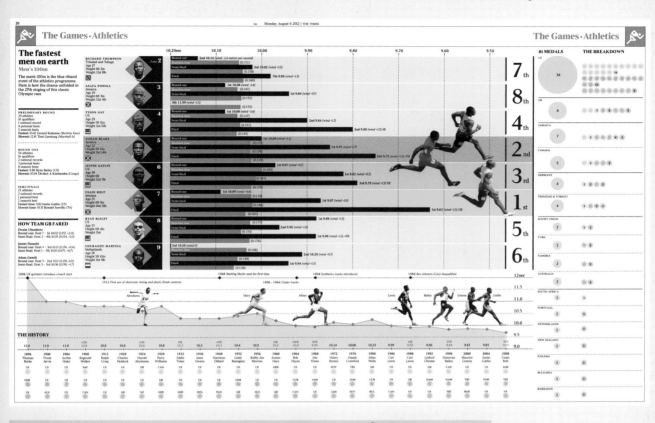

Images, have information on their websites about the legal issues surrounding rights and clearance.

Social media has ushered in a range of online photo-sharing sites. Some offer photo sharing for free others are subscription-based sites. Flikr, Pixable and Snapfish are all well known photo-sharing sites which offer a great source of images for designers.

Always check the resolution of an image is suitable for print reproduction, clear copyright and make sure you credit the image correctly.

Consistency without monotony

One of the editorial designer's most challenging—and enjoyable—tasks is creating a distinct, individual product or issue that is obviously part of a strong brand, but does not look or feel the same with every issue. How do they do it? With a good grid that is flexible, pagination that ensures similar spreads are interspersed with other pages, and inventive use of the design elements at their disposal.

A daily newspaper or weekly news-based magazine will have tight deadlines and short lead times, and the design has to be led by functionality and legibility. As a result, the designer has to develop and adopt a problem-solving approach, setting in place a grid and production system that enables fast layouts, fast repro and printing, and a design approach that is ordered and organized. But one need only compare a few of these titles to see that, within such order, there are still many opportunities for inventive structure, different directions and wholly distinct results, as seen here in these weekly news titles from Europe and America.

German weekly news magazine *Stern*'s cover, feature pages and photographic spreads all display a lively, populist approach to the news. Bold crops such as the face halved by the edge of the cover(above), along with the straightforward three-column grid on feature pages and ever-popular aerial photography, all appeal to a broad audience.

The cover on UK financial magazine *The Economist* (right) is witty and eye-catching—in contrast to the calm orderliness of its feature pages. Again, this illustrates how magazines can remain original and engaging from issue to issue and page to page.

The Economist

AUGUST 26TH–SEPTEMBER 1ST 2006   www.economist.com

Why Britain has soured on immigration

Ending Iran's spin cycle

Has America's housing bubble burst?

The limits of air power

A step forward for stem cells

WHO KILLED THE NEWSPAPER?

£3.25

3 4

9 770013 061169

Dan Rolleri

Dan Rolleri, editor and publisher of *Speak* magazine, rode the crest of the independent magazine wave when he came out of college in the mid-1990s. The desktop-publishing revolution ushered in by microcomputers and publishing programs had spawned thousands of magazines dealing with hundreds of specialisms, and Rolleri decided to follow suit.

Rolleri's first title – a music-video trade magazine – was, in his own words, "a horrible failure". His second attempt was the popular-culture magazine *Speak*, which is widely regarded as an excellent example of the genre. This success was due in no small part to the combative but collaborative relationship that existed between Rolleri and the publication's art director, Martin Venezky. And, from the outset, Rolleri had strong ideas about his magazine's designer:

> 'At the time, there was a glut of magazines on the news-stand, and I wanted Speak to stand out visually. It was important that the art director be willing to push the form. It was also important that the art director have an organic quality about his or her work. But more than anything, it was important that I liked the art director's work (not a small challenge because I didn't like much).'

Rolleri's ensuing stormy relationship with Venezky, which included the two suing each other, is well documented, but what is less well known are Rolleri's very strong feelings and understanding of the designer's impact on the magazine:

> 'It was important for me that the art director be intellectually driven and curious about the magazine's content, as opposed to only looking to follow a template or showcase his or her abilities separate from the magazine.'

Rolleri knew that Venezky had all that, and more:

> 'He reads, he thinks, he's extremely diligent. I wanted to match his effort, to get the editorial to live up to the design. I probably failed more times than I succeeded, but after my time with Martin I can't imagine ever working with another designer again.'

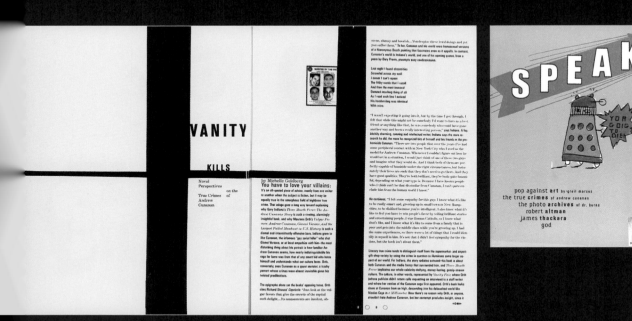

Chapter 7 : Looking back, looking forward

All designers benefit from an awareness of trends, cultural shifts and the contemporary zeitgeist, and this is doubly so for editorial designers, many of whom have to ensure that they are in the vanguard of visual fashion and culture. For this reason, we look at broad cultural and design trends and delivery media. But editorial designers can also gain huge insight into their craft – not to mention ideas and inspirations – by looking at work from the past, especially those designers and publications that were particularly influential, innovative or ground-breaking. Whether through an understanding of print techniques, a style of cropping, a certain grid or structure, a use of typography and symbols as a means of expression, or the ability to exploit the latest print technologies, designers over the last 80 years have created graphic ephemera that stand shoulder to shoulder with fine art in their ability to inspire visual delight and express cultural concerns in conceptual form. The designers who have done so are numerous, but in this chapter are gathered a handful of the best. In studying the work of these past masters, contemporary designers should focus on the following:

- motivating and underlying principles;
- reasons why a particular design works in a specific context (in any given period);
- how the past plays a part in mapping out future trends and directions.

Looking back – motivating and underlying principles

All designers look at other design work, but many focus exclusively on contemporary work. This is important in terms of being aware of cultural shifts and changing and emerging trends in typography, illustration, photography, stock and so on; but it is equally important to look at work that has gone before. What should you look for? Ideas and directions certainly, but you won't understand them unless you understand the principles underpinning them, which in the past were often closely aligned to movements in art and culture, which, in turn, were contextualized both politically and socially. So, for example, the ideas around mechanization and functionality, which formed part of the Bauhaus principles of the 1930s, reflected the industrialization of Western society and the rise of socialism in eastern Europe. When Neville Brody appropriated the typographical and geometrical styles of Russian constructivism in the mid-1970s, it was a cultural gesture that drew on the spirit of overthrowing oppression. An understanding and exploration of such principles, and how they relate to and reflect their cultural and political milieu, will give contemporary editorial designers a set of tools with which to develop their own cultural responses and connections, which are needed to acquire a true understanding of their publication's readership. So, study from the past often – not to copy great designers, but to understand their work.

Understanding why a particular design works in a specific context

Understanding how designers work involves an understanding of why a design works in its particular context. This means examining the broad picture—the underlying and motivating principles of a publication as outlined above – then focusing on individual layouts and understanding why they work for the publication in question and its readership. How do the layouts work to communicate the principles? Find out by deconstructing the layout, then looking at how the individual elements work alone and together. Using The Face as an example, Neville Brody understood that, in principle, a publication about alternative culture could draw on influences and styles outside its own cultural milieu, and give them a contemporary forward-looking twist to communicate its cool outsider status. But which styles to choose? He intelligently opted for an appropriate visual style with roots and connections that were abundantly clear to a youthful readership, whose political integrity was untainted and whose cultural cachet was assured. He conveyed these principles through layouts composed predominantly of type, shapes and geometrical elements – rules, blocks and scale. The effect was startling: new, bold, irreverent and absolutely right for the readership.

Exploring the past to map future trends and directions

It is clear from the influential designers and publications listed here that the intellectual, moral and cultural climates of an era play a part in creating key design movements, which in turn influence the styles of editorial design. Such movements and styles do not exist in a vacuum, and do not become meaningless or irrelevant as the zeitgeist shifts. They may go out of fashion, but through an understanding of their principles they always have something to offer.

The one key difference between the past and present is that inspirational design can now be shared more easily. Today, we have fast and reliable access to the vast array of images that exist in the digital cloud. More importantly, designers continue to use social media, such as Twitter, Facebook and blogs, as a sharing tool, giving everyone the opportunity to learn from highly-skilled practitioners. The generous spirit of editorial designers and art directors means that the design community is fuelled daily by news of good practice, talks and events. In the following section, we select some modern pioneers who are worth following, alongside the many figures from the past who have inspired generations of designers. These people form a 'Hall of Fame', each one providing a different source of inspiration.

Hall of Fame – designers and publications

M.F. Agha

Dr Mehemed Fehmy Agha (known as M.F. Agha) was one of the first 'art directors'. A Russian–Turkish constructivist working on German *Vogue*, he was discovered by Condé Nast, who was trawling Europe looking for designers to introduce the modern (European) style to his publications. In 1929, Agha took over the flagship Condé Nast title, American *Vogue*, and lived up to expectations; control of *Vanity Fair* (right) and *House & Garden* followed. What he brought to these titles was fresh, new and vital art direction. He pioneered the use of sans-serif typefaces and emerging print and photographic techniques such as montage, duotones and full-colour photographs, choosing photography over fashion illustrations wherever possible. He experimented successfully with photographic layouts, exploiting double-page spreads to take images across gutters and using full-bleeds to create an exciting sense of space and scale. His use of leading photographers, including Cecil Beaton and Edward Weston, was matched by his employment of artists such as Matisse and Picasso years before any other American magazine.

On *Vanity Fair* M.F. Agha adapted the stylistic tenets of European modernism to a US title and its market. He achieved this by simplifying and systemizing type use, recognizing the spread as a palette on which the various design elements – gutters, margins, headlines and white space – could be endlessly expanded and manipulated to create vibrant and varied spreads. He understood that by playing with the position and size of his design tools, such as floating small headlines on white space at the bottom of the page, he could create impact and energy – something hitherto unseen in editorial design. Hence, traditional decorative elements were pushed off the page in favour of sparse layouts in which scale and shape became the primary means of decoration.

Even at the height of the Depression, Agha was creating bold but elegant designs that communicated their message with humour and clarity.

Alexey Brodovitch

Russian émigré Alexey Brodovitch was art director at *Harper's Bazaar* from 1934 to 1958, and in that period initiated techniques that have set standards of art direction ever since. Indeed, he pioneered the notion of art direction as conceiving and commissioning visual material rather than simply laying out pages. In terms of style, Brodovitch introduced asymmetrical layouts, movement, stripped-down simplicity and dynamic imagery to magazines (and US editorial design in general), which had previously been dominated by static pages filled with decorative but irrelevant clutter. These innovations were based on the simple 'modern' graphic style he had helped develop in Europe in the 1920s, which, in turn, was based on an amalgam of modernist movements and styles in art and design – notably Dada and constructivism. Obsessed with change and new ideas, including early abstract expressionism, Brodovitch developed a style that by the 1950s was a byword for elegance, largely achieved through white space and understated colour, along with contrasts of scale, precise, restrained typography (often Bodoni), and photo shoots and spreads invested with lively drama.

Part of Brodovitch's skill lay in his ability to discover and nurture new photographic talent, including Irving Penn and Richard Avedon. He introduced the work of avant-garde European photographers and artists such as A.M. Cassandre, Salvador Dalí, Henri Cartier-Bresson and Man Ray to the American public. He used this photography as the backbone of spreads that were light, spacious, full of movement and, above all, expressionistic – something we take for granted today. To achieve this, he took shoots outside the studio, and made the models – what they were doing, where and why – as important as the clothes they wore.

A desire to innovate and experiment lay at the heart of Brodovitch's work: a very instinctive approach based on eschewing the rational and the dogmatic for the constant pursuit of change and modernity.

Cipe Pineles

Nowadays, it is a given that photographers, illustrators, artists and editorial designers are allowed to interpret a story personally; indeed, it's a practice that virtually guarantees a result that, whether conceptual, impressionistic, expressionistic or literal, will be original and unexpected. Its invention was the brainchild of Cipe Pineles, who in 1946 initiated the practice on *Seventeen* magazine when she began commissioning visuals for fiction.

Pineles began her career under M.F. Agha at Condé Nast, where in five years she learned enough to take her to *Glamour* in 1942 as the first autonomous female art director. Here, she took fashion shoots into galleries and open spaces, bled images off spreads, cleverly guided readers from four-colour to two-colour images, introduced drama and scale to photographs, and gave a personal twist to editorial design by integrating modernist principles of structure and abstraction with playful use of visuals and type. But it was on *Seventeen* (above), the first magazine aimed at teenage girls, that she really came into her own.

Both Pineles and *Seventeen*'s founder and editor Helen Valentine viewed their readers as serious, intelligent young adults, and gave them serious, intelligent content. Pineles did so by introducing them to some of the most thought-provoking art of the time: the radical politics of Seymour Chwast and Ben Shahn, among others. She also introduced a system for the use of type to define and shape individual sections, and brought American figurative typography into the fashion and editorial spreads, replacing type with objects to create visual puns, and manipulating and interacting with letterforms (scratching, tearing, hand-lettering and so forth) to add meaning and expression to a story. In this sense her work echoed what was happening in the American art world, where expression was moving away from the figurative to explore directions such as conceptualism and abstract art with the use of wildly varying media.

Pineles expanded her experimentation and intervention with type on *Charm* magazine in 1950. Once again, here was a thoughtful, intelligent publication, bearing the strapline 'for women who work', which consciously and firmly located its readers in the context of a working and changing world in which women played a vital part. Pineles responded to the magazine's remit with a modern realism that was refreshing and new. Fashion shoots were conducted against city backdrops and freeways to reflect the country's industrial revolution, vernacular type expressed the two-dimensional realism of urban space, and typography was used to give impact and emphasis. Above all, it was Pineles's ability to find and work with artists and photographers, treating them as friends as well as professionals, that marks her as one of the great art directors. She won every major design award possible during her lifetime, illustrating the importance of strong productive relationships with contributors and the ability to communicate effectively.

Tom Wolsey

Many of the big names of modernist design are Europeans who fled their homes to forge new careers and lives in America. A notable exception is Englishman Tom Wolsey, whose extraordinary art direction on tailor's magazine *Man About Town* (later *About Town*, then *Town*) during the early 1960s brought Swiss modernist ideals to the previously ornate, classical taste of English periodical publishing. His work was typified by the use of slab serifs and modern sans serifs such as Haas Grotesk – he aggressively combined the brute force of these faces with equally uncompromising, startling illustrations and set the two onto grid-free layouts that were all about horizontals and angles. The result was a form of

design that had immediate and forceful impact but was never monotonous, thanks to Wolsey's rejection of the grid, occasional playful integration of display fonts, masterly use of picture placement, unerring ability to create movement and dynamism, and instinctive knowledge of good photography. He commissioned some of the best photographers of the decade, among them Don McCullin and Terence Donovan, and employed excellent print production to reproduce their work, setting the standards and styles for magazine design in the 1960s and on.

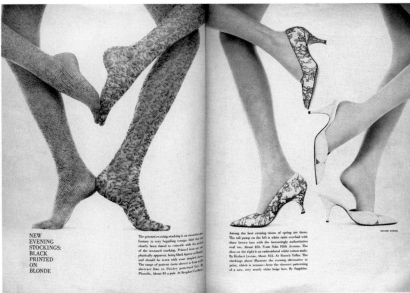

Henry Wolf

Austrian émigré Henry Wolf, who was art director of *Esquire* from 1952 to 1958, completely overhauled the design of this up-and-coming literary magazine, giving it a sophisticated and innovative style. In 1958, he became art director at *Harper's Bazaar*, succeeding Alexey Brodovitch. He remained there for three years, leaving in 1961 to start his own magazine, *Show*.

Wolf saw his task on all these titles as being to express their contents visually by integrating rigorous typography with expressive, eye-catching layouts. On *Harper's Bazaar*, where he inherited Alexey Brodovitch's stable of outstanding visual talent, Wolf built on this legacy, introducing simple, streamlined fonts and calm, spare compositions, which invested the layouts (illustrated left), and the magazine as a whole, with a measured pacing and flow. This was unusual for a designer who was more comfortable with opening spreads and covers than with the hard graft of lengthy features and their attendant problems of continuity and sustaining interest.

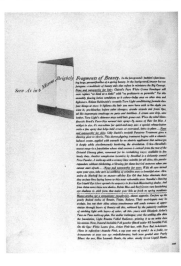

Not surprisingly, given his success in advertising, Wolf reigned supreme in creating the concept cover, often best seen in his work on *Show*, where he designed surrealist covers that were clever, witty and always original. Famous for the belief that 'a magazine should not only reflect a trend, it should help start it', Wolf was an intuitive designer who was instrumental in introducing Americans of the 1950s to European modernism.

Willy Fleckhaus

German designer Willy Fleckhaus is noted for his work on just two publications, but *Twen* (illustrated here) and *Frankfurter Allgemeine Magazin* (*FAZ*) are widely regarded as among the most influential titles in post-war editorial design. Fleckhaus's genius was to take the International Style, which dominated post-war graphic design, and give it an explosive 1960s energy created by the use of huge, tightly cropped pictures anchored to a rigid, grid-ruled approach to design. The resulting spreads offered a formal simplicity that he carried through to *Frankfurter Allgemeine Magazin* ten years after leaving *Twen*. This news magazine experimented and played with illustration in much the same way that *Twen* had done with photography, and retained the simple formalism of the earlier title, which was copied throughout Europe. In his book designs for publishing houses such as Suhrkamp, Fleckhaus's work shows as much aplomb and understated panache as that used in his magazines.

Twen

Twen launched in 1959 as a provocative youth title that combined erotic photography with thoughtful, intelligent articles. Its aim was to attract a new readership that demanded to be seen as distinct from its parents, an audience that was finding a language and style of its own: the emerging youth culture that was sweeping the West. This culture demanded a new graphic style, and designer Willy Fleckhaus provided it by combining elements of Swiss formalism –the rationalism of the grid and simple typography – with the witty and bold visual aesthetic of American publishing. To achieve this, he devised a 12-unit modular grid for the publication's large-scale format (265 x 335mm [10.4 x 13.2in]). The importance of this grid lay in its ability to combine units in a seemingly endless number of ways, enabling the use of two, three, four, or six columns, while horizontal units could be used to break down the columns into chunky blocks. What Fleckhaus put in place was a series of versatile coordinates on which to anchor his layouts – a brilliant solution that stood out from every other publication. Into this grid Fleckhaus then dropped some of the most striking imagery of the time, cropping and manipulating compositions to produce strange shapes

and massive close-ups that looked like weird landscapes, surreal portraits … anything went as long as it was dramatic, visually subversive and different. Combining the large format with distinctive black pages, minimal type (though a trained journalist, Fleckhaus didn't like writing and believed that visual storytelling had more impact) and some of the most eye-popping visual reportage of the day, *Twen* offered a dramatic shock-of-the-new publication that perfectly reflected its social and cultural milieu.

Combining the large format with distinctive black pages, minimal type (though a trained journalist Fleckhaus didn't like writing and believed that visual storytelling had more impact) and some of the most eye-popping visual reportage of the day, *Twen* offered a dramatic shock-of-the-new publication that perfectly relected its social and cultural milieu.

Nova

Founded in the UK in 1965, the radical women's monthly *Nova* saw its remit from the outset as being a women's version of a men's magazine – a title that would offer its readers intelligent conceptual content that went far beyond fashion and make-up. Art director Harri Peccinotti and editor Dennis Hackett were united in their determination to design a magazine that reflected this forward-looking stance, and drew on the American expressionist style developed by M.F. Agha and Alexey Brodovitch in the 1950s to do so. Covers, in particular, used a combination of unexpected image, space and text to reflect confrontational and often explosive topics such as racism, abuse, sex and politics. Photography was stark and expressive, both in content and cropping. But type was also innovative: stand-firsts in Times font covered half a page and demanded as much attention as the images. The legacy that Peccinotti left for David Hillman, who worked on *Nova* from 1969 until its demise in 1975, was ideal for documenting and exploring a period of intense social, sexual and political upheaval through bold, in-your-face visual elements (in particular photography, which he was highly skilled at using as reportage).

Hillman's ability to take design beyond defining a publication's identity to expressing its content, tone and stance was honed on *Nova*, highlighting the importance of being involved in all aspects of editorial. Acting as both deputy editor and art director, he was able both to interpret the magazine's identity as an uncompromising, individualistic title, breaking boundaries and taking risks, and to look at individual stories. Crucially, he believed photographs could tell stories, and commissioned many such 'stories' from photographers with different perspectives and even opposing stances. As a result, the magazine consistently broke new ground, but always in a way that was entirely appropriate to its identity and content.

Oz

Radical psychedelic magazine *Oz* was first published in Sydney, Australia, as a satirical publication edited by Richard Neville and co-edited by Richard Walsh and, crucially, artist, cartoonist, songwriter and filmmaker Martin Sharp. It was Sharp who drove the design direction of the magazine in its second incarnation as a London hippy magazine (from 1967 to 1973), where it garnered artistic kudos in equal measure with establishment opprobrium, and in 1970 a prosecution that would result in (at the time) the longest obscenity trial in British legal history. For the London issues of *Oz*, Sharp was able to take advantage of new advances in printing, stock and inks to design or show some of the most experimental and adventurous covers ever seen in editorial; many editions of the magazine included dazzling wrap-around covers or pull-out posters and were printed in metallic inks or on foil. With these covers and materials Sharp was pushing at the boundaries of print technology and offering a rich metaphor for *Oz*'s content, which was extending the limits of what was permissible by exploring accepted notions of pornography, libertarianism, obscenity and radical thinking.

Formats and sizes changed frequently, with Sharp as happy to explore the possibilities of landscape formats as he was portrait ones, but what remained constant was the ability of *Oz* to reflect and express brilliantly a subculture's shift from anti-authoritarian, drug-fuelled anarchy and experimentalism to dilution and eventual absorption in the establishment it had raged so hard against. It did this not just through its covers, but also through its design by Jon Goodchild. Working often with Sharp and other contributors, Goodchild turned the art room into 'a theatre of experiment', happily using paste-up to create collages and loose typographic layouts that moved editorial design away from the rigours and constraints of the prevailing Swiss style, with a lasting impact on graphic design.

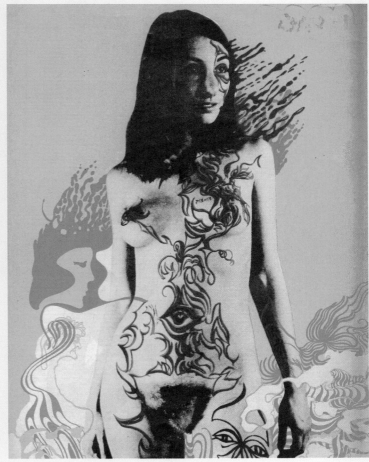

Neville Brody

Neville Brody joined *The Face* in 1981, and immediately established a design aesthetic rooted in, but not aping, the work of the twentieth-century art movements Constructivism, Dada and Expressionism. Here, once again, was typographic symbolism: playful experimentation that looked back to the mechanization of print and the opportunities it afforded the visual communicator, and utilized the expressionism inherent in stark, bold, geometric shapes and symbols. This was visual culture affiliated to political rebellion, which had a particular appeal for the overtly political designer. *The Face*'s anti-authoritarian, post-punk political and visual identity was a perfect match for Brody's experimental, individualistic approach to design because they shared the same rebellious spirit and helped define the look and feel of their time. Brody's main contribution to this youth-culture magazine was to break with traditional methods of type construction and establish it as a versatile, malleable design element that was barely distinguishable from imagery and could act as a vehicle for meaning.

The Face

Neville Brody's design of 1980s counter-culture magazine *The Face* revolutionized the editorial role of type and would have a lasting impact on graphic design. Brody's strength lay in using type to express meaning: by employing different faces within words to suggest nonconformity, positioning and angling type to echo the radical edginess introduced by Russian constructivism, and using graphic devices and symbols as page furniture to unify spreads and create visual cohesion. He also took a bold approach to images, cropping and framing to emphasize content visually. Full bleeds with just a portion of an image visible underlined the title's identity as anachronistic, anarchistic and thoroughly individual. As the magazine matured, so, too, did Brody's use of type and image, remaining in step with the readers, but always offering innovative and skilful design solutions. He was less successful in applying these same styles to other publications such as *City Limits* and *Per Lui*, but his work on *The Face* continues to stand out as a defining piece of editorial design.

Fabien Baron

For Fabien Baron, art direction runs in the family. After just one year of art school at the École des Arts Appliqués in Paris, he started work with his father, who art-directed a number of French newspapers (including Jean-Paul Sartre's radical left-wing newspaper *Libération*), later moving to *Self*, and then to *GQ* in the US. But it was on Italian *Vogue* in 1988, and then on *Harper's Bazaar* with Liz Tilberis, that he carved a reputation for strong, distinctive art direction that broke all the rules, including commercial ones. On Italian *Vogue*, for example, he simply ignored the accepted diktat of close-up figurative cover shots, and commissioned photographers such as Albert Watson to shoot arresting abstract portraits by reducing shapes to strong graphic devices that had real impact on the news-stand.

Baron's trademark style of bold graphic solutions was developed by minimizing the elements of design, as well as the range within those elements, drawing his colour palette from primary colours used sparingly and to startling effect with big blocks of black. Similarly, his illustration style is reduced to a few select artists (on Italian *Vogue* he only ever used illustrator Mats Gustafson, who created *Interview* magazine's logo) and his photos are mostly black-and-white images cropped in unusual ways to create striking results.

Above all, it is his use of typography as a constructive architectural element that Baron is famed for. On Italian *Vogue*, his use of huge full-page headlines to open a feature, combined with a minimalist style and large amounts of white space, created a new modern aesthetic. His letterforms echoed elements of an image; scale combined with a shape, a curve or a colour would act as the cornerstone on which to build a typographic solution. These became visual responses and connections that were perfectly adjusted to the magazine. On *Interview* he used this approach to strengthen textual portraits of interviewees, constructing type to express a sense of the person visually. In both cases, Baron presented the reader with visual solutions that were always coherent and exuberant pieces of editorial design. More than a decade later, his work on *Vogue Paris* (above) continues to do this, playing with image, text, space and scale to express the movement, action and vitality of fashion in a new century.

Mark Porter

Mark Porter was art director at *Colors* magazine, followed by the *Evening Standard*'s *ES Magazine*, and the first two issues of *Wired* in the UK. He is best known for his spectacular redesign of *The Guardian* newspaper during his time there as creative director there from 1996 to 2010. The redesign of that paper won a Design and Art Direction association Black Pencil award and a Society of Publication Designers design award, and was significant at the time as newspapers sought to break out of their old model into new formats. During his time at *The Guardian*, Porter also art directed the *Weekend* magazine and redesigned it six times with the assistance of Richard Turley.

Porter's passion for detail, and keen eye for a good image, has made his work very popular. He is a visual journalist first and foremost, reflecting his background as a language graduate. He now runs his own studio and recent work includes *Publico* and *Financiele Dagblad*. *Publico* is a Portuguese daily full colour newspaper, which has been praised for its very simple and bold design. The publication is graphic and features images throughout. Its smaller size makes it a modern version of a colour newspaper – almost a daily news magazine.

Financiele Dagblad is a daily financial paper produced in Amsterdam. It is designed first for print, but also appears in a website format and in a version for tablet. Porter has had to consider how the overall design format can be adapted for each different output.

Gail Anderson

Gail Anderson is one of the most prolific unsung design heroes and her work is a lasting inspiration to editorial designers. Born in the Bronx to Jamaican parents, she started at Random House after leaving the School of Visual Arts and then worked for the *Boston Globe* newspaper. However, it is for her years at *Rolling Stone* (1987–2002) that she is best known. Although she worked in a partnership with the esteemed Fred Woodward, it was Anderson who explored decorative letterforms and came up with double-page spreads that were good enough to be album covers in their own right. In his interview with her when she was awarded the 2008 AIGA MEDAL, Steve Heller calls this 'typographic eclecticism'. Her style at *Rolling Stone* shows a painstaking, craft-based attention to detail in densely designed pages, many featuring illustration that she had commissioned. Despite winning many awards for SPD and AIGA, she is a modest and quietly diligent person, and generous in crediting her influences as Paula Scher and Fred Woodward.

After *Rolling Stone,* Anderson joined the entertainment advertising agency SpotCo, where she designed stunning theatre posters for the entertainment industry. Her playful images combined great ideas, illustrative solutions and typographic play to create memorable images, some that have branded entire shows or plays on and off Broadway, such as the *Avenue Q* puppet. She designed a postage stamp for the US Postal Service as well as being on the Stamp Advisory Committee. The common thread in her work is good, strong ideas and skillful, attentive delivery, using both new and old letterforms in a contemporary mix-up. She describes the skill of having many ideas during her time at SpotCo to Steve Heller, her co-author on various books:

> 'You approach each project searching for a dozen great ideas, not just one or two,' Anderson explains how her work competes for the attention (and dollars) of theatregoers. 'After about seven designs, you realize there really are infinite ways to look at a problem. I now completely enjoy the process, though I'm keenly aware that all but one of those great ideas will eventually be killed off. It's strangely liberating.'

Anderson now teaches on the design programmes at the School of Visual Arts, New York and has her own boutique design firm.

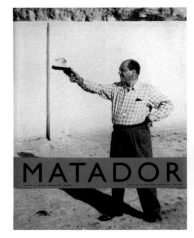

Fernando Gutiérrez

Everyone associates Benetton's *Colors* magazine with its original creators Oliviero Toscani and Tibor Kalman, but it is also very much the product of Fernando Gutiérrez, who became its creative director in 2000, adopting Kalman's original concept of visual reportage as honest, stark storytelling. A versatile designer, Gutiérrez has worked on everything, including book publishing, communications campaigns and editorial design, all produced by his own company within just seven years of graduating from the London College of Printing. Since then he has been quietly reshaping the landscape of editorial design in Spain and beyond, first on a government-department youth magazine, for which he created a format based on a double grid, but most notably on the Spanish fashion magazines *Vanidad* and *Matador* – a literary and a photography journal respectively – and on the newspaper *El País*. He has designed and art-directed a full range of daily sections and supplements for *El País*, including the youth-oriented *Tentaciones* (left and 'Conexión' spread opposite) and the Sunday *EPS*, which has a nationwide readership of 1.2 million. These are printed on low-grade newsprint, yet play to the strengths of the format and stock but are not confined by them. Gutiérrez was keen to design them as stand-alone magazines rather than as newspaper supplements, and the dynamism and panache with which he achieved this goal saw sales rocket.

On all these publications what is evident is Gutiérrez's ability to use design elements to express the title's identity and give readers an appropriate experience. Moreover, his work is infused with a cultural and national identity, which makes these magazines stand out from the crowd. On *Matador*, for which Gutiérrez plans to produce 29 issues by 2022 (each annual issue being 'numbered' with one letter from the Spanish alphabet, representing a homage to a different typeface), the key design elements are the high-quality stock, large-scale format and the printing. These combine with a formalism in the layout (*see* below) to create a dramatic and distinctly unique publication. Themes focusing on identity are overtly about nationality, but other less obvious topics also keep the title's Spanish parentage in evidence.

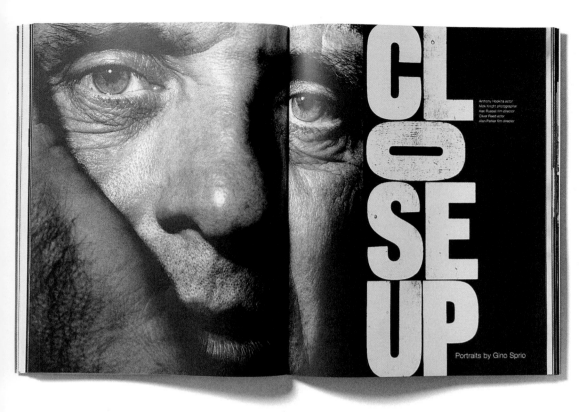

CLOSE UP

Anthony Hopkins actor
Nick Knight photographer
Ken Russell film director
Oliver Reed actor
Alan Parker film director

Portraits by Gino Sprio

Vince Frost

No designer since David Carson has used type in editorial as expressively as Vince Frost. The results could hardly be more different, but what unites the two is an inherent understanding of the need for editorial design – and particularly typography – to express the content and identity of a publication visually. For both designers, this has resulted in accusations of pointless obstruction in their visual solutions, but set against this is Frost's constant desire to intrigue and engage the reader through vibrant, exciting design.

Along with art-directing *The Independent on Saturday* newspaper's magazine in the UK during the mid-1990s, Frost devised the design for the *Financial Times*'s weekend magazine *FT The Business*. Both reveal a delight in intelligent conceptual design. Frost favours simplification and 'tidy' designs, which may explain his extraordinary ability to work with letterpress and woodblock typography as decorative elements that are always wholly related to content – though perhaps not always appropriate to its tone and style. By reducing the number of design tools in his palette, Frost is able to focus on making each element work extra hard to arrive at clean, bold solutions. On

Big magazine (below), an alternative style title printed in Spanish and English, he worked with letterpress guru Alan Kitching to produce type that he employed playfully as skyscrapers, speech bubbles, a mask and various other objects, all responding to the stunning accompanying photography, which in turn echoed the work of seminal New York photographer William Klein. And on the UK magazine *Zembla*, a literary magazine that wanted us to 'have fun with words', Frost literally interpreted that fun on every page, with bright, energetic, irreverent and playfully unpredictable designs centred in most cases on type as decoration.

Frost's skill goes beyond individual page solutions, however, to incorporate another, equally important aspect of editorial design: the ability to handle the flow of a publication so that the whole product is an exciting, constantly unexpected experience for the user. Nowhere is this more evident than on *Zembla*, where stunning photography, much of it black-and-white, was combined with letterpress to surprising and delightful effect, and where the regular editorial department—letters, reviews, news and so on – was given as much attention as feature pages.

Janet Froelich

Janet Froelich is well known for her strong art direction for The New York Times Magazine and Real Simple, and for her passion for photography and design. Over her long career, her ability to work with diverse creative partners has helped her strive for the best images and the best ideas. Froelich began her career as a painter, and studied fine art at Cooper Union and at Yale University.

Froelich was art director of *The New York Times Magazine* from 1986 to 2004, becoming creative director in 2004, and has won over 60 design awards from the Society of Publication Designers, the Art Directors Club and the Society of Newspaper Designers. Under her direction, *The New York Times Magazine* won the Society of Publication Designers "Magazine of the Year" award in 2007. In 2004, she became the founding creative director of *T: The New York Times Style Magazine*, an award-winning publication filled with beautiful fashion and design content which she helped develop. In 2006, she also became founding creative director for *Play: The New York Times Sports Magazine* and *Key: The New York Times Real Estate Magazine*. As we go to press, Froelich is the creative director of *Real Simple* magazine where she heads the creative team on this lifestyle, food and home title for Time Inc. She oversees design for print and tablet, mobile and web, as well as product packaging, all of which benefit from her clear vision of design and commitment to excellence in photography and typography. The images in *Real Simple* are beautiful and striking, and often succeed in telling a whole story in a single image, even when it is downsized into an icon for mobile media.

In 2006, Froelich received the Art Directors Club Hall of Fame award, and she has inspired many young designers through her work, and through teaching at the School of Visual Arts, New York. She has served on the boards of the Society of Publication Designers and the Art Directors Club, and was the president of the New York chapter of the American Institute of Graphic Arts (AIGA), organizations that each help to raise the profile of design.

Froelich's passion for fine art has informed many of the choices she has made, and has helped her to collaborate with artists and designers to make memorable images.

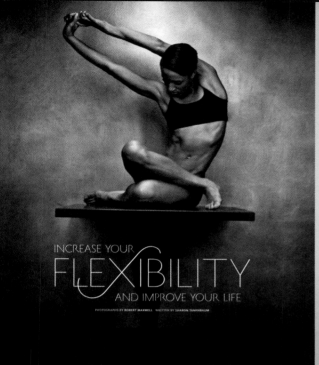

INCREASE YOUR
FLEXIBILITY
AND IMPROVE YOUR LIFE

PHOTOGRAPHS BY ROBERT MAXWELL WRITTEN BY SHARON TANENBAUM

THE SIMPLE ACT OF STRETCHING DOES A LOT MORE THAN
MAKE YOU LIMBER. IT MAY HELP PREVENT INJURIES OR EVEN ILLNESS.
AND YOU DON'T HAVE TO BE PRETZELIAN TO REAP
THE BENEFITS—ALL IT TAKES IS 10 EASY MINUTES A DAY.

WHEN YOU'RE LIMBER,
YOUR BODY CAN MORE EASILY ADAPT
TO PHYSICAL STRESSORS.

Scott Dadich

Originally from Texas, Scott Dadich worked on the beautifully crafted *Texas Monthly* before arriving at *Wired* magazine in 2006. After winning many awards for groundbreaking design, characterized by his can-do attitude to the magazine format and innovative engagement with the readership, Dadich became one of the pioneers of good magazine design during the transitional period from print to iPad. He initiated the concept of the Wired app and led the entire team in its development. Wired was the very first app built in the framework that would become DPS. He also designed the second app, which was for *The New Yorker*, and in 2012 this app became one of the most successful in terms of sales in the entire industry. With the backing of the renowned Condé Nast publishing company, Dadich's team also launched *The New Yorker* for iPhone in 2012.

Dadich investigated the transition from flipping through magazine pages as linear PDFs in early apps to include digital pages too. He called it the 'stack' system where pages of both digital and print are arranged as if on a clothesline. With the investment of Condé Nast behind his team of designers and developers, he explored the format when it was still in its infancy.

Dadich's thirst for innovation continues to drive him on in his role as Vice President, Editorial Platforms & Design at Condé Nast. His passion and eloquence for the medium, and his generosity in sharing has made him an outstanding contributor to the design community as it moves through the greatest transition since the invention of the printing press.

For print

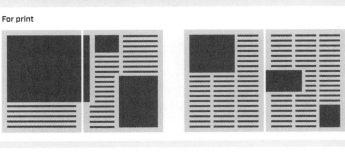

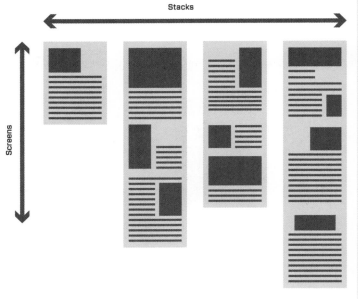

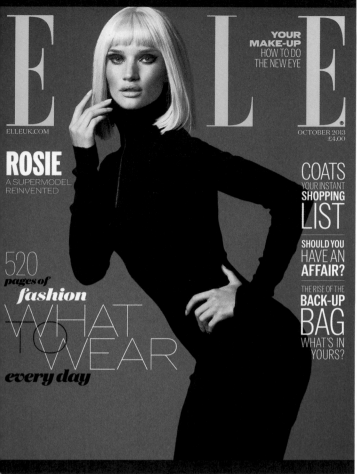

Suzanne Sykes

Suzanne Sykes is a British art director known for her work in reinventing fashion magazines. She was the launch designer for *Marie Claire UK* in 1989 with editor Glenda Bailey. Her various D&AD design awards came for her work on *Grazia*, which took the glamorous fashion monthly aesthetic and translated it into a fast-paced, newsy weekly formula. At the time this was a revolutionary approach to top-selling fashion brands. The look was dramatic and divided opinion, but changed the fashion magazine landscape with its layered pages and coloured panels.

After a stint in New York as art director of *Marie Claire US* (2007–12), Suzanne tackled an ambitious redesign of *Elle UK*, which had its heyday in the supermodel-dominated '80s. Sykes recognized the need to respond to a changing readership, now less likely to buy glossy magazines, but keen to use social media for their fashion advice. With art director Mark Leeds she created a publication both online and in print that directly connected both platforms – unlike the competition, which produced sibling versions from the master print title.

Talking about digital and print in March 2013 she said: 'Print is the hero brand. We set our stall in print, driving readers to the digital arena.' In 2013, *Elle* sold 177,094 copies in print; website readership was 450,000 unique users per month. *Elle* was the first UK women's mag to have 1.13 million Facebook followers. Sykes says that with editor Lorraine Candy she is 'aiming for the reader to be able to buy directly from the page'.

Suzanne's design follows the bold mother brand but expands to the enhanced app version, (elle.com page). Here, the cover model Rosie Huntington appears in a video on ElleTV, giving the reader a variety of ways of exploring and sharing content.

Looking forward

While it is almost impossible and perhaps foolish to try and predict emerging trends in design, it is useful to touch on technological and other changes which are affecting design practice. All the figures listed above have benefited from the new technologies of their era, be that the increased availability of colour printing or the flexibility of phototypesetting. Today, the Apple computer on the desk of every editorial designer enables them to be a true multi-disciplinarian: part printer, part art director, part image-maker, part coder, part editor, part blogger, part marketer ... but he or she must be more than the sum of all these parts. Designers must be aware of economic, cultural and technological shifts in different media, and be ever-ready to adapt to new technologies in order to survive.

In this section, we look at the challenges that may be coming up in the near future and reveal insights from industry experts.

Technological shifts

The tablet magazine
As we go to press, the biggest challenge to the editorial design industry is the variety of channels that magazines face across print, tablets and social media. The 2010 launch of the Apple iPad triggered a race to make app versions of print magazines in the hope that these would be the answer to monetizing digital content. Adobe, Woodwing, Mag+ and others quickly developed plug-ins for InDesign that allowed print designers to adapt their layouts for the iPad and other tablets. Overnight, a whole new stage in the editorial workflow was introduced. The print edition completed, the design team would adapt the final pages to the smaller tablet screen, reformatting everything and adding interactive elements – animation, video, audio. It remains to be seen how genuinely successful such apps might become, but the production process has led editorial designers to add interactive skills to their ever-increasing list of responsibilities.

Responsive design
Initially developed to cope with the multiple screen sizes on which a website might be viewed (desktop,

tablet, phone), responsive design means the width of the browser window triggers an algorithmic change of layout to suit each environment. The broad multi-column screen design for desktop browsing automatically changes to single-column design for the smartphone.

To help the designer cope with the changes in the workflow discussed above, it has been proposed that a similar algorithm-based responsivity might be developed to account not only for the change between print design and tablet design, but also to account for the more subtly varied tablet screen sizes and formats.

Automated content

With RSS feeds, the automatic magazine is a reality with algorithms (calculation/problem-solving processes performed by a computer) working out the content the reader wants and delivering it via application software to different mobile devices. In 2012, the most popular provider of aggregated content was Flipboard, which was founded in the US two years previously by Mike McCue and Evan Doll. Flipboard is a digital social magazine that aggregates content from social media such as Facebook and Twitter and displays the content in magazine format on an iPad or Android mobile device. Users can also "flip" through feeds from websites that have partnered with the company, for example, subscribers of *The New York Times* can now read the publication's content on Flipboard. As Jeremy Leslie, creative director of magCulture, notes:

'There is no art director in that sense, there is an algorithm. Flipboard is the first that has brought some sense of scale and space. I use it on my phone for my social network feeds. Twitter is a great example and it works well with Flipboard. The way the pages turn on Flipboard is also worth a mention. Traditionally page turning on devices was an unhappy aesthetic between purpose and function, looking very uncomfortable. The way that Flipboard splits the iPad screen down the middle is very clever, it refers to a magazine without directly mimicking it.'

Combining print and digital

Another algorithm-based project demonstrates one of the most interesting recent themes in publishing, the combining of traditional print and new digital technologies. The Newspaper Club developed from its founders desire to open up print production to non-designers. They developed a bespoke software called Arthr and negotiated good rates with printers based on using their press downtime. The result was a service where anyone could upload words and text, have the software lay it out as pages, and order a small run of newspapers (design-literate users could upload their own designs as PDFs).

A more personal form of print-digital crossover came with Little Printer, developed by London-based studio Berg. Rejecting the traditional publishing model that you print editorial, distribute it and hope somebody buys it, Little Printer offers a selection of material to choose from via a web dashboard. The content arrives via WiFi to be printed on receipt paper by the Little Printer (see pp.232–33). Bearing some similarities to Flipboard, it is a typically playful experiment from Berg. Principal Jack Schulze, explains:

'Little Printer is a product that has a couple of qualities to it and behaviours that are very different from Flipboard. One is that everything is archived in the cloud. It has a history of its behaviours if you want to look at it. Second it schedules a release of small poignant personal data and information for you. You ought to be able to access it with just a single point of interaction. Some of this output is usual content e.g. puzzles, weather, some is social media content, plus a mix of broadcasters and big publishers like The Guardian. *It is just junk being sent around in pixels. The point is that it is at 8.15am and it is my friends. The Big M media and the small media all come out in the same language. Little Printer does not differentiate.'*

Finite publishing

A recent focus of interest has been the notion of presenting digital content – usually endless in its open, linked, internet guise – within a finite boundary to echo the way a printed publication is limited by the number of pages. Instead of an infinite quantity of website content, a website or app might flaunt an exact finiteness. One such experiment is The Magazine, an iPhone app launched by Marco Arment (founder of reading app Instapaper) that presents four technology-orientated pieces of writing to subscribers every two weeks. Available exclusively via Apple's Newsstand and not in print, there are no visuals or decoration, simply readable text delivered in small volumes with a clear end, or 'edge'.

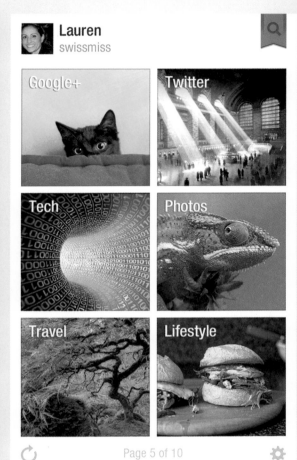

Available on both Apple and Android devices, the automotically produced content of Flipboard has a magazine-like feel, with sharp black text appearing on a clean white background along with images and links, and clean white text appearing over images as shown here.

Another start-up, Aeon Magazine (aeonmagazine.com), publishes one original long form essay every weekday, again concentrating on the quality of content rather than quantity. The material is highly progressive, thought-provoking and written by specialists, the aim being that readers focus on this daily serving of valuable content rather than drown in endless 'must reads'. Aeon essays are published daily on the web, as well as being available via a subscription email on a daily or weekly basis, and aadapt respnsively to desktop, iPad and smart phone screens.

Availability of data Many companies, such as *The Times* newspaper, can use increased data availability to their advantage. Jon Hill, design editor at *The Times*, says:

> *'..new developments in data availability can be pushed further, of which GPS is just one part of what we can do. The other exciting thing is that we can contextualize stories and show picture galleries using our archive, which goes back 225 years, in an interesting way. This project has great potential for an organization like The Times .... We have a lot of feedback now for the editions too, telling us how much time the readers spend. There is now microdata on our work, with analysis showing which infographics people spent time looking at. Before, if you put it out and if people looked at it then that was great, but now we have detailed feedback telling us what was actually successful.'*

Changing business models The sharing of ideas and editorial opinions used to be person-to-person, but is now done via social media networks such as Twitter and Tumblr. These tools help to bring audiences back to print and are part of the multi-channel network of support systems that publications use to share their content.

News media companies like NewsCorp are working on how to sustain their large organizations via a mix of multi-channel products and services. Some of these prove to be lucrative business models, while others consist of more traditional and historic parts that don't generate high income. As Jon Hill says:

> *'..the big thing is with the paywall and the digital editions. We have to look at our workflow at The Times and see how we produce these things*

> *efficiently and make sure the design team are having proper input. We are working hard to try to sustain all the different platforms at once, 24 hours a day. We can't make bespoke editions for every single new tablet or mobile platform that comes up so we will prioritize our design efforts. We want to make a difference to the design of each part of the output.'*

So can magazines survive just in print? Simon Esterson, co-publisher of *Eye* magazine answers:

> *'... too hard to generalize. Smaller publishing companies have been cleared out as supermarkets take over distribution of a selection of titles. Small newsagents are no longer able to compete. At one end you have got big publishing in print and at the other you have got a fertile area of self-publishing.*

> *... The difference the web makes is that you can actually purchase back copies and subscriptions from abroad and have them delivered to your home. Instead of schlepping to specialist collectors, you can find them online. Small publishers like* Eye, *can keep in touch with readers once they find us and let them know about events and new issues. For small publishers, their titles may not be in the shops but that's not a problem."*

It appears that the iPad is really loved by many of its users as a unique object. However, it cannot be assumed that this tablet or other cheaper Android tablets will continue to have the same appeal to consumers in the future, or that these or any new devices will remove paper from our lives.

Jack Schulze

While Jack Schulze has one foot in the future, he also has an interest in designing beautiful aesthetic work, influenced by his passion for typography and respect for a good idea. His work for *Mag+* showed a simple way of navigating through different types of content within a magazine app.

The idea of new software and exploring different deliveries for editorial continues to interest BERG, a company founded by Schulze and Matt Webb in London in 2005 (they were later joined by Matt Jones).

In February 2012, Fast Company ranked BERG one of the 'World's 50 most innovative companies'. This annual guide to companies whose innovations have made an impact in technology and culture, applauded BERG for 'wildly imagining the marriage of physical and digital'. Through its playful and off-the-wall thinking, BERG helps companies to realize their potential with digital technologies and offers innovative products, such as Little Printer, as an alternative to usual publishing thinking.

In the following interview, Schulze puts forward his views on the role of big media companies and what might happen in the future.

How can the big media companies stay agile and keep in touch with what consumers want?

They need to become software companies. Steve Jobs and Amazon have changed the rules of the relationship with consumers. There are two big games in town: one is experience, the other is data. Basically media companies need to be making software, it is not enough to be making content.

Where does this leave the big media companies?

Those big media companies do still have value. Alan Rusbridger (editor of *The Guardian*), for instance, is clever and understands collaboration. However, Big Media are in trouble. Historically if you are a successful media company you want to be the largest. Media is used to owning stuff (assets) and having a lot of output and reach into TV, into hotel rooms, etc. In the software sector you want to be three dudes in a basement. What you want to be is small.

What those businesses rely on is the value of their infrastructure. If you are a broadcaster you own many buildings and on the top of hills you have 40-foot (12 metre) antennas scooping up electricity and signals and beaming out TV and radio. It was enough when there wasn't any other alternative, but now we can just check Facebook. Broadcasters have all that huge hardware and business just for mundane content. If you are a news company and let's then say you own buildings and all these printing presses. You would also have trucks that drive the newspapers and distribute them, just in case someone might happen to want to spend 90 pence on a fixed piece of paper that they then have to carry home and read cover-to-cover. It is a very expensive way to do things. When there was no alternative it was fine. Now it seems ridiculous and a waste of energy and money.

How does Little Printer work?

When I need to configure it then I go online to subscribe to one of the publishing streams. I say these are the things that I want and it delivers them once a day. For me, for instance, I want it delivered in the morning. On the top is a button. If a delivery is sent, the light gently flashes, a bit like an answering machine. If you don't print it out and the next delivery comes, then you just get one, not two. If you go away for a couple of days then on your return you don't get everything, just the new delivery, but the rest is still stored on the cloud.

Take this for example: the content stream *How many people are in space right now?* tells you that there are six people in space right now. If you subscribe to this stream then you get news only when it changes. You only need to know an update when there are seven people in space. Daily newspapers have to come out every day. They always have to fill space with their columnists, even on a slow news day, and rely on habits of readers. Here we can create content only when it matters. Some days there is not much to say. There are ways of creating publishing only when there is something to publish. Why not publish something only when something happens because that is when it matters. Why publish every day? Media companies don't work like that.

What is your prediction for the future?

This ubiquitous cheap Android tablet device made in China is going to look like the USB key or a CD in a few years time. They will be giving them away with a film on it or a book on it. It will be in your fruit bowl at home and when you want to check your email you won't go to your computer but will be picking up one of these.

It is literally a cheap factory-made tablet device. Google make Android as an open system so that Samsung, Nokia and Apple could use the Android system on their hardware. Apple matters because people want it. The difference is that people want the Apple product.

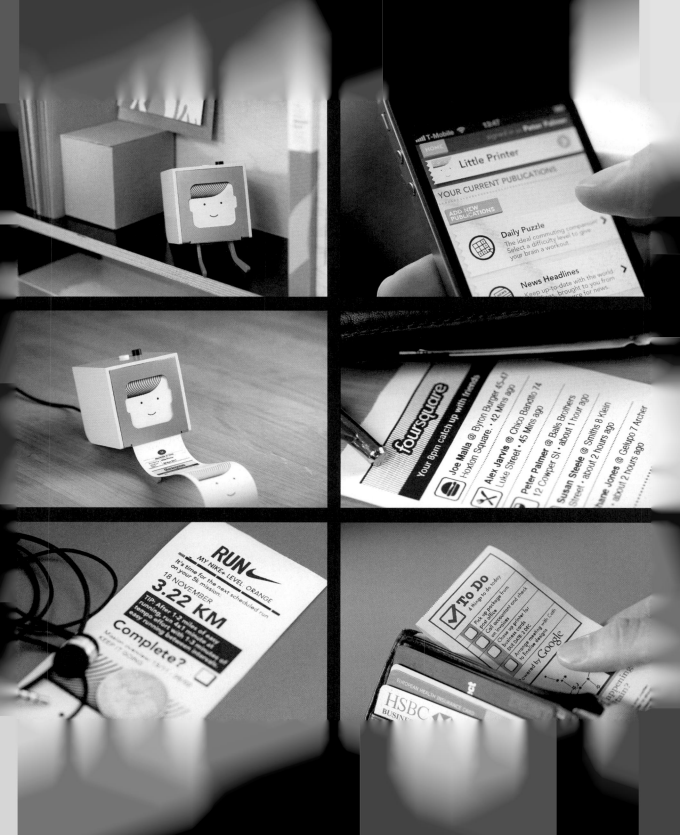

Cultural and behavioural shifts

The boundaries between what is marketing, publishing, broadcasting and advertising have blurred. People now consume more media in their daily lives; often using mobile and television, or web and music, at the same time. Global web traffic statistics from marketing data services, such as Neilson BookData, show that consumers seem to be hungry for more.

Journalists can share their ideas on social media. Editors no longer have control over the journey that the reader once took when a magazine or newspaper was a more linear experience. Increasingly editors need to look for more ways for their publication to stand out.

The blurring of print and digital outputs also continues. Jeremy Leslie says:

'We are at the stage of print and digital where you can say what is the difference? You have to just understand the difference between making a pamphlet of your own, having a Twitter feed, a blog or a magazine. Ask yourself how does your voice decrease or diminish in different worlds? Now it is all publishing, it is communicating opinion.'

One example of this is the travel and culture magazine *Monocle*, known for its innovative approach to magazines and the blurring of boundaries between advertising and editorial. In 2011, editor Tyler Brûlé launched a television show on Bloomberg network and an internet radio station, *Monocle 24*. Both of these channels seek to broadcast an intimate experience for the magazine's jet-setting readership and reflect Brûlé's keen understanding of his readership, borne out by 2.5 million downloads a month. Radio adds an intimate touch and nostalgic quality to the brand using a faintly BBC World Service style of broadcasting.

Economic shifts and new world markets

While the emerging 'BRIC' markets (Brazil, Russia, India and China) were thought to offer the big media (Big M) companies new markets, we have seen evidence that the freedom of the press is not what it was in the US or the UK. This affects news organizations such as *The New York Times* and the BBC as they struggle to make their services pay.

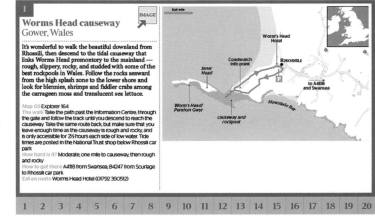

As Jack Schulze from BERG observes:

'American Big M media is interested in the Chinese market. The difference in the market is scale. If they can get 5 per cent of that market, it would be significant and a way to sustain their business model back in the US. There is nothing unique or sensible about trying to launch a media platform in China. (It is just desperation in my view). Likewise, The Guardian *is interested in the US because it prolongs their UK-based business model ... In Africa SMS is significant because any kind of connectivity be it social or whatever can be exploited for social and economic gain. Stef Magdalinski runs businesses in Africa and runs a Yellow Pages service via SMS,*

which is very popular. He is one to watch as he aims to bring information and data to many people.'

The use of a simple solar panel device can bring electricity to populations who do not have power to charge a computer or a mobile device. However, the network coverage available in remote, poorer regions is insufficient to enable publishing to be downloaded, so there is still a cap on the expansion until mobile networks catch up. The networks need to see a financial reward for their investment in infrastructure before they will bring network availability to remote areas.

Real benefits of using social media

The next generation of publishing talent will still need to tell the stories which need to be told, but will use their natural ease with social media as part of their output tools. At the point of writing, it is a myth that there is a singular 'next big thing' which will replace print. Instead, editors and designers are now telling stories in every medium that readers can consume in. Janet Froelich, creative director at *Real Simple*, relates one example of this:

*'*Real Simple *was the first magazine to gain over 100k followers on Pinterest. Most of our images are re-posted on readers' blogs and on personal favorites pages. Our photo and art teams have been shooting what they find visually stimulating, and posting these images on Instagram. We often get hundreds of "likes" on each of them. Those photographs expand our audience, keep the dialogue going, and showcase the vision and talent of our team. We are always working to create a more seamless integration of print, digital and social media.'*

Readers are no longer static while they read. They are more likely to be on the move or doing two things at once. In the 'Wild Summer Walks' feature (opposite) from *The Times*, interactive content is provided in App form. The reader can use the content to guide their walk, as here on the Welsh coastline, for example, where the reader will use the location to enhance their interaction with the content.

Real Simple magazine is often used in the kitchen on the iPad, as the user follows recipes. Content is interactive, and can be used to follow step-by-step instructions. Other media may often be consumed at the same time – TV, email, social media. The way we enjoy magazines is constantly evolving.

The evolution of the printed page

AD 105 Paper is invented in China.

770 Relief printing is practised in China.

868 The world's earliest dated printed book, a Chinese Diamond Sutra text, is created using woodblocks.

Early 15th century Professional writers join the ranks of monks in writing books as trading and wider education lead to more books for the upper and middle classes in Europe. In Paris, these writers form themselves into a guild – publishing has arrived.

1450 In Mainz, Germany, goldsmith Johannes Gutenberg invents movable type (also known as 'foundry type' or 'hot type'), and five years later uses it to begin a print run of 180 copies of the Gutenberg Bible.

1457 *Gazette*, claimed to be the first printed newspaper, is printed in Nuremberg, Germany. The earliest example of colour printing arrives with the *Mainz Psalter* by Johann Fust and Peter Schöffer.

1476 William Caxton returns from Cologne, Germany, with a range of typefaces and sets up a printing press in Westminster, London, having already produced the first book in the English language, *The Recuyell of the Historyes of Troye*, in Bruges.

1486 The first English, colour-illustrated book is printed in St Albans, England.

1494 Typographer, teacher and editor Aldus Manutius establishes the Aldine printing house in Venice, Italy.

1500 Approximately 35,000 books have been printed, 10 million copies worldwide.

1501 Italic type, designed by Francesco Griffo, is first used in an octavo edition of Virgil printed by Manutius's Aldine Press.

1588 Englishman Timothy Bright invents a form of shorthand.

1605 The first regularly published weekly newspaper appears in Strasbourg.

1622 Nathaniel Butter, the 'father of the English press', publishes *Weekly Newes*, the first printed English newspaper, in London.

1650 Leipzig in Germany becomes home to the first daily newspaper.

1663 *Erbauliche Monaths-Unterredungen* ('Edifying Monthly Discussions'), considered the world's first magazine, is published in Germany.

1690 America's first newspaper, *Publick Occurrences Both Forreign and Domestick*, is printed in Boston, Massachusetts, and subsequently suspended for operating without a royal licence.

1702 The first daily news-sheet, *The Daily Courant*, is published in England.

1703 *Sankt-Peterburgskie Vedomasti* newspaper founded by Peter the Great in Russia.

1709 The Copyright Act is passed in England. *Tatler*, the first major magazine, is launched in London.

1714 Henry Mill is granted a patent for a writing machine in London.

1719 German engraver Jakob Le Blon, granted a privilege by George I of England to reproduce pictures and drawings in full colour, produces the basis of modern four-colour plate printing.

1731 *The Gentleman's Magazine*, considered the first modern magazine, published in England.

1741 Benjamin Franklin plans to publish America's first magazine, *General Magazine*, but *American Magazine* comes out three days earlier.

1764 Pierre Fournier of France develops the point system to measure type sizes. His system is further refined by François Didot, establishing consistency in type measure throughout the world.

1784 *The Pennsylvania Evening Post* is America's first daily newspaper.

1785 *The Daily Universal Register* is founded in London by John Walter. Three years later it is renamed *The Times*.

1790s Lithography is invented by Alois Senefelder in Bavaria, Germany, streamlining the reproduction of images by eliminating the need for engraving or carving.

1791 *The Observer*, the country's first Sunday newspaper, is launched in England by W.S. Bourne.

1814 An early version of the cylinder press is used to produce the London *Times* at a rate of 1,100 copies an hour, but it is not refined and taken up universally until 1830, when Richard March Hoe perfects the drum-cylinder press, capable of producing 2,500 pages per hour. By 1847 he has expanded this to a five-cylinder press.

1828 *The Ladies' Magazine* is launched to become the first successful American magazine for women.

1842 *The Illustrated London News* is founded in England by Herbert Ingram and Mark Lemon. Using woodcuts and engravings, it prompts the growth of illustrated publications.

1844 *The Bangkok Recorder* is the first newspaper published in Thailand.

1845 *Scientific American* launches in America. It has been published continuously since that date, making it the longest-running magazine in American history.

c.1845 Paperbacks are introduced in America (four years after their appearance in Germany) as newspaper supplements, and soon appear as small-sized reprints of existing books.

1850 Heidelberg's first press is made by Andreas Hamm in the Palatine city of Frankenthal in southwest Germany.

1851 *The New York Times* launches, priced at one cent.

1854 *Le Figaro* newspaper is launched in Paris, France.

1856 The first African-American daily, the *New Orleans Daily Creole*, is published.

1867 The first Japanese magazine, *Seiyo-Zasshi*

('The Western Magazine'), is published.

1874 E. Remington and Sons in Illinois manufactures the first commercial typewriter, invented seven years earlier by Wisconsin newspaperman Christopher Latham Sholes. It has only upper-case letters but a QWERTY keyboard. The machine is refined the following year to incorporate lower-case letters.

1875 Offset litho printing – printing onto etched metal plates from a smooth surface rather than letterpress – is introduced.

1878 In the United States, inventor William A. Lavalette patents a printing press that greatly improves the quality of printing, particularly in terms of legibility and quality. In Scotland, Frederick Wicks invents the typecasting machine.

1886 The Linotype typesetting machine is invented by Ottmar Mergenthaler. Combining keyboard unit, matrix magazine and caster in one unit, it can cast letters at the rate of 17,000 per hour by compositors pressing keys to create 'slugs' – lines of matrices combined then redistributed for reuse.

1900 An estimated 1,800 magazines are being published in America, where total newspaper circulation passes 15 million a day.

1903 The first offset printing press is used by Ira Washington Rubel in America, and, separately, by Caspar Hermann in Germany.

1911 Typesetting is refined further with the introduction of the Ludlow typesetting machine, developed by Washington I. Ludlow and William Reade in Chicago, Illinois.

1912 *Photoplay* debuts in America as the first magazine for movie fans.

1917 The first 'op-ed' (opinion and editorial) page appears in *The New York Times*.

1923 *Time* magazine debuts in America.

1933 *Esquire* launches in America as the first men's magazine.

1934 Alexey Brodovitch is hired to work on *Harper's Bazaar* in New York, bringing a visual flair and dynamism to the layouts.

1936 Allen Lane's Penguin Press reintroduces the paperback book in the UK. In America, photojournalism magazine *Life* is founded by Henry Luce for Time Inc. It was to dominate the American news market for 40 years, selling more than 13.5 million copies a week.

1941-44 Documentary photography reports back from WWII and magazines publish stories led by reportage. Some images are restricted and questioned.

1945 *Ebony*, the first magazine for the African-American market, is founded in the US by John H. Johnson.

1953 The first issue of *TV Guide* magazine hits the newsstands on April 3 in ten American cities, with a circulation of 1,560,000.

Playboy magazine appears, its cover featuring Marilyn Monroe.

1955 Dry-coated paper is developed at the Battelle Memorial Institute, Columbia, Ohio.

1955 *Esquire* magazine in the US publishes bold cover with minimal cover lines due to the strong sense of brand. Only a few other publications are able to use colour.

1958 Henry Wolf becomes Art Director at *Harper's Bazaar* and pushes graphic language to connect photoshoots and typography.

1956 The first hard-disk drive is created at IBM.

1962 British national newspaper *The Sunday Times* launches a full-colour magazine supplement designed by Michael Rand.

1964 In America, statistics show that 81 per cent of adults read a daily newspaper.

1965 Teen magazine *Twen* is launched by German publishing giant Springer. Designed by Willy Fleckhaus, it comes to be regarded as a ground-breaking example of editorial design. In the UK, the *Daily Mirror*'s magazine division launches *Nova*, with Dennis Hackett as editor and David Hillman as designer.

1967 The ISBN (International Standard Book Number) system starts in the UK. *Rolling Stone* debuts in the US, followed by *New York Magazine* in 1968, spawning the popularity of special-interest and regional magazines.

1969 Andy Warhol launches *Interview* magazine.

1971 Newspapers worldwide begin the switch from hot-metal letterpress to offset.

1975 *Nova* magazine closes.

1977 Apple Computer launches the Apple II microcomputer.

1980 At the European Organization for Nuclear Research (CERN) in Geneva, Switzerland, Tim Berners-Lee takes the first steps towards a worldwide web, creating a software program called 'Enquire Within Upon Everything' after a Victorian-era encyclopaedia remembered from his childhood.
The Face is launched in the UK by Nick Logan as a style and culture alternative to women's glossy magazines

1981 The cover of *Rolling Stone* shows a naked John Lennon and clothed Yoko Ono. This iconic Annie Leibovitz image epitomizes the power of magazines within the music business.

1982 Daily newspaper *USA Today* launches. Taking its visual lead from television, it uses colour throughout, features numerous graphics, and is an immediate success. Innovative techniques assist distribution, enabling the final edition to be printed in multiple locations across the country.

1983 The Apple Lisa is launched by Apple Computer, ushering in a new Graphic User Interface (GUI) that makes home computing – and publishing – accessible and affordable.

1984 The Apple Macintosh, or the Mac, is introduced, marking the first successful commercial implementation of a GUI, which is now used in all major computers.
Emigre magazine launches in California and is soon to be a creative showcase for digital fonts and imagery.

1985 The first desktop-publishing program, Aldus Pagemaker 1.0, is created by Paul Brainerd and Aldus and released for the Macintosh. This desktop-publishing program leads to a new type of publishing and puts design and editing tools into the hands of everyone.

1987 QuarkXPress is launched. Despite the release of Aldus Pagemaker two years earlier, it quickly becomes the pre-eminent desktop-publishing program.

1991 The World Wide Web debuts. Using Tim Berners-Lee's HTML (hyper-text mark-up language), anyone can now build a website and share it with at first hundreds, but quickly millions, of people worldwide.

1994 In Italy, an A5 handbag-sized version of *Glamour* is launched by Condé Nast.
In America, the first beta version of the Netscape browser Mosaic is released.
The first wiki is developed in Portland Oregon by Ward Cunningham. Wikis enable users to create and link pages of content in a non-linear and collaborative way on the web.

1995 *Salon*, a US liberal magazine published in online form only. This format challenges the traditional business model for print media.

1997 *The New York Times* introduces colour photos to its news pages.

2004 In the UK, *The Independent* newspaper moves from a broadsheet to a tabloid format. Within a year, *The Times* also produces a daily tabloid.

2005 *The Guardian* newspaper moves to a Berliner format and to full colour.
The First Post online news magazine launches in the UK.

2006 Video-sharing website YouTube purchased by Google for $1.65 billion in stock.
Online newspaper websites in the US attract over 58 million readers, according to a report for the Newspaper Association for America.

2007 UK online publication *Financial Times* reports a 30 per cent increase in advertising sales.
The wireless Kindle e-book reader goes on sale.

2008 In America the number of adults who say they read a daily newspaper the day before is 30 per cent.

2009 Newspaper sales fall following world financial crisis. *The Faster Times* is launched in the US by Sam Apple as an experiment to find a model for 'on-demand journalism'.
thetimesonline.co.uk has a daily readership of 750,000

2010 The Apple iPad goes on sale; 3 million units are sold within 30 days.
Amazon Books announces that sales of ebooks have surpassed the sale of paperbacks for the first time.
WIRED magazine releases its tablet edition for the iPad.
The Times launches an interactive issue for the tablet market.
Wikileaks publishes classified documents from anonymous new sources and upsets the news media by bypassing usual established practices. In light of the demise of large news publishers the validity of news stories on the web is challenged by this activism.

2011 *The Guardian* tablet editions launches.
iPad2 goes on sale. Over 15 million units are sold in the first year.
The New York Times' publisher announces that it will charge frequent readers for access to its online content in the US.
News International introduces a paywall for the London *Times*.

2012 Cross-platform magazines like *Little White Lies* and *Letter to Jane* branch out into different formats and leave print behind.

2013 Independent magazines start to thrive due to low cost of production on the internet. Following the Leveson Inquiry into press misconduct in the UK, a Royal Charter aimed at underpinning self-regulation of the British press is proposed and meets opposition from many editors.
At the Modern Magazine Conference in London, the term 'Golden Age' is used to refer to the industry as publishing activity starts to normalize following the impact of three years of the iPad. Large publishers and small independents develop the freedom that digital media brings to the industry.

Further reading

Editorial art direction

Theodore E. Conover, revised by William W. Ryan, *Graphic Communications Today*, fourth edition, Clifton Park, New York: Thomson Delmar Learning, 2004

Stephane Duperray and Raphaele Vidaling, *Front Page: Covers of the Twentieth Century*, London: Weidenfeld and Nicolson, 2003

Roger Fawcett-Tang (ed.), *Experimental Formats: Books, Brochures, Catalogues* Crans-Près-Céligny, Switzerland and Hove, Sussex: RotoVision, 2001

Peter Feierabend and Hans Heiermann, *Best of Graphis: Editorial*, Zurich: Graphis Press, 1993; Corte Madera, California: Gingko Press, 1995

Chris Foges (ed.), *Magazine Design*, Crans-Près-Céligny, Switzerland and Hove, Sussex: RotoVision, 1999

Sammye Johnson and Patricia Prijatel, *The Magazine from Cover to Cover: Inside a Dynamic Industry*, Lincolnwood, Illinois: NTC, 1999

Stacey King, *Magazine Design That Works: Secrets for Successful Magazine Design*, Gloucester, Massachusetts: Rockport Publishers, 2001

Jeremy Leslie, foreword by Lewis Blackwell, *Issues: New Magazine Design*, London: Laurence King Publishing Ltd, and Corte Madera, California: Gingko Press, 2000

Jeremy Leslie (ed.), *MagCulture: New Magazine Design*, London: Laurence King Publishing Ltd, and New York: HarperCollins, 2003

Jeremy Leslie (ed.), *The Modern Magazine: Visual Journalism in the Digital Era*, London: Laurence King Publishing Ltd, 2013

Horst Moser, *Surprise Me: Editorial Design*, translated from the German by David H. Wilson, West New York, New Jersey: Mark Batty Publisher, 2003

William Owen, *Magazine Design*, London: Laurence King Publishing Ltd, 1991

B. Martin Pedersen (ed.), *Graphis Magazine Design*, volume 1, New York: Graphis Press, 1997

Jan V. White, *Designing for Magazines: Common Problems, Realistic Solutions*, revised edition, New York: Bowker, 1982

Jan V. White, *Editing by Design: For Designers, Art Directors and Editors – The Classic Guide to Winning Readers*, New York: Allworth Press, 2003

Kaoru Yamashita and Maya Kishida (eds.), *Magazine Editorial Graphics*, Tokyo: PIE Books, 1997

Typography

Phil Baines and Andrew Haslam, *Type and Typography*, London: Laurence King Publishing Ltd and New York: Watson-Guptill Publications, 2002; revised edition, 2005

Andreu Balius, *Type at Work: The Use of Type in Editorial Design*, Corte Madera, California: Gingko Press, 2003

Robert Bringhurst, *The Elements of Typographic Style*, Vancouver: Hartley and Marks, 1997

Carl Dair, *Design with Type*, Toronto: University of Toronto Press, 2000

Steven Heller and Mirko Ilic, *Handwritten: Expressive Lettering in the Digital Age*, London and New York: Thames & Hudson, 2004

David Jury, *About Face: Reviving the Rules of Typography*, Hove, Sussex: RotoVision, and Gloucester, Massachusetts: Rockport Publishers, 2002

Ellen Lupton, *Thinking with Type: A Critical Guide for Designers, Writers, Editors, & Students*, New York: Princeton Architectural Press, 2004

Ruari McLean, *The Thames & Hudson Manual of Typography*, London and New York: Thames and Hudson, 1980; reprinted 1997

Rick Poynor (ed.), *Typography Now: The Next Wave*, London: Booth-Clibborn Editions, 1991

Andrew Robinson, *The Story of Writing: Alphabets, Hieroglyphs and Pictograms*, London and New York: Thames and Hudson, 1995

Erik Spiekermann and E. M. Ginger, *Stop Stealing Sheep & Find Out How Type Works*, Berkeley, California: Adobe Press, 1993; second edition, 2002

There are many great sources for typographic inspiration on the web. The photo-sharing website Flickr (www.flickr.com) has numerous groups devoted to type, such as the excellent Typography and Lettering group to be found at: www.flickr.com/groups/type.

Layouts

Gavin Ambrose and Paul Harris, *Layout*, Lausanne: AVA Publishing, 2005

David E. Carter, *The Little Book of Layouts: Good Designs and Why They Work*, New York: Harper Design, 2003

David Dabner, *Graphic Design School: The Principles and Practices of Graphic Design*, London and New York: Thames & Hudson, 2004

Kimberly Elam, *Grid Systems: Principles of Organizing Type*, New York: Princeton Architectural Press, 2004

Gail Deibler Finke, *White Graphics: The Power of White in Graphic Design*, Gloucester, Massachusetts: Rockport Publishers, 2003

Allen Hurlburt, *The Grid: A Modular System for the Design and Production of Newspapers, Magazines and Books*, New York: John Wiley, 1982

Carolyn Knight and Jessica Glaser, *Layout: Making It Fit – Finding the Right Balance Between Content and Space*, Gloucester, Massachusetts: Rockport Publishers, 2003

Lucienne Roberts, *The Designer and the Grid*, Hove, Sussex: RotoVision, 2002

Timothy Samara, *Making and Breaking the Grid: A Graphic Design Layout Workshop*, Gloucester, Massachusetts: Rockport Publishers, 2003

Imagery

Gavin Ambrose, *Image*, Lausanne: AVA Publishing, 2005

Charlotte Cotton, *The Photograph as Contemporary Art*, London and New York: Thames & Hudson, 2004

Geoff Dyer, *The Ongoing Moment*, London: Little Brown, and New York: Pantheon Books, 2005

Angus Hyland and Roanne Bell, *Hand to Eye: Contemporary Illustration*, London: Laurence King Publishing Ltd, 2003

John Ingledew, *Photography*, London: Laurence King Publishing, 2013

Scott Kelby, *The Photoshop CS2 Book for Digital Photographers*, Indianapolis, Indiana: New Riders, 2003

Robert Klanten and Hendrik Hellige (eds.), *Illusive: Contemporary Illustration and its Context*, Berlin: Die Gestalten, 2005

Gunther Kress and Theo van Leeuwen, *Reading Images: The Grammar of Visual Design*, London and New York: Routledge, 1996

Susan Sontag, *On Photography*, New York: Farrar Straus and Giroux, 1977; London: Allen Lane, 1978

Susan Sontag, *Regarding the Pain of Others*, New York: Farrar Straus and Giroux, and London: Hamish Hamilton, 2003

Julius Wiedemann, *Illustration Now!*, Cologne: Taschen, 2005

Lawrence Zeegen, *The Fundamentals of Illustration*, Lausanne: AVA Publishing, 2005

Inspiration

Lewis Blackwell and Lorraine Wild, *Edward Fella: Letters on America*, London: Laurence King Publishing Ltd, and New York: Princeton Architectural Press, 2000

Lewis Blackwell and David Carson, *The End of Print: The Grafik Design of David Carson*, revised edition, London: Laurence King Publishing Ltd, 2012

David Carson, *Trek: David Carson – Recent Werk*, Corte Madera, California: Gingko Press, 2003

David Crowley, *Magazine Covers*, London: Mitchell Beazley (Octopus Publishing Group Ltd), 2006

Alan Fletcher, *The Art of Looking Sideways*, London: Phaidon Press, 2001

Richard Hollis, *Swiss Graphic Design: The Origins and Growth of an International Style, 1920–1965*, London: Laurence King Publishing Ltd, and New Haven, Connecticut: Yale University Press, 2006

Cees W. de Jong and Alston W. Purvis, *Dutch Graphic Design: A Century of Innovation*, London and New York: Thames & Hudson, 2006

Tibor Kalman and Maira Kalman, *Colors: Issues 1–13*, New York: Harry N. Abrams, 2002

Barbara Kruger, *Barbara Kruger*, Cambridge, Massachusetts: MIT Press, 1999

Beryl McAlhone and David Stuart, *A Smile in the Mind*, revised edition, London: Phaidon Press, 1998

The Society for News Design, *The Best of Newspaper Design 27*, Gloucester, Massachusetts: Rockport Publishers Inc., 2006

Martin Venezky, *It Is Beautiful … Then Gone*, New York: Princeton Architectural Press, 2005

Printing and colour use

Josef Albers, *Interaction of Color*, revised and expanded edition, New Haven, Connecticut: Yale University Press, 2006

Leatrice Eiseman, *Pantone Guide to Communicating with Color*, Cincinnati, Ohio: Grafix Press, 2000

Mark Gatter, *Production for Print*, London: Laurence King Publishing Ltd, 2010

Johannes Itten, *The Art of Color: The Subjective Experience and Objective Rationale of Color*, revised edition, New York and Chichester: John Wiley & Sons Inc., 1997

Naomi Kuno and FORMS Inc./Color Intelligence Institute, *Colors in Context*, Tokyo: Graphic-sha Publishing, 1999

Alan Pipes, *Production for Graphic Designers*, fifth edition, London: Laurence King Publishing Ltd, 2009

Michael Rogondino and Pat Rogondino, *Process Colour Manual: 24,000 CMYK Combinations for Design, Prepress and Printing*, San Francisco: Chronicle Books, 2000

Lesa Sawahata, *Color Harmony Workbook: A Workbook and Guide to Creative Color Combinations*, Gloucester, Massachusetts: Rockport Publishers Inc., 2001

Journalism and communication

Harold Evans, *Editing and Design*, five volumes, London: William Heinneman (Random House Group Ltd), 1972–1978

Harold Evans, *Essential English for Journalists, Editors and Writers*, London: Pimlico (Random House Group Ltd), 2000

Stephen Quinn, *Digital Sub-Editing and Design*, Oxford: Focal Press (Elsevier Ltd), 2001

Mike Sharples, *How We Write: Writing as Creative Design*, Oxford: Routledge (Taylor & Francis Books Ltd), 1998

General design books

Joshua Berger and Sarah Dougher, *100 Habits of Successful Graphic Designers: Insider Secrets on Working Smart and Staying Creative*, Gloucester, Massachusetts: Rockport Publishers Inc., 2003

Charlotte Fiell and Peter Fiell, *Graphic Design Now*, Cologne: Taschen, 2005

Lisa Graham, *Basics of Design: Layout and Typography for Beginners*, Clifton Park, New York: Thomson Delmar Learning, 2001

Richard Hollis, *A Concise History of Graphic Design*, revised edition, London and New York: Thames & Hudson, 2002

Johannes Itten, *Design and Form: The Basic Course at the Bauhaus*, revised edition, London: Thames & Hudson, 1975

Michael Johnson, *Problem Solved: A Primer in Design and Communication*, London: Phaidon Press, 2002

Ellen Lupton and J. Abbott Miller, *Design Writing Research. Writing on Graphic Design*, New York: Kiosk Press, 1996

Quentin Newark, *What Is Graphic Design?*, Gloucester, Massachusetts: Rockport Publishers Inc., and Hove, Sussex: RotoVision, 2002

Rick Poynor, *Design Without Boundaries. Visual Communication in the Nineties*, London: Booth-Clibborn Editions, 2000

Adrian Shaughnessy, *How to Be a Graphic Designer, Without Losing Your Soul*, second edition, London: Laurence King Publishing Ltd, 2010

Edward R. Tufte, *Visual Explanations. Images and Quantities, Evidence and Narrative*, Cheshire, Connecticut: Graphics Press, 1997

Index

Page numbers in *italics* refer to captions

About Town 80, 173 see also Town
Abrahams, Stefan *151*
Adbusters 30, 62, 65, 81
Adobe Creative Suite 19, 186 *see also* InDesign; Photoshop
Aeon Magazine 229
Agha, M.F. 207, 209, 214
Amelia's Magazine 186
Anderson, Gail 219
Anorak 47, 126
Another Magazine 183
Ansel, Ruth *102*
apps 23, 24, 29, 37, 47, 59, 165, 167, 224, 226
Arena 73
Arment, Marco 227
art directors/editors 14, 18, 21, 32–3, 60, 99, 128, 153, 165, 196
Arthr (Newspaper Club) 227
Autukaite, Sandra *202*

Bar, Noma *42*
Barnes, Paul *180*
Baron, Fabien 55, *84,* 179, 217
Bass, Saul 148
Bauhaus 139, 140, 179, 206
Beach Culture 55, 57, 179
Belknap, John 21
Benezri, Kobi *199*
BERG Design *164,* 186, 227, 230
Big 221
Black, Roger 156
Blah Blah Blah 70
Blitz 56, 124, 126
blogs 35, 48, 60, 91, 124, 126, 146, 206
Bloomberg Businessweek 32–3, 190
Blueprint 146
body copy 8, *83,* 85, 87, 88, *90,* 96, 114, 116–17
Bonnier R&D 164
Boston Globe 29, 59, 219
Boston Sunday Globe 46
box copy 82, 88, 90, 121, 140, 176
branding 35, 42, 57
    covers 30, 41, 42, 44, 44, 45, 47, *50, 57,* 65, 98
    logos 42, 69–70, *85*
    style 35, 42, 73, 83, 91, 141, 142, 143, 156
    supplements *31,* 34, *85*
    typography 42, 88, 177, *182,* 183
    see also identity
Brodovitch, Alexey 50, 179, 208, 211, 214
Brody, Neville 55, 57, *82,* 92, *97,* 141, 179, 206, 216
Brown, James *64*
Brûlé, Tyler 10, 232
budget issues 34, 97–8, 127, 128, 188, 197
Burrill, Anthony 48
Business 2.0 82
business-to-business (B2B) magazines 35
bylines *27,* 87, *88, 110, 113,* 114, 121, 163, *177*

captions *88,* 89, 90, 98, *110,* 120–1, *166,* 174
Carlos 36, 62, *103,* 104, *145*

Carson, David 55, 57, 70, 91, *115, 122,* 141, *173, 178,* 179, 221
Chambers, Tony 10
Charm 209
City Limits 56, 216
Cleland, Thomas Maitland 190
collage *50, 64,* 215
Colors 18, 218, 220
colour printing *27,* 34, 50, 52, 55, 57, 187, 188, 190
colour selection *37,* 42, *46,* 72, 85, 92
columns *27,* 83, 96, 110, *113,* 114, 130, *150,* 158, 160, 163
Condé Nast 24, 50, 52, 68, 207, 209, 224
Constructivism *70, 82, 97,* 179, 206, 207, 208, 216
consumer magazines 30, 35, 57, 60, 125–6, 172
Cook, Gary 82, *127*
copy *see* body copy; box copy; panel copy
Corbin, Lee 143–4, *173,* 183, *185,* 198
Cottrell, Ivan *182*
cover lines 30, 47, 55, *64,* 69, 70, 73, *86*
covers 41, 44
    abstract 65–6
    and branding 30, 41, 42, 44, 44, *45,* 47, *50, 57,* 65, 98
    brief 74–5
    celebrity covers 55, *56,* 57, 59
    components *64,* 69–73
    custom-made 48–9, *65*
    design approaches 62–7
    development of 50–61
    digital media 41, 44, 47, 60, 68, 98
    figurative 62–3, *65*
    importance of 44, 50, 52, 98
    logos *50,* 62, *64,* 65, 66, 69–70, 73, 86
    magazines 44, 47, 50–7, 59
    newspapers 45, *101*
    photography 50, 52–3, 55, 62, *64*
    supplements 52, 55
    text-based 66–7
Creative Review 124, 126, 143
credits 87, *88, 110, 121 see also* picture credits
cross-heads *see* subheads
customer magazines 35, 36, 57, 124

Dadaism *97, 115,* 179, 208, 216
Dadich, Scott 68, 224
Dagens Nyheter (DN) 130, 174
Daily Mirror 163, 174
Dazed & Confused 48, *57,* 62, *139*
deadlines 127, 128–9, 154, 187, 190, 194
design directors 14, 21
design skills 7, 95
    artwork skills 153, 186–7 *see also* images
    brief 202–3
    concepts 38–9, 153, *157, 190*
    consistency 153, 194, 197
    digital design 32, 160, 164–5, 168
    monotony, avoiding 135, 153, 156, 194, 197, 201
    production issues 153, 186–7
    visualization 153, 154
    see also page design; typography
Deuchars, Marion *102*
digital media 24–5

automated content 60, 227
covers 41, 44, 47, 60, 68, 98
data availability 229
digital design 32, 160, 164–5, 168
finite publishing 227, 229
the future 226, 227, 229, 230, 232
grids 126, *151,* 160, *161, 162*
magazines 19, 20, 29, 36–7, 59, 164, 166, 224, 226 *see also* named magazines
navigation 8, 16, 29, 60, 160, 164, 166–7, *168*
newspapers 28, 29, 59, 166, 167 *see also* named newspapers
print crossover 227
print media compared 29, 124–5, 126
responsive design 226–7
terminology 29
see also tablets; websites
Diprose, Andrew and Philip 12, *47*
Dixon, Chris 81
Docherty, Jeffrey *133, 158, 182*
Doll, Evan 227
Domus 146
Douglas, Sarah 10, 12–13, 167
Draper, Richard *191*
Driver, David *191*
drop caps *34,* 92, *110, 116,* 117–18, *123,* 140, *174, 179*
Duff-Smith, Rebecca *151*
Dvorani, Jetmire *75*

Eat 105
The Economist 31, 143, *194*
Editions 37
editorial, defined 7, 8
editorial design
    defined 7, 8
    design factors 18, 129–38
    designers 18, 98 *see also* design skills
    the future 226–9, 232–3
    key staff 14, 18–21
    the past, exploring 205, 206
    purpose 8, 10, 18
editors 14, 18, 21, 60, 92, 98
Edwards, Neil *48*
Elle 53, 225
Ellis, Darren (Sea Studio) *104*
Emigre 55, 91, 99, *173, 178*
ES Magazine (Evening Standard) 218
Esopus 136, 186
Esquire 50, 52, 66, 211
Esterson, Simon (Esterson Associates) 15, 35, 146–7, 229
Eureka magazine *(The Times)* 92, *168*
Evans, Harold 27
Expressionism 208, 214, 216
Eye 146, 229

The Face 55, *82, 97,* 126, 141, 179, 206, 216
Facebook 37, 44, 206, 225
Fact 66
fanzines 30, 48, *103, 145*
Fassett's theorem of legible line length 114, 156, 158, *159*
Feltier, Bea *102*
Financiele Dagblad 218
Fire & Knives 48, 126
Fishwrap 112, 116, 121, 176

Flaunt 69, 89, 123, 139, 143–4, *171, 173,* 183, *185,* 198
Fleckhaus, Willy 18, *84,* 212, *213*
Flipboard 37, 60, *61,* 227, *228*
fold-outs *186, 187*
Folha de S. Paulo 142, *192*
folios *88,* 90–1, *110,* 121, *172*
fonts
    digital media 24, 55, 91, 92
    print media 50, 82, *90,* 91, 92, 172, *176,* 177, *178, 199*
Fortune 190
Frankfurter Allgemeine Magazin (FAZ) 212
Frere-Jones, Toby *178,* 183
Froelich, Janet *24,* 34, *65, 66, 70, 79, 114, 116, 117, 123, 135, 149, 178,* 188, 222–3, 233
Frost, Vince 8, 18, 57, *59, 64, 115,* 117, 179, *181,* 182, 221
FT The Business Magazine 70, 82, 101, *127, 183,* 221

Garcia, Mario *31,* 45, *46,* 97, 134–5, *142,* 144, *172,* 200
Gentile, Massimo *142*
Glamour 173, 209
golden section 134
Goodchild, Jon 215
GPS (Global Positioning System) 8, 16, 28, 29, 37, 229
GQ 24, 73, 217
Graphic International 121
Grazia 225
grids 55, *80, 84,* 85, 110, *127,* 135, *151,* 155–62, 212
The Guardian 15–17, *45,* 59, *60, 101, 102,* 103, 124, 146, *155,* 160, *162, 164,* 177, 183, *192,* 218, 232
Gustafson, Mats 70, 217
Gutiérrez, Fernando 65–6, *73,* 156, *182, 185,* 220

Hackett, Dennis 214
Hall, Alistair (We Made This) *49*
Harper's Bazaar 50, 70, *102,* 179, 208, 211, 217
Harrison-Twist, Jordan 108
headings *13,* 113–14, 119, 128, *162,* 165, 174, *203 see also* subheads
headlines 8, *13, 16, 26,* 45, *64, 83,* 87, *88, 89,* 96, *110,* 113–14, *131,* 173–4, *175 see also* running headlines
Hill, Jon 92–5, 160, *161, 168,* 229
Hillman, David 15, 18, 146, *178,* 214
Holley, Lisa Wagner *176*
Hort 48
House & Garden 207
Huck 47
the human eye and how it scans a page *128*

ICC Profile 187
icons 81, 82, *119, 192*
i-D 48, 55, 62, 124
I.D. 104, *105, 137, 138, 199*
identity 14, 15, 28, 34, *36,* 42, 47, 110, 197 *see also* branding
The Illustrated Ape 104
Illustrated News 52
illustration *48,* 62, *63, 91, 102,* 103–4
images
    bleeding 85, *123*
    cropping *8, 100,* 104, 122, *138, 185,*

194
    cut-outs *27, 64,* 85, 201
    finding 98–9, 190, 194
    full-bleed *8,* 66, 83, 85, *98,* 136
    importance of 98, 121, 122, 188
    from the Internet 98–9, 190, 194
    originals, evaluating 188, 190
    and text combination 99, 122, *133, 175*
    working with 97–8, 121–2, *123,* 188–94
    see also illustration; photography
The Independent on Saturday 64, 221
independent publications 14, 30, 32, 47
InDesign (Adobe) 21, 167, 183, 186, 226
infographics 14, 28, 190–3
initial caps *116,* 117–18, *178*
Inner Loop 113, *182*
Inside 158, *182, 197*
Instapaper 29, 227
International Style 212
interns 19
Interview 53, 70, 217
intros *see* stand-firsts
iPads 10, 16, 23, 24, 68, *99,* 124, 160, 226, 229
iPhones 20, 60, 94

The Jewish Chronicle 21
Jones, Dylan 18
Jones, Jasmine *151*
Joyce, James 48
jumplines *119,* 120, *142*
junior designers 19, 85

Kalman, Tibor 18, 220
King, David 52, *56*
King, Scott 66
Kitching, Alan *183,* 221
Kuhr, Barbara 65, 68

Lappin, Criswell *80, 100,* 103, *122, 135, 137,* 140, 143, *157, 177*
Lasn, Kalle 81
Lawyer 35
layouts *197*
    alignment *110, 113,* 116, 135, 139
    balance *27,* 114, 129, 130, *133,* 134, 137, *139, 150, 185*
    brief 150–1
    colour, use of *110,* 128, *131,* 134–5, 137, *145, 197*
    components 110–19, 143–4
    construction 127–38
    contrast 85, *113,* 136, 145
    depth *83, 123,* 137, *171*
    discord *117,* 130, 139, 140–1 *see also* tension *below*
    flow 78, 130, 135, *197*
    format 129, 143, *145,* 155, 172, *173, 176*
    harmony 122, 130, 135, 139–41, 144, *182*
    inspiration, finding *50, 79, 115,* 148
    leading 110, *114,* 116, 139, 174, 179
    movement, implied *83, 98, 105, 123,* 138
    placement issues 73, *112, 131, 132,* 139, 155
    repetition *54,* 135

scale issues *27, 42*, 98, 110, 135–6, *185*
shape 82, *90, 113*, 114, 116, 130, 134–5, 145
spatial issues 124, 129–30, *131, 132 see also* white space
stock 143, *145*, 155, 170–2, *176*
structure 143
tension 110, 122, *123*, 135, *136*, 139 *see also* discord *above*
type/typefaces *110, 112*, 114, *133*, 134, 143–4
see also grids; page design; style
Leeds, Mark 225
Leslie, Jeremy 10, 35, *63*, 66, *103*, 124–6, *145*, 154, 168, 227, 232
Libération 217
Licko, Zusanna *55*
Liebermann, Alexander 50, 52
Life 52
Little Printer (BERG) 227, 230
Loaded 64, 73, *83*, 87, *128*
Logan, Nick *82*, 124
logos
  branding 42, 69–70, *85*
  covers *50*, 62, *64*, 65, 66, 69–70, 73, 86
  typography *34*, 70, 73
Lois, George 66
Lowe, Rob *48*
Lubalin, Herb 66

M-real 35, *63*, 124, 143, *169*
MacUser 55
Mag+ software (BERG and Bonier) *165*, 230
The Magazine 227
magazines 8, 14, 18, 23, 30–7
  automated content 60, 227
  back sections 78, 85–6
  contents pages 78–81, *82*
  covers 44, 47, 50–7, 59
  digital 19, 20, 29, 36–7, 59, 164, 166, 224, 226
  feature well 78, 81, 83–5
  front sections 78, 82
  independent publications 14, 30, 32, 47
  news pages 78, 81, 82
  section openers *85*, 86
  typography 55, *57*, 70, *82*, 83, 173–4
  see also named magazines; supplements
magCulture 124, 126
Magdalinski, Stef 232
Marchbank, Pearce *64*, 66
Marie Claire 73, 225
Marshall, Joseph *150, 151*
Martinesva, Esa 19
mastheads 38, 47, 69, 82, 96 *see also* logos
Matador 143, 156, 220
McCall's 179
McCue, Mike 227
McNay, Mike 15
Metropolis 80, 100, 103, 122, 135, *137*, 140, *157*, *177*
mobile devices *see* mobile phones; tablets
mobile phones 14, 16, 23, 60 *see also* iPhones
Modernism *122*, 208, 210, 211
Monocle 126, 232

montage 62, *191*, 207
Morla, Jennifer *65*
Murray, Peter 146

navigation
  digital media 8, *16*, 29, 60, 160, 164, 166–7, *168*
  print media *27*, 78, 81, 91, 121
Neal, Christopher *103*
Nest 70
Net-a-Porter 20, *166*
The New York Times 24, 47, *113*, 227, 232
The New York Times Magazine 32, *34*, *65*, *66*, *70*, *79*, *90*, *102*, *114*, *116*, *117*, 135, *136*, *149*, *159*, *178*, *188*, 222
The New York Times Style Magazine 34, *70*, 222
The New York Times T: Travel Magazine 85, *123*
The New Yorker 59, 224
Newspaper Club 29, 227
newspapers 8, 18, 21, 23, 26–8
  Berliner format 15, 28, 130, 160, *172*, *200*
  broadsheet format 15, 28, 57, *172*, *200*
  content 78, 82
  covers 45, *101*
  digital media 28, 29, 59, 166, 167
  horizontal and vertical design *27*, *45*, 130, *162*
  sizes 28
  tabloid format 15, *27*, 28, 130, *172*
  typography 15, 16, *27*, 28, *47*, 92, 174, 176, 177, *180*
  websites 57, 166
  see also named newspapers; supplements
Newsweek 29
Nova 10, 53, 70, *178*, 179, 214
NZZ 146

The Observer 134–5, *200*
The Observer Music Monthly 112
Oh Comely 47
Oliver, Vaughan 57
Oz 10, *52*, 215

page design 153, 155
  digital design 164–5
  double-page spreads (DPS) 52, 53, 110, 150–1
  flatplans 14, 155, 163, 168–9
  format 143, *145*, 155, *172*, *173*, *176*
  gutters 96, 110
  pagination 155, 162–3, 168, *169*, 194
  signalling *16, 34, 113, 131, 132, 162*, 163
  stock selection 143, *145*, 155, 170–2, *176*
  templates 82, 85, 110–11, 162, 167, 197
  see also grids
page furniture *64*, 82, 90, *165*, 216
El Pais 45, 65–6, *89*, *113*, 220
panel copy *27*, 88, 90, 121
paper, selecting 170–2
Pariscope 145
Het Parool 118, *128*
Patterson, Christian *104*
paywalls 29, 57, 92, 229

Peccinotti, Harri 179, 214
Per lui 216
photography 99–101
  close-ups *63*, 104, *105*
  covers 50, 52–3, 55, 62, *64*
  reportage 16, 52, 55, 96, *130, 131*, 212, 214, 220
  selecting photographs 99, *101*, 188
Photoshop (Adobe) 20, 186, *188*, 190
picture credits 98–9, 121, 194
picture editors 14, 99, 101
Pineles, Cipe 209
Plunkett, John 65, 68
Pop 63
Port 19, 47
Porter, Mark 14, 15, 16, 18, 27–8, 32, *45*, 103, 130, 160, 166, 177, *180*, 198, 218
print media
  digital crossover 227
  digital media compared 29, 124–5, 126
  fonts 50, 82, *90*, 91, 92, 172, *176*, 177, *178*, *199*
  the future 29, 206, 229, 232
  navigation *27*, 78, 81, 91, 121
  see also magazines; newspapers
printing and printers 47, 52, 55, 57, 96, 143, 187, 188
Pritchard, Meirion 10, 12–13, 24, 48–9
production managers 14, 18, 162
proofs/proofing 14, 57, 128, 185, 186, 188
Publico *27*, 146, 218
pull quotes 85, 87, *88, 89*, 110, 118–19, 163, *174, 175, 176, 179*

QuarkXPress 21, 167, 183, 186
Queen 179
quotes 118 *see also* pull quotes

Radio Times 190, *191*
RayGun 55, 57, 70, 91, 99, 141, 179
Read, Steve *64, 83*
Real Simple 36, *37*, 222, 233
redesigning 15, 32, 45, *142*, 146, 198, 200
The RiDE Journal 12, 47
Ripoli, Paula *142*
Robinson, Nigel 48
Roinestad, Eric 148
Rolleri, Dan 196
Rolling Stone 53, *55*, 219
rules 81, 82, 86, 119, 121, 134, 135, *172*, *175*
running headlines *88*, 119, *128*, 139, 140
Ryan, Rob *186*

Salomi *38, 39*
San Francisco Chronicle Magazine 31
Schulze, Jack *164*, 227, 230–1, 232
Schwartz, Christian *180*
Schweizer, Nico *199*
screen calibration 186, 190
Self 217
Self Service 126
sells *see* stand-firsts
Seventeen 209
Sharp, Martin *52*, 215
Shively, Hudson *151*

Show 211
sidebars 88, 121, 135, 138
Silvertown, Ben *203*
Sims, Michael *104*
Sleazenation 57, 66, *80*
slugs *13*, 120
social magazines 37, *61*, 229
social media 35, 47, 48, 146, 167, 194, 227, 229, 232, 233 *see also* Facebook; Twitter
soDA 143, *145, 157, 171*
Speak 90, 91, *115*, 141, 179, *181*, 196
Der Spiegel 53
spines 73, 110, 122, *136*
Stack Magazines 47
stand-firsts 83, 85, 87, *88*, *110*, 114
Stark, Gemma 20
Statements 143
Stern 194, *201*
Storch, Otto 179
straplines 119, 209
studio managers 18, 166
style
  advertising style 144
  and branding 35, 42, 73, 83, 91, 141, 142, 143, 156
  defined 142
  design style 143–4
  editorial style 143
  house style 83, 197
  style sheets 21, 82, 106–7, 114, 197, 201
sub-decks *see* stand-firsts
subeditors 14, 21, 87, 114, 118, 129, 160, 185
subheads 87, *110, 114*, 118, 158, *175*
Substance UK 70
Sudic, Deyan 146
The Sunday Times Magazine 34
SuperCal (BERG) 186
supplements 23, *31*, 34, 52, 55, 65 *see also* named supplements
Sykes, Suzanne 225

tablets 23, 230
  development of 23, 59, 60, 226
  importance of 10, 14, 16, 19, 29
  navigation 16, 60, 166, *167*
  see also iPads
tag-lines *64*, 87, 117
Tang, Kam 48
Tank 173
Tentaciones (El Pais) 65–6, 220
Texas Monthly 224
3D techniques *171, 186*
Time Out 64, 66, *67*, 124
The Times 26, 92, 160, *161, 168, 192*, 229, *233*
Toscani, Oliviero 220
Town (prev. *About Town*) 179, 210
Turley, Richard 32–3, 218
turn arrows *119*, 120
Turner, Jim *69, 171*
turns *45*
Twen 53, *80, 84*, 100, *119*, 187, 212, *213*
Twitter 12, 32, 37, 126, 146, 206, 227, 229
type/typefaces
  capitals *see* drop caps; initial caps

custom-designed 183, *185, 199*
  expressive use of 177, 179, *181, 182*, 216, 221
  finding 182
  in layouts *110, 112*, 114, *133*, 134, 143–4
  myths about 96
  selecting 70, *112*, 139, 143–4, 156, 173–7, *184*
  serif *vs.* sans serif 118, 121, 139, 174, 176, *180*
  woodblock 70, 182, *184*, 221
  see also fonts
typography 86–91, 95, 96
  branding 42, 88, 177, *182*, 183
  brief 106–7
  digital media 29, 86, 91, 92, *161*
  digital techniques 48, 55, 57, 59, 183, 185
  interpreting text 116–17, 179, *181, 182*, 217
  letterpress 182, *183*, 221
  logos *34*, 70, 73
  magazines 55, *57*, 70, *82*, 83, 173–4
  newspapers 15, 16, *27*, 28, *47*, 92, 174, 176, 177, *180*
  playing with 70, *117*, 177, 179, 219
  style sheets 106–7, 197
  supplements *31, 34, 90*
  see also fonts; type/typefaces

VanderLans, Rudy *55*, 91
Vanidad 73, *182, 185*, 220
Vanity Fair 24, 73, 207
Venezky, Martin 10, 87, *90*, 91, *115*, 121–2, 141, 148, 179, *181*, 182, 196, 197, 198
Visionaire 143
Vogue 50, 55, *59*, 73, 179, 207, 217
Vogue Paris 84, *173*, 217

WAD 65, 87
*Wallpaper** 10–13, *42*, 48–9, 73, 87, *98, 99*, 167
Warhol, Andy *53*
Watson, Steve 47
Watts, Michael 99, 101
the web 8, 21, 24, 59, 82, 98–9, *119* *see also* websites
Webb, Matt 230
websites 23, 24, 29, 44, 57, 95, 166, 226–7 *see also* named websites
Weekend magazine (*The Guardian*) 218
Weidmann, Micha *67*
white space 15, *46*, 83, *84*, 85, 99, 114, 129, 130, *135*, 201
WIRED 12, 18, 24, 59, 65, 68, 82, 190, 218, 224
Wolf, Henry 50, 70, 211
Wolsey, Tom 179, 210
Woodward, Fred 219

Zembla 59, *79*, *115*, 117, 179, *181, 184*, 221
zines 30, 48

Picture Credits

6, 73, 182b, 185b, 204, 220 Courtesy Fernando Gutiérrez; 8, 65tr Courtesy *WAD* magazine; 9tl, 86 Courtesy *Numéro* magazine; 9tr *Paper Sky*; 9bl Courtesy Time Out Group, August 11-18 1993, no. 1199; 9br *FT Business* cover 26.02.00. Photographer: Gareth Munden; 11-13, 49, 98 Courtesy *Wallpaper** magazine; 14 Photographer: Cath Caldwell; 15 © Guardian News & Media Ltd 2013; 16t © Guardian News & Media Ltd 2013. Photographers: Darren Kidd and Erci Ogden / Retna; 16b © Guardian News & Media Ltd 2013. Photograph © www.lfi.co.uk; 17, 162, 165t © Guardian News & Media Ltd 2013. Courtesy Mark Porter. Creative Director: Mark Porter@ Mark Porter Associates. Designers: Andy Brockie, Barry Ainslie; 19, 99, 102bl, 125b Courtesy: *Port* magazine. Designer: Jeremy Leslie. Coding: Tim Moore. Design Assistant: Esa Matinvesi; 20 Courtesy Gemma Stark, Net-a-Porter; 21 Courtesy John Belknap, *Jewish Chronicle*; 22, 34tr, 34b, 65bl, 65br, 66r, 79r, 85b, 90, 113br, 114, 116b, 117, 123t, 135, 136t, 149, 159, 178t, 189 *The New York Times Magazine*. Courtesy Janet Froelich; 25, 37bl, 37br *Real Simple* magazine. Courtesy Janet Froelich; 26, 92-94, 160-161, 168, 193, 232 Courtesy Jon Hill, *The Times*; 27, 199tr, 218 *Publico*: Creative Directors: Mark Porter and Simon Esterson. *Publico* Design Director: Sonia Matos; 30, 62, 65tl Courtesy www.adbusters. org; 31t Courtesy *San Francisco Chronicle Magazine* February 12 2006 A Serosorting Story by Christopher Heredia; 31b © *The Economist Newspaper* Limited, London, November 17, 2012; 32 Creative Director: Richard Turley. Photo Illustrator: Justin Metz; 33t Creative Director: Richard Turley. Graphics Director: Jennifer Daniel; 33bl Creative Director: Richard Turley. Illustrator: David Folvari; 33br Creative Director: Richard Turley. Illustrator: Noma Bar; 34tl *The New York Times Magazine*. Courtesy Janet Froelich. Photographer: Raymond Meier; 35, 63l, 169b Courtesy *M-real* magazine. Graphics Director: Richard Turley; 36, 103t, 144 Courtesy *Carlos* magazine; 37tl, 37tr, 60-61, 228 Courtesy *Flipboard*; 38-39 Designer and Photographer: Salomi Desai (sdesai1.workflow.arts.ac.uk); 40, 42-43 Courtesy *Wallpaper** magazine. Illustrator: Noma Bar; 44, 89b, 113bl Courtesy *El Pais*; 45 © Guardian News & Media Ltd 2013. Photograph: Reuters / Namir Noor-Eldeen; 46 *Boston Sunday Globe*; 47 Courtesy Andrew Diprose, *The Ride Journal*. ILoveDust / Shan Jiang; 48t Courtesy *Fire & Knives*. Art Director: Rob Lowe. Illustrator: Marie Claire-Bridges. Editor: Tim Hayward; 48b Courtesy *Pop Sox* Designed and printed by Mr Edwards; 50, 66l Images courtesy of *Esquire* magazine / Hearst Corporation; 51, 102t, 208, 211, 217tl Images courtesy of *Harper's Bazaar* magazine / Hearst Corporation; 52, 215 Courtesy Hapshash and the Coloured Coat; 53 *Interview* magazine, August 1972, Liza Minelli. Photographer: Berry Berenson. Designer: Richard Bernstein. Courtesy Brandt Publications, Inc.; 54 Cover image by Annie Leibovitz, *Rolling Stone*, No. 335, January 22, 1981, © Rolling Stone LLC 1981. All Rights Reserved. Reprinted by Permission; 55, 172b, 179b Designer: Rudy VanderLans / *Emigre*; 56l Courtesy Jeremy Leslie; 56r David King Collection. Designer: David King; 57t Courtesy *Dazed & Confused*. Photographer: Rankin; 57b, 81b ©www.PYMCA.com; 58 Photographer: Lachlan Bailey, MAO/Model: Magdalena/*Vogue Paris*/ Vogue.fr © Condé Nast Publications Ltd; 59, 78-79, 115t, 181t, 184, 221 Courtesy Vince Frost, Frost Design. Editor: Dan Crowe. Creative Director: Vince Frost. Designer: Matt Willey; 63r Courtesy *Pop* magazine; 64tl, 83, 128 Courtesy *Loaded* magazine / Blue Publishing Ltd; 64tr Courtesy Time Out Group, January 13-19 1978, no. 406; 64br, 172tl Courtesy *The Independent*; 67l ©www.PYMCA. com. Art Directior and Designer: Scott King and Earl Brutus; 67r Courtesy Time Out Group, December 14-21 2005, no. 1843; 68 Courtesy Scott Dadich. *WIRED* © Condé Nast Publications Ltd; 69, 89t, 123b, 139t, 170r, 185tl, 185tr Courtesy *Flaunt* magazine; 70tl, 71 *The New York Times Magazine*. Courtesy Janet Froelich. Photographer: James Wojcik; 70tr *The New York Times Magazine*. Courtesy Janet Froelich. T by Philippe Apeloig; 70b *The New York Times Magazine*. Courtesy Janet Froelich. Photographer: Stephen Lewis; 74-75 Designer: Jetmire Dvorani (jetmiredvorani.wordpress.com); 76 Photographer: Nick Knight. Vogue © Condé Nast Publications Ltd; 80, 85t, 100b, 119t, 119m, 119br, 187, 212-213 *Twen* magazine; 81tl, 173b, 210 Collection Tony Quinn; 81tr, 122, 137b, 157b, 177 Courtesy Metropolis; 82, 97, 141t, 216 Courtesy Neville Brody, Research Studio Ltd; 84 *Vogue* par Sofia Coppola, Sofia Coppola. Photographer: David Sims, Art Partner – © Vogue Paris © Condé Nast Publications Ltd; 88, 96, 118, 129 Courtesy *Het Parool*; 91 Courtesy Speak magazine. Photographer: Ira Nowinski; 100t Courtesy *Metropolis*. Photographer: Sean Hemmerle; 101 © Guardian News & Media Ltd 2013. Photograph: Allsport/Getty Images; 102br © Guardian News & Media Ltd 2013. Illustrator: Marian Deuchars; 103b Courtesy *Metropolis*. Illustrator: Christopher Silas Neal; 104 Image courtesy Paul Davis/*Illustrated Ape* magazine www.theillustratedape.com; 105t Courtesy Eat Creative. Creative Director: Steve Martin. Art Director: Tin Brown. Writer: Antony Head, Photographer: Satomi Ono; 105bl, 105br, 137t, 136bl, 199tl, 199b Courtesy *I.D.* magazine; 106-107 Photographer: Jordan Harrison-Twist; 108 © Guardian News & Media Ltd 2013. Courtesy Simon Esterson; 112t © Guardian News & Media Ltd 2013. Courtesy *The Observer*. Photographer: Murdo MacLeod; 112b, 116t, 121, 176 Courtesy *Fishwrap* magazine; 113t, 182m Courtesy *Inner Loop*; 115b, 181b, 196bl Courtesy Speak magazine; 119bl iStock; 120 *Graphic International*; 124, 125t Courtesy *Port* magazine. Designer: Matt Willey; 127 *FT.Business*. Photographer: Sasha Gusov; 130, 174t Courtesy *Dagens Nyheter*; 133, 158, 182t, 197 Courtesy (*inside*) magazine www.australiandesignreview.com; 134 Courtesy *Metropolis*. Photographer: Michelle Litvin; 136b Courtesy *Esopus*. Photographer: © 2004 David Michalek; 139b Courtesy *Dazed & Confused*; 140 Courtesy *Metropolis*. Photographer: Conrad Kiffin; 141b Courtesy Speak magazine. Illustrator: Brad Holland. Photographer: Steve Sherman; 142, 192t, 226 Courtesy Mario R Garcia, *Folha de S.Paolo*; 145l Courtesy *soDA* www.soDA.ch, Benjamin Güdel www.guedel.biz; 145tr Courtesy *Pariscope*; 146-147 Courtesy Simon Esterson; 150 Designer: Joseph Marshall (www.josephbisatmarshall.co.uk); 151t Designers: Stefan Abrahams, Rebecca Duff-Smith, Jasmine Jones and Hudson Shively; 152, 219 Courtesy Gail Anderson; 156 © Guardian News & Media Ltd 2013; 157t Courtesy *soDA* www.soDA.ch, Alex Capus - www. alexcapus.de / Benjamin Güdel - www.guedel.biz / Marc Kappeler - www.moire.ch; 163, 174b Courtesy Mirrorpix; 164, 165m, 165b, 167, 231 Berg Ltd and Bonnier AB; 166 Courtesy Jon Hill; 170l Courtesy *soDA* www.soDA.ch, Courtesy soDA. Marc Kappeler - www.moire.ch; 172tr Courtesy *Tank* magazine. Thierry van Biesen; 173t *Vogue Paris* © Condé Nast Publications Ltd; 178b, 179t, 214 Courtesy David Hillman; 180t © *Guardian* News & Media Ltd 2013. Photograph: Francesca Yorke 2006; 180b © *Guardian* News & Media Ltd 2013. Photograph: Getty Images; 183 *FT Business*. Courtesy: Alan Kitching; 186t Courtesy *Amelia's Magazine*. Art Director: Amelia Gregory. Illustrator: Rob Ryan; 186b Courtesy *Esopus. Ghost Form*, 2004 © William Christenberry; 190, 191tl Courtesy *Radio Times* © BBC Worldwide Limited; 191tr Courtesy *Radio Times* © BBC Worldwide Limited. Illustrator: Lyn Gray; 191b Courtesy *Radio Times* © BBC Worldwide Limited. Illustrator: Richard Draper; 192b © *Guardian* News & Media Ltd 2013. Grundy Graphics 2006; 194 Courtesy *Stern*; 195 © *The Economist Newspaper* Limited, London, August 26th-September 1st 2005; 196br Courtesy *Speak* magazine. Illustrator: Austin Cowdall / New Studio; 200 © *Guardian* News & Media Ltd 2013. Courtesy *The Observer*; 201t Courtesy *Stern*. Photographer: Vincent Laforet/Polaris; 201b Courtesy *Stern*. Photographer: Volker Hinz; 202 Designer: Sandra Audukaite; 203 Joint project by Ben Silvertown (bensilvertown.com), Iliana Dudueva, Manon Dafydd and Violetta Miller. Portrait of Haley Ma: © Tate; 207 *Vanity Fair* © Condé Nast Publications Ltd; 209 Courtesy *Seventeen* magazine / Hearst Corporation; 217tr *Vogue Italia* © Condé Nast Publications Ltd. Photographer: Barry McKinley. Stylist: Krizia; 222t, 222m *Real Simple* magazine. Courtesy Janet Froelich. Photographer: Rodney Smith; 222b *Real Simple* magazine. Courtesy Janet Froelich. Christopher Griffiths; 223 *Real Simple* magazine. Courtesy Janet Froelich. Photographer: Robert Maxwell 224t Courtesy Scott Dadich, *The New Yorker* © Condé Nast Publications Ltd; 224m, 224b Courtesy Scott Dadich; 225 © *Grazia* magazine. Courtesy Suzanne Sykes; 233 *Real Simple* magazine. Courtesy Janet Froelich. Photographer: David Meredith

Author Credits

Special thanks to:

All those who contributed images and profiles, in particular to Janet Froelich, Jon Hill, Mark Porter, Sarah Douglas, Jeremy Leslie, Richard Turley and Scott Dadich.

To all at Laurence King Publishing for their keen editing skills, particularly Peter Jones and Susan George, and to Mari West for pictures.

Thanks to all my students at Central Saint Martins Graphic Design who shared their projects from my design briefs with generosity: Stefan Abrahams' team, Sandra Adukuaite, Oliver Ballon, Salomi Desai, Iliana Dudueva, Jetmire Dvorani, Jordan Harrison-Twist, Joseph Marshall, and Ben Silvertown's team.

Thanks to my father Eddie Caldwell, a compositor who encouraged me to draw and love print, and to my husband John Belknap for his advice and endless cups of tea, and to Sam, Ed and Daisy for their patience. Thanks to Karen Sims and the Highbury Book Club for support.

Also thanks to Yolanda Zeppaterra, a Central Saint Martins graduate who wrote the excellent first edition of *Editorial Design* back in the print age of 2007.